Dear Reader:

The book you are about to read is the latest bestseller from the St. Martin's True Crime Library, the imprint the *New York Times* calls "the leader in true crime!" Each month, we offer you a fascinating account of the latest, most sensational crime that has captured the national attention. St. Martin's is the publisher of bestselling true crime author and crime journalist Kieran Crowley, who explores the dark, deadly links between a prominent Manhattan surgeon and the disappearance of his wife fifteen years earlier in THE SURGEON'S WIFE. Suzy Spencer's BREAKING POINT guides readers through the tortuous twists and turns in the case of Andrea Yates, the Houston mother who drowned her five young children in the family's bathtub. In Edgar Award-nominated DARK DREAMS, legendary FBI profiler Roy Hazelwood and bestselling crime author Stephen G. Michaud shine light on the inner workings of America's most violent and depraved murderers. In the book you now hold, Brenda Gunn details how the man she had a storybook marriage with plotted to have her killed . . .

St. Martin's True Crime Library gives you the stories behind the headlines. Our authors take you right to the scene of the crime and into the minds of the most notorious murderers to show you what really makes them tick. St. Martin's True Crime Library paperbacks are better than the most terrifying thriller, because it's all true! The next time you want a crackling good read, make sure it's got the St. Martin's True Crime Library logo on the spine—you'll be up all night!

Charles E. Spicer, Jr.
Executive Editor, St. Martin's True Crime Library

**FIRST, BRENDA GUNN MARRIED THE MAN
OF HER DREAMS . . .**

THEN THE NIGHTMARE BEGAN.

Dear Sheriff Gilbert,

If you're reading this then I'm already dead. I suspect that someone is plotting to kill me. Too many strange things have been happening around my house and to me. I can think of no other explanation.

I am giving the key to the safe-deposit box where I'll keep this letter to my sister. I will tell her to deliver it to you upon my death.

Sincerely,
Brenda Brumbaugh

DEADLY DECEPTION

A True Story of Duplicity, Greed, Dangerous Passions and One Woman's Courage

Brenda Gunn
and
Shannon Richardson

St. Martin's Paperbacks

NOTE: If you purchased this book without a cover you should be aware that this book is stolen property. It was reported as "unsold and destroyed" to the publisher, and neither the author nor the publisher has received any payment for this "stripped book."

Dedicated to every woman who has had to fight for her life and the sacrifices it cost her.   —Brenda Gunn

To my loving family, Gene, Danielle, Justice and Ashton, who have sacrificed so much to support me during my writing career.
—Shannon Richardson

Published by arrangement with New Horizon Press

DEADLY DECEPTION

Copyright © 2001 by Brenda Gunn and Shannon Richardson.

Cover photograph of Glen and Brenda courtesy Brenda Gunn; landscape courtesy Panoramic Images.

All rights reserved. No part of this book may be used or reproduced in any manner whatsoever without written permission except in the case of brief quotations embodied in critical articles or reviews. For information address New Horizon Press, P.O. Box 669, Far Hills, NJ 07931.

Library of Congress Catalog Card Number: 00-132568

ISBN: 0-312-98103-1

Printed in the United States of America

New Horizon Press hardcover edition published 2001
St. Martin's Paperbacks edition / July 2003

St. Martin's Paperbacks are published by St. Martin's Press, 175 Fifth Avenue, New York, NY 10010.

10 9 8 7 6 5 4 3 2 1

If you do good, good will be done to you;
But if you do evil, the same will be
Measured back to you again.

— Fables of Bidpai

TABLE OF CONTENTS

	Prologue	xi
Chapter 1	The Perfect Man	1
Chapter 2	"Till Death Do Us Part"	13
Chapter 3	A Capsule of Peace	27
Chapter 4	A Nest Egg	31
Chapter 5	Monday Morning	37
Chapter 6	The Carnival	51
Chapter 7	A House in the Country	57
Chapter 8	A Fiery Plan	65
Chapter 9	Of Suspicious Origin	71
Chapter 10	Insurance	79
Chapter 11	Bad Business	89
Chapter 12	The Honeymoon Is Over	99
Chapter 13	Suspicions	111
Chapter 14	The Hunt	121
Chapter 15	Sour Melody	127
Chapter 16	Spoiled	137
Chapter 17	Red Light Special	145
Chapter 18	Lovesick	149

Chapter 19   Anniversary Waltz 161

Chapter 20   A Bad Omen..175

Chapter 21   Confessions 187

Chapter 22   No Idle Conversation...207

Chapter 23   A Doubtful Future 215

Chapter 24   A Call in the Night 231

Chapter 25   Proof Positive 239

Chapter 26   In Her Own Hands 245

Chapter 27   Watch and Wait...251

Chapter 28   No Protection...265

Chapter 29   Of Dreams, Delusions & Nightmares 275

Chapter 30   Fatal Deceit 293

             Epilogue 301

PROLOGUE

She was lying on a pristine white sandy beach on the island of St. Martin. It was one of those deliciously hot and sunny Caribbean days, when the aquamarine sky shone like a jewel. Brenda was lying on her back and Glen had brought her an icy Piña Colada to drink.

Suddenly, just as she opened her mouth to take a sip, the gentle wind whipped up, making the beach umbrella beside her sway back and forth spraying sand. Startled, Brenda began to choke.

Her coughing woke her. The Caribbean faded. She opened her eyes but couldn't see anything through the billowing clouds surrounding her. Her chest began to ache and another severe bout of coughing overtook her. She tried to sit up and catch her breath. That's when she knew this wasn't a dream and they weren't clouds at all, but smoke. The temperature was rising in the room. The smoke grew thicker, leaving a bitter, acrid taste in her mouth.

Wet with perspiration, Brenda felt a trickle of sweat run into the corner of her mouth. It was salty, but her mouth was so parched from the heat that any moisture was welcome. She tried to look around her bedroom, but smoke stung her eyes. She couldn't see anything. *Which direction is the door? Wait! If it's smoky in here, the fire isn't from outside the house. I need to find the window so I can get out!*

Why did she feel so groggy? What had she drunk last night? *It was only one glass of wine.* Struggling to her feet, Brenda felt around for the edge of the bed. If she could follow its perimeter, she'd find the window. It was getting tougher to breathe. Her chest hurt, her eyes stung and she was getting weaker by the moment.

Brenda held her hand in front of her face but couldn't see it through the smoke. *This must be what it's like to be blind.* Unable to see, she collided with the wall. She hadn't realized how dependent she was on her sight. *I've never been so disoriented,* she thought. *I have to picture the room in my mind,* she told herself. But she couldn't get her mind to function. *It's as if I've been drugged.* She tried to pull herself together and felt along the wall, hoping to find some landmarks, but if there were any, she missed them.

She decided the best thing to do was continue following the wall. When she got to the door frame, she realized she'd gone in the wrong direction. The door itself felt like a hot iron. Wafts of black smoke pungent with the smell of charcoal filtered under it, and she could hear timbers crackling and popping on the other side. *I have to get out of here fast.*

Brenda turned around, stood up and bolted across the room as fast as her wobbly legs would take her. She hoped she was running in a straight line but had no way of knowing. When she hit the end of the wrought iron canopy bed, it knocked the wind out of her. She fell face forward. It took her a few seconds before she could try to get up on her hands and knees and crawl to where the window should be.

Suddenly, there was a loud crash! Then a roar and the door she'd just left disintegrated into a fireball. It was as if a bomb had exploded! Flames rumbled in...

"I'm going to die!" Brenda murmured as she frantically searched for the lamp that sat on a small table next to the window. *Where is it?* She didn't have much time! Waving her outstretched arms, she accidentally hit the shade and knocked it over. It crashed to the floor. She felt along the floor in wide sweeping motions. *God, please don't let me die!*

Suddenly her fingertip nicked the bottom of the lamp. She grabbed the base and threw it through the window. Fresh air whipped in while the fire swelled at her back. She could smell her hair burning. The air rushing in through the window was fanning the flame. Without a moment to waste, she crashed through the broken window.

Brenda heard the noise of firemen yelling, water splattering on the roof and bouncing off, covering her with a fine mist. She could literally feel it lowering her body temperature. Suddenly, she was being dragged across the lawn, coughing and sputtering. When they had moved her to safety, the paramedics slapped an oxygen mask on her face and told her to breathe. She was trying, but the harder she tried, the more she coughed. And then, there was nothing...

When Brenda opened her eyes, the sun was too bright. Everything was blurry. *Where am I?* She caught only glimpses of colors and moving forms that must have been people. In the distance, she thought she saw her husband, Glen, with a garden hose standing next to her best friend, Jane, who was busy tying animals' leashes to far off trees. Then she remembered the fire.

Brenda was numb. She didn't even feel the paramedics put an intravenous needle in her arm, but she did hear the fire chief yell to his men, "We've got to contain the blaze on the west side of the house. Get in there and form a barrier between the flames and the east side of the house before the rest of the structure goes."

A loud crack hurt her ears. The entire roof above the bedroom crashed to the ground. Brenda felt the ground beneath her vibrate from the noise. Smoke and cinders mushroomed into the sky. Flickering embers floated through the air like fireflies. *If it wasn't so devastating, it would be beautiful,* she thought.

Thank you, God, for getting me out of there before the roof caved in. I'd have been trapped.

Tears spilled out of Brenda's scorched eyes. The salt stung, but the tears were also soothing. She could feel them washing away the smoky grit. When she tried to rub her forehead, she felt her eyebrows. They were wiry from being singed.

Glen's voice drifted closer to her. She tried to look in that direction but kept slipping in and out of consciousness. The paramedics were trying to keep him away, but he wasn't cooperating.

"She's my wife!" Brenda heard him yell. "I'll stay out of your way, but I'm damned-well going to see her!"

Glen's shadowy form shoved past the paramedics. He took her limp hand in his, looked at the paramedic and asked in a grim tone, "Is she—?"

"No, she's hanging in now, but she came close to dying in there. She's suffering from smoke inhalation and there may have been lung damage. We're going to take her to the hospital," the paramedic said.

Brenda looked into Glen's face and thought she saw tears forming in his eyes. She was so moved by his concern that she tried to reach up to hug him. When she did, she saw the bedroom, bathroom and guest bedroom burning beyond control. She buried her face in Glen's chest and cried, "All my hard work is going up in flames."

Glen stroked her hair to comfort her. "Baby, I'm so-o-o sorry."

The sheriff, Dan Gilbert, who had just arrived on the scene, strode over. He cleared his throat noisily to make his presence known. Glen gently laid Brenda back on the stretcher and looked up at him questioningly.

"Mr. and Mrs. Brumbaugh? I need to speak with you.

Do you have insurance?" the huge, stocky man asked in a deep baritone voice.

"My wife works for an insurance company. They'd kill her if she didn't have plenty of insurance," Glen answered curtly.

"Do you smoke?" the sheriff asked.

"Glen does, but he wasn't home," she wheezed.

"You two have any enemies?" the sheriff asked.

Brenda shook her head no. Even through the oxygen mask, she could smell the foul odor of his rattlesnake skin boots.

"No one that I know of," Glen said.

Brenda saw the sheriff look at her then Glen. Brenda could tell the sheriff was trying to size them up.

"The fire chief thinks that because of the odor and intense flames, it might have been started by chemicals, so he called me."

"Chemicals," Glen echoed.

"It can't be," Brenda shook her head.

"More likely it was electrical or gas or something else," the sheriff shrugged.

Brenda gasped for breath between each word. "It has to be an accident. I can't think of anybody who'd want to do this to us."

"Wait a minute." Glen scratched his chin. "What about the renters at the house your Grandma gave you? They were two months behind on their rent," Glen said.

Brenda nodded and tried to say something, but Glen put his hand on her shoulder to indicate she should rest.

"Brenda had to get ugly with them yesterday and threatened to evict them," he told the sheriff.

"I'll question 'em. Can you think of anybody else—ex-spouses, angry relatives or neighbors, disgruntled employees?" the sheriff asked.

"There's this one guy that keeps following me," Brenda

said hoarsely. "He's one of our company's clients. He made a pass at me when I was giving him a physical but I turned him down. Also, I had to give the company a negative medical report on him. I don't know if he's learned of the bad report yet but it means he he won't get a million dollar policy. Anyway, ever since the day he came on to me, I've been seeing his car everywhere I go, even here at the house."

"What's his name?" the sheriff asked.

"Something...Morgan. My boss will know," she said.

"Say, I saw a blue car with 'Morgan' on the license plate just this morning," Glen said.

"We'll check it all out," the sheriff said and walked over to his deputy.

"Mr. Brumbaugh, we're ready to take your wife to the hospital. You'll need to take your own car and follow the ambulance," the paramedic said.

Brenda felt Glen squeeze her hand as he said, "I'll be right behind you, darlin'."

As the paramedics lifted Brenda onto a new, stark white stretcher, she saw the devastation the fire had wrought and began to weep again. They raised the stretcher and locked it into place with a snapping sound. As they wheeled her toward the ambulance, Brenda saw that Glen had walked back toward Jane. Their heads were bent together and Jane's voice wafting back sounded angry. She hoped Jane wasn't blaming Glen for not having been home. It would be just like her protective best friend. But it wasn't Glen's fault, Brenda wanted to tell her. He was fixing a neighbor's fence to earn some extra money so they could take a long, romantic weekend away. Glen was the best thing that had ever happened to her.

On the way to the hospital, as the ambulance's siren careened in and out of her ears, Brenda's groggy mind drifted back to the happiest day of her life.

CHAPTER ONE

THE PERFECT MAN

It was the day she had waited for, dreamed about, for years. Now everything would be sublime. Brenda had polished the house to a high gloss and worked day and night to get caught up at work so she could take some time off.

After applying a little gray eye shadow and some lip gloss, Brenda checked her watch and fluffed her shoulder length brown hair with her fingertips. She kept her hair long enough to dress up when she had a date yet short enough to sweep back out of her way when she wore her nurse's uniform. The movement was just enough to release the scent of her shampoo—vanilla.

She took an Art Deco hair comb from the vanity. It was gold, shaped into a fluted leaf and highlighted with five diamonds. Her grandmother, who had given the comb to her, said she had bought the ornament in 1940 from Cartier and Brenda should wear it as "something old" on her wedding day. Now Brenda swept the comb through the side of her hair, then flipped its direction and pushed it in. The comb held the lock of hair in the perfect position. The diamonds sparkled, adding a nice contrast to her dark hair.

Brenda was finally in love and she would show off her man to her family and friends. Those people who hadn't met Glen would be shocked that *she* could land such a good-looking guy. She heard the voices in her head of the kids at school chanting, as they had so many years before, their own version of the Carly Simon song; "You're so plain, you probably think this song is about you, Brenda."

"Glen thinks I'm pretty," she told herself and shoved the memory of her classmates' cruel words and how they had hurt aside.

Brenda gazed into the mirror where her milky white skin, pale blue eyes with flecks of gray and the strong jawline she had inherited from her father's side of the family were reflected. But Brenda shook her head. All she could ever see when she looked in the mirror were her flaws. She thought her skin was too pasty, her hair too limp and stringy, her face too angular and her hips too broad.

When she was in high school, her big sister had told her she would grow out of her self-conscious nature, but Brenda never did. Even though she had read *Our Bodies, Ourselves* six times, along with a ton of other self-esteem books, she still was over-critical of her face and body, especially today. She wanted to look perfect for *him.*

She let her fingertips dance across the form-fitting bodice she was wearing. She closed her eyes and wondered if her great-grandmother had felt this aroused on her wedding day. Had this outfit made her feel sexy? Had she been nervous, too? Had her body ached for her lover's hands to cup her breasts? Stroke her inner thigh? Had she longed to be in her lover's arms?

Brenda let out a deep breath and opened her eyes. She hadn't worn this outfit just because it was an heirloom. No, she really liked the gown and hoped to hand it down to her daughter someday. It would be wonderful to say that five generations had worn this same outfit.

The dress was beautiful. Made of creamy ivory lace, it had a high collar and tiny, peach-colored satin roses lining both the collar and the mutton sleeves. Brenda fluffed the sleeves, then tugged at the corseted waistband of the skirt. She wished she'd had the time to lose ten pounds. She told herself the pale, peach-colored chiffon skirt flowed smoothly over her hips and made her look taller and thinner, but nevertheless she agonized that he might think her heavy.

Brenda imagined the man she loved and was marrying making love to her. Because she had wanted this to be so special she had convinced him to wait. He was tall and muscular from lifting weights each day and she had no doubt she would enjoy making love to his body. The question was, would he enjoy hers?

She nervously twisted the platinum engagement ring on her finger and the light caught the diamond, making it sparkle. She couldn't believe they were actually going to be married.

"Billy Gunn's old-maid daughter is finally going to get married," she said and thought back to the day she had first suspected that Glen might propose.

She had gone to visit him in Kansas City. Two months before that day, he and Brenda had met almost serendipitously. Glen had arrived in Kansas City only a few days before, and was reading a map while driving. Brenda's car was in front of him and when she suddenly stopped he rear-ended her car. Since it wasn't serious and only her bumper was damaged, they didn't bother calling the police but did exchange insurance information. Brenda had been feeling lonely and overworked that day and Glen was charming, assuming full responsibility for the accident, promising to have her car fixed and seeming to care so much that she might be injured. They began to see each other regularly. The first time she realized that he might be getting serious was at the ice-cream shop, when they were picking out the flavors of their cones. Brenda had ordered cookies-n-cream and Glen had requested rocky road then turned to her and said something that stuck with her all the next day: "I have something very important about our future to talk over with you tomorrow." Then he had smiled, looking into her eyes. When she had questioned him, he had refused to tell her what he was referring to. "It's a surprise!" he'd said.

She wondered all the next day. *Is he going to ask me to marry him? No, that can't be it. It is way too soon. We've only been dating for two months. But, what if he does? What will I do?*

That night, he did propose and presented her with the engagement ring she now wore.

She had wanted to throw her arms around him and scream at the top of her lungs, "Yes!" But instead, she remained calm saying, "You know this is crazy. We hardly know each other."

"Do you love me?" he asked.

"Yes."

"Then how can it be too soon? We aren't teenagers. We know what true love is."

She couldn't argue with that. She was thirty-five and had never been married. In fact, she'd never even been a bridesmaid. He was forty, had been married and divorced, but that didn't bother her. She knew the chances at her age of finding a man who hadn't been married before were unlikely.

He grinned. "I'd like to go to a Justice of the Peace tomorrow."

"No," she answered softly.

His face dropped.

"I want to wear my great-grandmother's gown and have a real ceremony—small, but perfect."

He smiled. "Then I guess you'd better introduce me to your father so I can formally ask for your hand." She'd nodded, brimming over with emotion.

And now they would start a life together. She loved him—everything about him. She liked how his tan made his teeth seem stark white, the way he always sent presents, cards and flowers for no special reason. The way he always knew what she was thinking. In fact, they often said the same thing at the same time. They were perfect for each other.

We're getting married and I'll never be lonely again. We'll never be apart.

Glen's eyes scanned the houses along the street. *Pretty nice, considering it's such a tiny town,* he thought. He glanced at the address on the piece of paper he held—234 Sunshine Street. Glen muttered the numbers and looked over at his buddy driving the car. Manfred Simmons, or Manny, as he preferred being called, liked fast cars and even faster women, but he and Glen usually got along well and had been friends for years.

"Do you see her house?" Manny asked.

"We want 234. The evens are on your side." Glen saw the number and yelled, "Stop! There it is. I recognize her car." Glen pointed out the car window for his friend to see.

The Cadillac skidded to a stop and left black tire marks about eight feet long on the street. Manny often boasted that he'd never been passed by any car and only two trains. The motor of the car had been souped up and it could move.

"Back up," Glen said.

Manny put the car in reverse and stopped in front of Brenda's house.

"Well, isn't this cozy?" Manny said, looking around.

The ranch style house bore a fresh coat of white paint on the wooden shingles and an antique red swing hung from the porch ceiling swayed in the breeze. A garden full of red and pink flowers decorated the front yard. In its center was a very large stone birdbath with a long crack in it, so it held almost no water. "She definitely needs a handyman around here. I can fix that like new," Glen murmured.

He reached in the back seat and tugged the tuxedo hanger. The plastic wrapping was caught on the car's garment hook and he was having trouble getting it loose.

"Thanks for the ride," Glen said, finally ripping the plastic free. "Just be back at five-thirty sharp so you're early for the ceremony, Manfred."

"Don't call me that! Nobody calls me that but my mother."

"Sorry," Glen said. Usually, he would have told Manny where to go, but he didn't want to get into a hassle and provoke his friend's quick temper. Not today. "I didn't mean anything by it, Manny. I'm just a little nervous," Glen said, and pulled up on the door's handle.

"Nervous about what? Maybe you're afraid your big score won't go down," Manny winked.

"What are you talking about? There's no score here," Glen said, trying to assure him. "I'm a changed man. I'm marrying Brenda because I love her. That's all there is to it," Glen said, darting him a *You don't know what you're talking about* look.

Manny grinned. "Just wanted to be sure you're sure."

When Glen didn't say anything, Manny continued.

"Remember you and I have a rich history." He slurred the last words, toying with Glen. His friend looked at him.

"Would you stop razzing me. I'm nervous enough." Glen slammed the door behind him. "Dammit! You may be my best friend, but you can be a pain." With the tuxedo slung over his shoulder, Glen walked up the sidewalk to the front of the house. He didn't turn back, but heard the sound of the Cadillac's revved-up motor racing away.

The doorbell startled Brenda and the dogs in the backyard started a cacophony of barking. She took a calming breath, put her hand to her mouth and blew into it to check her breath. It smelled okay. She straightened her shoulders, put on an air of confidence and went to open the front door.

Taped to the back of the door was a 'to-do' list. Brenda scanned it: flowers, balloons, wine and champagne, wedding cake and rice. She hoped she had remembered everything. She snatched the list off the door, wadded the paper up and hid it discreetly behind a vase on a nearby table. She grasped the brass door handle. It felt cool from the air-conditioning and she wondered if she had the thermostat too low. Then she realized that *she* was running hot because of her racing heartbeat.

Brenda paused briefly to steady herself, then opened the door. Framed in the doorway and glowing in the afternoon sun was Glen. His handsome, chiseled features, emphasized by a mustache and dark brown eyes, contrasted nicely with his light brown, wavy hair. *What a perfect man*, Brenda thought and sighed. She doubted that he knew just what a hunk he was, because he often seemed shy and unsure of himself.

He offered her a skittish smile and said, "You look beautiful." He paused a moment looking at her, then went on, "Are we really doing this?"

Brenda flung her arms around him and shouted "yes."

Startled by the sudden gesture, Glen stepped backward, taking her with him, but she didn't care. She was too excited. He took control of the moment, raised her chin and kissed her gently on the lips as she closed her eyes. It was odd, she thought, how he always knew just the right thing to do to calm her fidgetiness.

The heavenly kiss sent her soaring. When Glen broke away, she opened her eyes and he stood back staring at her. She saw the stain of her lipstick on his face. It reminded her of a Picasso painting. He looked funny and she giggled.

"I guess you better get in here, before we give the whole neighborhood something to talk about," she said and gave him a little tug.

Glen stepped inside the house. He stood in one spot as if glued to the floor and scanned the room. He had never been to her house before. He had been living in Kansas City and since she worked there, they had always met at his place.

Suddenly, Brenda realized it was all strange to him.

"This is home," she told him and looped her arm through his.

Brenda looked around the house, trying to see it through Glen's eyes as she led him into the living room. Things she had never thought about before, she suddenly realized, had her personality stamped all over them. One whole wall held a mahogany bookcase filled with her books, her porcelain doll collection and the glass incense burners that wafted her favorite vanilla aroma into the room. In one corner stood a pink wrought iron birdcage and the exotic blue parrot in the cage squawked at Glen. Even he knew Glen was a stranger to this house.

Brenda hadn't realized before how feminine the place was until she looked around now. Suddenly, she saw through a man's eyes her delicate figurines—mostly of animal figures—

scattered around the room and the canopy of flowering plants that hung from the ceiling. Each plant's perfume saturated her nostrils as she walked under them.

When Glen reached up and felt a leafy fern, she said, "It's real."

"Why wouldn't it be?" he asked.

"You might have thought it was silk."

"What? Silk comes from worms, not flowers," he said.

"I'll explain later." *Glen seems more nervous than I am. I never thought about the groom having last-minute jitters. I need to think of something to help him relax.*

He took her hands in his and looked in her eyes. "Brenda, I love you and I don't want any secrets between us."

"Oh, alright," Brenda said. "I'll tell you now. A lot of people have ferns made out of plastic or silk. I..."

He cut her off. "No, I wasn't talking about that. I have something I've got to tell you before we get married. When I was younger and stupid, I made some mistakes..."

They hadn't known each other but a couple of months. Her mind was racing ahead of him. *Did he have AIDS? Was he not legally divorced? Did he have ten kids that she didn't know about?*

"I ran into a little trouble," he said. "I got into debt and wrote some hot checks...It was more than just one check...It was..." he paused and looked at her. "Now my credit is ruined."

Well, if that's the worst thing about him...I didn't dare tell him about the time I miscalculated my checkbook and bounced seven hundred dollars worth of checks. I had never been more embarrassed than calling all those people and trying to convince them it had been an honest mistake.

She could see the concern in his eyes. *Isn't it sweet? He wants to start our life together with a clean ledger.* "Glen, we all make mistakes," she said. "I wish it hadn't happened, but over time you can get your credit back. I'll help you."

He picked her up and twirled her around. "I love you. You just made me the happiest man in the world."

They kissed and Brenda was certain she could forgive him just about anything—she loved him so much. Maybe even too much if there was such a thing. A loud lion's roar parted them.

"What was that?" Glen asked.

"That was Katula, my mountain lion. Remember I told you I take in abused animals and raise others for zoos?"

"Oh, right. I forgot," Glen said. The mantle clock chimed a sweet tune. He looked at it. "It's getting late. I'd better change clothes. Where's the bathroom?"

"Would you like to tour the place first?" Brenda asked.

Glen nodded. "But we'd better hurry," he said, then stuffed his hands in his pockets and nervously jingled his change.

She showed him the kitchen area. Old farm implements hung around the ceiling—a cotton scale, sickle, horse shoe, ice tongs, a wagon wheel. The walls were painted a cheerful yellow and white eyelet curtains adorned the windows. The room was cozy and rustic.

"Would you like something to drink?"

"Iced tea, if you have it."

"Peach or lemon?"

"Peach or lemon what?"

"Tea."

"I've never had either. I'll take what you're having," he said.

She made them each a glass of peach tea. Glen took a sip and grinned. "It's good."

Brenda swallowed some of hers. The sweet, fruity bouquet drifted up from the glass and added to the flavor.

An antique curio cabinet in the corner housed her salt and pepper shaker collection. Glen bent down. "I've never seen so many salt and pepper shakers in my life."

"I have almost four hundred pairs," Brenda said with pride. "I started collecting them when I was eight years old. These were my first," she said, pointing to a pair of pink pumpkin-shaped porcelain ones with hand-painted roses on the sides.

They continued on the tour and the last place she took him was her bedroom.

The walls were papered in a tan palmetto pattern. To give the feel of the tropics, gauzy curtains covered the windows and filtered the sunlight. Centered on one wall sat a wrought iron bed, encased by a sheer canopy.

Glen looked away. She offered an embarrassed smile and quickly changed the subject. "Do you like our bedroom?"

He shrugged. "Kind of frilly, isn't it?" Glen fingered the sheer netting draped over the bed.

Brenda glanced at the alarm clock that sat on her nightstand. "The Justice of the Peace will be arriving any minute. You can change in here and then I'll show you the backyard."

"The backyard?"

"Remember we're going to make our vows out there as the sun goes down. If that's still okay with you."

"Sure," he said.

She left him alone to change into his tuxedo and went into the bathroom to touch up her lipstick. Somehow, his disclosure about his bad credit nagged at her. After all, if it didn't matter, why hadn't he told her from the start? Still, she truly loved him. She told herself the credit thing didn't really matter. Their love was the most important thing in the world. They would make their marriage work.

When she turned around, he was standing in the doorway staring at her.

"I can't believe, you wonderful woman, that you are going to be my wife," Glen said, a bashful smile playing about his lips.

"Wow! You look great in that tuxedo!" she said, and ran her hand through his silky brown hair to smooth out a wayward strand. "Perfect." Glen was lean, athletic. His expensive watch and clothes made him look like a model. Only, he didn't have the conceit of such an attractive man. He was caring and a little shy. That's what she liked about him.

He took her hand in his and rubbed it. "God, your skin is soft."

Smiling, she led him through the house and out the back door to the patio.

"Surprise!" her father and mother, who were ensconced in two beribboned seats set near the flowered canopy, and a host of people shouted. Manny was among them, smiling.

Glen's shocked face had a dazed look. Brenda reassuringly wrapped her arm around his slim waist.

"I wanted to have my family and some friends come to our wedding."

Glen paled and broke away, bolting back inside the house.

CHAPTER TWO

"TILL DEATH DO US PART"

The wedding guests stopped talking and gawked at each other in an uncomfortable silence.

"Go ahead and please help yourself to the hors d'oeuvres. I'll be right back," Brenda told her guests and followed Glen inside.

She found him pacing in the kitchen like a caged leopard. She tried to wrap her arms around him to reassure him, but he shrugged her off. She felt helpless.

"Glen, what's wrong?"

"You should have told me all those people were out there!" he said.

The music of Billy Joel's, "Just the Way You Are," filtered in from the backyard. Brenda peeked out the window, relieved that her guests were mingling and seemed to be having a good time. She turned her attention back to Glen.

"Why did you invite all these people?" he asked, continuing to pace. He kept rubbing his hands on his pants in an attempt to find the pockets, but there were no pockets on the formal pants.

"It's a wedding party. It wouldn't be much of a *party* if I didn't invite people, now would it? I've never seen you like this. What's wrong?"

He stopped pacing and faced her. "I haven't been around strangers very much. I don't know how to act."

"You don't have to act any way. Just be yourself and have a good time," she said, caressing the side of his face. "These people will be your friends, Glen. You just haven't met them yet."

"Brenda, I'm agoraphobic. Crowds petrify me. I'm not used to having a lot of people around," he told her desperately.

She gently turned him to face her and looked him in the eyes. "Glen, remember family and friends who care are good for and to each other."

He hugged her. She held him tightly.

"Nobody's ever been as good to me as you are," he said. They held each other a long time. All the while, Brenda stroked his back as a mother would to calm a frightened little boy.

Finally, he pulled back to look at her. "Sorry I ran out on you, Brenda. I'll never do that again."

"I love you," she responded gently.

Glen nodded and smiled.

Brenda tapped on the window to give her sisters, Suzy and Emily, the cue and the wedding march began to play. Brenda looped her arm through Glen's. Her dad and mother had not been well and she had decided she and Glen would walk down the aisle together, setting up their own new custom.

"Wait," she whispered to him, "Sniffer goes first."

Glen shook his head and frowned. "Honestly, Brenda, I know you love animals, but that bundle of bones and fur looks more like a rat. Are you sure you want your dog in our wedding?"

"Please, Glen," Brenda said.

He managed a forced smile. "Oh, if it pleases you, I guess I can live with it."

Outside, Suzy deposited the Yorkshire puppy on the ground. He wore a collar of carnations and apricot-colored tulle and a puffy bow on his wagging tail. In his mouth he carried a basket of rose petals. As he pranced down the peach satin draped aisle, the rose petals spilled over to form a trail for the wedding couple. Sniffer marched up to the Justice of the Peace and stopped, just like he knew what he was doing. The guests *ooh-ed* and *aah-ed*.

Next, Brenda and Glen came out the door and followed Sniffer down the aisle. The guests' murmurs turned to silence as Brenda and Glen stopped in front of the Justice of the Peace. It was a lovely November day. The weather was perfect and exceptionally mild for that time of year. The skies were blue and clear, but for a few wispy clouds above them that were shading to pink as the sun set. The gentle rustle of deep red leaves on the maple trees was the only sound.

Glen took Brenda's hands in his and looked lovingly into her eyes. His voice had a nervous edge to it as he recited the poem he had written.

"When I lay down to sleep at night,
I want you by my side.
Through good and bad and thick and thin,
I want you as my bride."

Brenda gave his hand a reassuring squeeze and he squeezed hers back as he continued,

"I promise to love and cherish you,
And harm will come to you never.

For richer or poorer, in sickness and health,
I promise to love you forever."

Glen smiled lovingly at Brenda. She gazed into his adoring eyes and began her vow.

"From this day forward, for the rest of my life,
I'll promise to care for you, as any good wife.
As the sun rises and I wake up each morning,
Always know that my love is dawning.
If by human standards, we turn out to be poor,
We'll still have each other, I won't ask for more.
When there comes a day we don't get along,
I'll remember this promise, this lovely song.
I promise to love you, till death do us part,
And this I mean with all of my heart."

The Justice of the Peace opened his Bible and recited the rite that made them husband and wife. As he rambled on, Brenda didn't hear half of what he was saying. She was entranced by the man at her side. It was as if she was Sleeping Beauty and when Glen kissed her, she would awake to a whole new world and a bright new life.

"You may kiss the bride," the Justice of the Peace said.

Glen bent down and kissed her softly. Brenda wrapped her arms around him and pulled him close. She wanted this to be a kiss she would remember the rest of her life.

First they walked over to her father and mother and Brenda saw tears in both their eyes as they kissed Brenda and hugged Glen. Then guests swarmed around them offering "Congratulations" and "Best wishes." Brenda was the happiest she had ever been. If her heart held another drop of happiness, she thought it would burst.

Brenda's boss, Cal Langley, brought over a magnum of champagne which, in the delay, some of the guests had already opened. He refilled the glasses of her parents and the nearby guests. Everyone raised their glasses and toasted the nuptial couple.

The atmosphere was joyful and growing louder by the moment. Sniffer yipped and pawed at Brenda's legs in an attempt to get her attention.

"No, no, Sniffer. You'll tear my dress," she admonished as she picked up the little dog and tried to calm him. She didn't want Glen to be annoyed by his behavior.

A smiling young man with curly hair stepped up to Glen and stuck out his hand. "I'm Brenda's brother, Dave."

Glen shook his hand.

"You gave us quite a scare when you went back in the house," Dave continued. "We figured Brenda was gonna stay an old-maid for sure."

Brenda's face reddened. "My brother likes to tease."

Glen narrowed his eyes and said, "Watch out who you call an old-maid. That's my beautiful wife you're talking about."

"Just brotherly-sisterly ribbing. She knows I love her."

Glen laughed, though his eyes had an angry look and he changed the subject. "This is quite a shindig. I wasn't expecting anybody to be here except Brenda, the Justice of the Peace and two witnesses. Suddenly, I saw about a hundred people jump out at me yelling 'Surprise!'"

"There's only thirty-five or so," Brenda corrected.

"Well, it seems like a hundred."

"We have some more champagne over there. Do you want a glass?" Dave asked.

Brenda glared at Dave. She had told him about Glen's drinking problem, but guessed that he had forgotten about it due to the excitement.

"That's nice of you to offer," Glen said. "I don't drink, but I'll take a club soda if you have one."

"Well, that's a weak toast for your wedding," Dave said looking at his new brother-in-law appraisingly, "but you got it." He set off for the bar.

Suzy and Emily, Brenda's two sisters, walked up to them. Emily, blond and petite in a powder blue suit, was the youngest. She looked at Brenda adoringly and kissed her cheek. Brenda was fond of Emily, who was the quiet, conservative one in the family. It had broken her heart when her baby sister took a job in California the year before, but she was thrilled that Emily could come back to town for the wedding.

Suzy was Emily's opposite. She always spoke her mind and never shied away from even the most sensitive or racy of topics. The hem of Suzy's expensive-looking pink silk dress had a beaded fringe and she wore a pink straw hat set at a sassy angle. Suzy stuck out her hand to shake Glen's. "I'm Brenda's older sister. I'm the one she complains about all the time and Emily's the one who used to tag after her like a puppy—that is, until she moved far away and abandoned us all! Welcome to our screwy family," she teased.

"Now Suzy, tell the truth. You're the only one in the family that's nutty," Brenda joked. She wrapped her arm around her sister's shoulder and squeezed.

"Brenda, you look beautiful. Doesn't she, Emily?" Emily nodded and Suzy went on. "See, I told you great-grandma's dress would look great on you. Who was right?"

"You were right, as always, Suzy," Brenda chanted with Emily. This was banter they had indulged in since sixth-grade when Suzy had told Brenda how to get the cutest boy in the class to kiss her.

Suzy was standing with one of her stiletto heels stuck

in the ground, rocking casually back and forth as she talked. Sniffer, who had been enjoying the rapture of Brenda's arms, noticed the swaying fringe and watched it intently. His head went back and forth as if he were watching a tennis match. Suddenly, it got the best of him and he lurched out of Brenda's arms to the ground and playfully swiped at the fringe. A claw snagged a string of the fringe and he yelped. Sheepishly, he scampered under the food table and hid. Emily went to fetch him and carried the little dog back.

Brenda's friend, Jane, sauntered over to them, a bottle of champagne tucked under her arm, tulip glasses dangling from her fingers. "That's some watchdog you've got there," Jane said, pouring a glass of bluish-tinged champagne and offering it to Brenda.

"Blue champagne?" Brenda asked, looking at the sparkling liquid.

"It's blueberry. I wanted the finest for my best friend on her wedding day," Jane said, giving Suzy a side glance. Suzy and Jane sometimes tangled. Brenda thought Suzy didn't want Jane usurping her role as big sister and adviser.

"It's delicious," Brenda said as she took a sip. The tiny bubbles tickled her nose as she took another one.

Turning to her new husband, Brenda noticed Glen looking at Jane. He saw Brenda watching him, looked away from Jane and smiled reassuringly at his new wife.

He's just trying to be friendly after that talk I gave him, Brenda told herself. *I have to stop being paranoid he'll find someone else more attractive than me.*

Brenda took Glen's elbow. She had been looking forward to introducing these two people to each other. "Glen, this is Jane Leach. She's been my best friend since we met. In fact, she sold me this house almost six years ago."

"Listen, buddy, you better take good care of her or

you'll have to answer to me," Jane said to Glen, in a mock-threatening tone.

Brenda thought it odd that Jane hadn't offered Glen any champagne. *How does she know he doesn't drink?* She shook off the thought. *I'm so suspicious of my own good fortune, I'm imagining things. Jane has just forgotten her manners.*

"Drink a little too much champagne already?" Glen asked Jane sharply.

"Perhaps you need a little. Too bad you'd better not," Jane shot back at him.

She must have overheard Glen tell my brother he doesn't drink. Puzzled by her angry behavior, Brenda touched Jane on the shoulder. "Jane, what's going on? What's the matter?"

"I'm sorry, Brenda. My divorce from Marshall is final today and the fact that he's gotten into trouble and been sent away only makes it worse. I just visited him in prison for the last time. I keep telling myself to get on with my life, but..."

"Out with the old," Suzy intoned, "in with the new."

Brenda mouthed "Cut it out!" to Suzy and wrapped her arm around Jane. Suzy was too outspoken. True, Jane was a bit of a flirt, but this was hardly the time to comment on it.

"Let's go in the house and freshen up," Brenda suggested, wanting to change the subject.

Jane nodded as Dave reappeared and handed Glen a glass of Perrier with lime. Glen smiled his thanks.

"Glen, I'll be back in a minute. Will you be okay?" Brenda asked.

He nodded that he would. Brenda gave him an encouraging smile and the three women headed toward the house with Emily tagging along.

As Dave and Glen watched them leave, Dave said, "Brenda and Jane couldn't be any more opposite. It amazes me they're such good friends."

"You can say that again," Glen agreed.

"I like my women just like Jane—bleached blond hair, dynamite figure and a deep, sexy voice. Hell, I even like her sarcastic tongue and that sexy, flowery perfume she wears."

Glen gave him a scouring look. "I favor women like Brenda. She has that wholesome quality. The first time I saw her, I went into meltdown," Glen offered.

Dave chuckled, "You make her sound like a Palmolive commercial."

Dave was still watching Jane as she went up the back steps.

"Down boy!" Glen interjected with a short laugh.

The women disappeared into the house and Dave sighed.

"If we want some of that buffet, we better get in line. It's disappearing fast," Glen said to Dave.

"Sounds good to me," Dave replied.

They went to the end of the serving line.

Glen looked around. "This backyard would be huge if Brenda didn't line the entire perimeter with animal cages."

"You better not let her hear you say that. Brenda would really like to let the animals roam, but the neighbors would call the authorities," Dave said. "Well, at least she keeps the cages spotless," he added.

"That's why the yard doesn't have that muggy animal smell," Suzy said as she joined them in line.

"What are you doing back so soon?" Dave asked.

"Oh, I'm not much for girl-talk. I want to enjoy the celebration." She turned to Glen and pointed to the white and peach-colored heart-shaped balloons tied to the bars of the cages. "Guess how many balloons I put up there?

"I don't know. Fifty?" Glen guessed.

"One hundred and twenty-three. I was trying to make these cages more cheerful," Suzy said.

Glen grinned and scratched his cheek. "It looks really nice."

"The place is like a zoo," Suzy grumbled.

"Well, Brenda's got quite a variety of animals," Glen said diplomatically.

"Did you know the wildlife shelter brings her some of theirs?" asked Dave.

"Do you like animals?" Suzy asked Glen.

Glen frowned. "Well, uh...personally...I don't, but if they make Brenda happy, then I'm happy."

Suzy smiled and changed the subject. "I hope you can slow Brenda down. Lord knows, she won't listen to me," Suzy said. "All that girl does is work—fourteen, fifteen hours a day—then she comes home, takes care of these animals and studies."

"I know. I think it's great that she wants to better herself," Glen said with a weak grin.

"I do too," Suzy responded defensively. "I'm just amazed she had time to fall in love."

"She fit me into her schedule between work and studying on Tuesdays and Thursdays," Glen joked.

"You won't think it's so funny when you're living with her all the time and she does nothing but work." In a confidential tone, Suzy said, "That's why the insurance company gives her so many policies as bonuses."

Glen's eyebrows raised. "I like an independent woman," he said quietly.

An animal growled and Glen jumped.

"That's Katula, the mountain lion," Suzy said. "She was being starved by some carney troupe when the humane society brought her to Brenda. That growling would drive me crazy, but Brenda likes it. *Queen of the Beasts* and all that."

"It probably wants to go to the buffet, too," Dave added.

"How many other wild animals does she have beside the mountain lion?" Glen asked.

"Haven't you been here before?" Suzy asked.

"No, I haven't. I knew she had a lot of animals, but I assumed they were all cats and dogs," Glen said.

"Heck no!" Suzy said with a chuckle. She pointed to the first cage in the line. "That's Lady Godiva, a golden retriever who someone tried to stuff into a garbage can. She lived on the streets. Brenda's trying to civilize her into being a house pet. And next to her are the Rottweilers she's been trying to breed."

"The retriever might make a good hunting dog," Glen said.

"Oh Gawd, does Brenda know you're a hunter?" Suzy asked.

"Well, I guess the subject never came up," Glen said.

"The next cage holds my favorites, the birds," Suzy said, pointing toward it. "They flutter around and chirp all day long. Course, the only one I recognize is the yellow parakeet."

"The cobalt-blue one is unbelievable," said Glen, squinting. "His feathers are so bright it almost hurts my eyes to look at him."

"Watch this," Dave said.

He picked up a slice of apple someone had dropped on the ground and walked over to a cage containing a Rhesus monkey. It swung on the bars and chattered at Dave, who held out the piece of apple. The monkey snatched it from Dave's hand and hid in the corner to eat it.

"That's Sammy. Isn't he cute?" Dave said, returning to the line. "He lives in the house half the time, so you'll be seeing a lot of him."

Suzy tugged on Glen's arm. It was their turn. Glen moved forward and picked up two plates.

"Are you hungry?" Dave teased.

"One's for me and one's for Brenda," Glen said.

"That's so sweet," Suzy said.

The spread before them was a sea of varying shades of peach—shrimp, white asparagus with peach Hollandaise sauce, salmon, sliced peaches, Royale Peach Meringue dessert, peach pudding, peach ice-cream, peach-colored deviled eggs, peach sherbet punch...even the French bread had a peach-colored swirl through it.

"I never would have guessed what half of this stuff is. It's lucky there are name cards in front of each dish," Dave said.

Suzy smiled. "Isn't this beautiful? Brenda asked me to be in charge of the food since all this happened on such short notice. I was lucky to get the best caterer in town. Of course, when I told him to make everything he could peach-colored, he looked at me like I was crazy."

Glen grinned. "It's very nice," he said as he made his way down the buffet line, putting a little bit of everything on one plate and very little on the other. He didn't want any of that peach-colored stuff. Glen lifted the lid off a heated dish. "It smells good, but I don't believe I've ever seen peach-colored creamed potatoes before." He placed the lid back on the tureen without dishing any onto his plate.

Suzy frowned.

"Sir, would you like roast beef or ham?" a young man behind the buffet asked.

Glen nodded happily. "Both, please."

Suzy shook her head. "Meat-man, I see."

He nodded. "This looks great," Glen said, then headed over to the head table, which was covered with a lacy peach tablecloth. He set both plates down next to his new in-laws and gave each of them a hug. Then he sat down and began to eat. Looking up, he saw Brenda, Jane and Emily come out of the house and walk toward him.

"There she is, the love of my life, till death do us part," Glen called out.

Brenda smiled tremulously, almost giddy with pride, happiness and love.

CHAPTER THREE

A CAPSULE
OF PEACE

Excusing herself from Emily and Jane, Brenda walked over to Glen. He stood up and embraced her. "I'm starving. I got you a little bit of everything on the buffet table so you wouldn't have to stand in line."

Brenda smiled at him. "How did I get so lucky?"

"It's just a plate of peach-colored food," he shrugged.

"I meant you, silly. I'm so lucky you married me."

"No, I'm the lucky one," he said.

Jane had walked up behind him, holding a plate of food.

"Hi, Jane, would you like to join us?" Brenda asked, then added proudly, "Glen got me my plate."

Jane glanced at Glen and walked around the table to sit by Brenda. "Yes, thank you," she said coolly. She turned her plate to the left, then to the right, where the food was in *just the right place*, picked up her napkin and placed it in her lap. "Could you pass the salt and pepper, please?" she asked Glen.

He scanned the table and saw the shakers hiding behind a bouquet of peachy roses. He looped his fingers around the necks of both shakers and picked them up in one hand, passing them to Jane.

She mumbled "thank you" and sprinkled the salt on her peachy potatoes. Glen was still holding the pepper shaker and he set it down in front of her.

"Brenda says you have a degree in psychology and can practically read her mind," Jane said.

"No. I've just had a few college courses and Brenda's easy to read. Everything she does is to gain love," he said.

"You seem pretty astute to me for just a few courses."

"I wouldn't say that," Glen said to Jane, defensively, "but the courses come in pretty handy in sizing up people." He wiped some barbecue sauce from his hand onto his napkin and continued. "Take you, for instance, a beautiful woman with a chip on her shoulder who flirts with every man in sight. I'd say your daddy probably abandoned you as a child."

Brenda knew he'd struck too close to home. Jane threw her napkin in her plate.

"I don't like this," she said and stomped off.

Brenda started to stand up. She was going to chase after her, but Glen grabbed her hand. "Let her go. She'll come back."

Maybe Glen was right. "How'd you know about her father?" Brenda asked.

"Lucky guess," he said, raising Brenda's hand to his lips. "This is *our* day, not hers."

Brenda looked into his eyes and wondered how she could ever possibly love anyone this much.

Over the next three hours, the wedding guests drank, sang, danced and polished off most of the food. Finally almost everyone had gone home. Glen had been right and Jane had returned. She apologized to Brenda—but not to Glen, although they were polite to each other from then on. They'd all had a good time, but Brenda was ready to be alone with her new husband. She felt the flutter of butterflies in her stomach, just from the anticipation. She wanted their first married night to be special, but she was also nervous about it.

Suzy walked out of the house carrying a large garbage bag. She was going around throwing plastic glasses in it. *Suzy doesn't know when to go home. She still thinks her little sister needs her protection.*

"Suzy, you don't have to do that. You're paying a baby sitter," Brenda said, barely veiling her desire for Suzy to leave.

"Oh no. I'm not leaving you with this mess," she insisted.

"We have someone coming to clean up tomorrow," Brenda said, "and I'm taking tomorrow off."

"You don't want to be paying them a fortune or cleaning on your day off. Besides, I'm too tipsy to drive right now. I'll start covering the food and you clean off the tables," Suzy ordered.

Brenda raced around cleaning counters, sealing food in Saran Wrap and washing dishes as fast as she could. Now, there was only one thing left to do. She didn't like to wash antiques in the dishwasher. They were too easily chipped. So Brenda pulled the antique platter out of the slippery dish water, washed it, rinsed it and placed it in the drainer. She gazed around the kitchen, which was now spotless, and removed her apron.

Suzy came in from outside carrying a paper plate. "I gave Katula the leftover ham scraps. I think I'll be her friend for life."

"Thanks for the help, Sis," Brenda said, giving her sister a hug, "but it is awfully late and your kids are waiting." Brenda walked over and opened the glass door and flipped on the porch light, so there could be no doubt in Suzy's mind that it was time to leave. Suzy picked up her purse and coat and hugged Brenda with her free arm. The fringe on Suzy's sleeves tickled Brenda and she giggled. Suzy told her, "Just remember I love ya," and Brenda answered by rote, "Me too." Brenda didn't wait to see Suzy leave. She swung around and went back in the house. Glen was waiting for her and she went to him.

He brought her a glass of wine. "I have to bathe," she said, smiling shyly and he nodded. Brenda took a warm shower, smoothing the gardenia gel over her body and put on the filmy blue negligee she'd bought. As she came out of the bathroom, she saw the lights were dim. Romantic music was playing. In her dreams, she had seen him pick her up and carry her into the bedroom. Now her dream would become reality.

Brenda took a deep breath. She ran her fingertips over the satin that covered her breasts. She loved the smoothness of satin. It always reminded her of her Senior Prom dress.

Glen sauntered over to her and kissed her neck, her shoulders, her breasts. It felt good. His lips caressed her body as he gently guided her to bed. It had been a long time since anyone had made love to Brenda and she hadn't realized until this moment how much she'd missed it. She wanted him so badly. She felt herself getting moist and recognized the natural scent. Her breathing quickened. The weight of his body increased her pleasure as he climbed on top of her. He rode her, pumping harder and harder until every muscle in her body ached with passion. And in a glorious instant, they climaxed together. She felt their spirits soar into the heavens and float back down to earth in a vibrating capsule of peace.

CHAPTER FOUR

A Nest Egg

During those next few weeks, they settled into married life. Brenda went back to work and Glen began job hunting. At first he seemed confident, but then he began looking discouraged. A month passed, then two, without job offers. Since nothing came through for him, he started fixing up their house and the ranch house Brenda had bought as an investment the year before from her friend Jane, who was now living in it and paying Brenda rent.

On Tuesday, when she had a few free hours, Brenda went over to the ranch house both to see her friend and to look at Glen's handiwork.

"I can't believe all the work Glen's done," Jane said showing Brenda some moldings Glen had replaced. "You know he and I mix like oil and water. You know I don't think he's good enough for you, but he does work hard to improve your life."

Brenda smiled, her pride evident. "You wouldn't believe all he's done at our house. He practically built a three-car garage single-handedly. The only things we had to pay out were for one guy to help spread the cement and a couple more to help with the roofing. The rest Glen did by himself."

"Well, even I will have to admit he's pretty good if he finishes building that barn for my horse," Jane said. "He may really be a good find, Brenda."

Brenda's face turned serious. "He is. I just wish he'd find a job. He's getting antsy. I bought him a brand new Dodge Ram truck and even that hasn't improved his mood."

Jane looked at her. "Where'd you get all of your money? Glen boasted to me that you have two more houses. You never told me any of that."

"I didn't want to brag, especially with all your marital and money problems."

"Brenda, you're always thinking of others first. Maybe you ought to start taking care of you."

Brenda blushed. "I have been taking care of myself, Jane. At least, financially. I'm heavily insured and a while back I started a retirement package savings account. My parents thought it was funny for someone to do that in their twenties, but now I have a tidy nest egg, so when this house came up at a good price, I decided to buy it for a rental property."

"That's using your head. Just how much insurance do you have now?"

"Too much. Because of my bonuses, I have over half a million, and a full million if I die from an accident. And if I don't die, I'll be prepared to retire at age fifty and start an animal sanctuary—larger than the one in my backyard. It's what I've always wanted to do."

"I'll bet you'd be good at that," Jane observed.

Brenda shook her head. "Meanwhile, especially with Glen not bringing in money, I need to work my head off and I'm studying for my biology degree to boot," she sighed.

"Working all the time like this must be hard on your relationship with Glen, especially with him not having regular employment. I wonder why he can't find a job?" Jane's face was inscrutable.

"It seems to be getting harder all the time. Glen is feeling miserable about not working and he says he wants to move to the country. I don't, but—"

Jane broke in, "Well, just remember, I'm a real estate agent, so let me make the commission if you move."

As they sat in the kitchen drinking tea, Brenda was surprised to see Glen walk in.

"Hey honey, what are you doing here?" she said as he bent down to kiss her.

"Finishing the fence. This property is so big it goes on forever. I think Jane's increasing the acreage to keep me busy. Anyway, I came in to get something cool to drink. Jane said I didn't have to die of thirst even though I'm the handyman."

"I'm all heart," Jane said nodding.

Glen took a 7UP from the refrigerator, kissed Brenda again and left saying: "I'll be home before dark."

"He's a pain, but he does have a cute butt," Jane said.

Brenda shook her head. "You think so? I think he's gotten too skinny. He's lost a lot of weight doing all this outdoor work."

"Nope, he certainly is looking good."

"And I think you've been alone too long," Brenda laughed self-consciously, trying to make a joke. She really didn't like her friend making remarks about Glen's body. But she told herself it was just Jane's way of being cute and let the thought go.

"Jane, I've got a long day, so I'll be on my way," Brenda said. "Come over real soon."

"Sure," Jane said as Brenda gathered her things and headed for her car.

At 8:00 P.M., when Brenda got home from her appointments, to her surprise Glen wasn't there, despite his saying he'd be home before dark. She got her biology book, grabbed a sandwich and decided to devote the extra time to study. A short time later she looked up to see Sniffer cock one ear and growl while the dogs outside went into a barking frenzy.

Glen walked in, looking weary and discouraged. Seeing Brenda studying, he complained, "I think you love those damned books and grimy animals more than you do me."

His sudden outburst of anger surprised her. "Glen, I love you more than anything. I'm just trying to better myself."

"Excu-u-use me!" His voice was hurt.

"What's wrong?"

He blurted out, "If you were ever here, you'd know what's wrong."

"I'm here now. Tell me," she said, closing her book.

"Brenda, I have to get a job soon but nobody'll hire 'cause my family hasn't lived here for four generations. This town's so snooty. We've got to get away from here."

"You want to go somewhere for a three-day weekend?" she asked, as she filled a cup with water and put it in the microwave.

"No. I mean move away from here."

"We can't move. Where would we go?"

"To the country where it's quiet and there's nobody around—just you, me and the fireflies."

"We can't afford to buy another house, Glen."

"We could sell this house." His voice had a forlorn tone to it.

"No!"

"Then take $50,000 out of your nest-egg and we'll borrow the rest."

"I don't know." Brenda didn't like dipping into her retirement for anything, especially for something she didn't really need nor want. The microwave timer went off. She took the cup of hot water out and stirred in some Café Vienna coffee. She held it out to Glen.

"Please. I know it's this uppity town that's making me edgy," he said, looking at her with desperation in his eyes.

"I'll think about it," she said softly.

"Please do that," Glen said in a flat tone, staring into his coffee. "I'm going back to our room and try to relax."

She nodded. She knew that asking her for money was hard for him. After all, *he* was the man and he felt *he* should control the finances. *What an archaic notion*, she thought, but she understood that his pride was hurt.

A short while later her thoughts were interrupted when Glen came up behind her and began rubbing her shoulders. It felt good and she rolled her head in an arc to relax the muscles in her neck. Glen moved his hands off her shoulders and onto her neck. That felt good, too.

She stood up and took his hand and led him back to their bedroom. As they undressed, Brenda said, "By the way, Jane thinks you have a cute butt."

He turned and began to tickle her. "You think that's funny, don't you?"

"Maybe she's after you."

He walked over to the bed and lay down. "She'll never

even get near my butt if I have something to say about it," he said curtly. "That...that *woman* treats me like a servant."

"Well, she is a lot of talk, but she's beautiful," Brenda sighed, "and a flirt."

"The only one I want to flirt with is you," Glen smiled. "Come here." He crooked his finger.

"So, you think that's all you have to do to get me, don't you?"

"Come a little closer and I'll show you that you're my wife and I can do anything to you I want because I love you."

Brenda lay down beside him. "I love you, too," she said.

CHAPTER FIVE

MONDAY MORNING

Brenda checked her watch; it was 8:45. She climbed out of her car and pulled a roll of quarters out of her pocket. She fed quarters into the parking meter in front of the Crown Center and surveyed the structure. It was a classic mixture of grayish brick and glass. Just then, an old couple walked past her. The old man was hunched over, holding the old woman's arm. Brenda noticed she had an obvious limp and used a cane.

"You must watch out for that crack," the old man warned his wife.

"Oh, Harry," she said, "I'm not a child."

"But I still want to protect you," he said. They were walking toward a place in the sidewalk where the cement had a two-inch rise. Brenda watched the old woman stop as her husband tightened his arm supportively and helped the woman place her foot up along the crack, feeling until her footing was steady on the other side. Then she stepped over.

Brenda smiled. *They're so sweet together. Glen and I will be like that some day.*

Brenda took a small black suitcase on wheels out of her trunk and hurried toward the building.

Once inside the marble foyer, she made it into a waiting elevator, punched twenty-three and waited for the door to close. When she reached the twenty-third floor, the bell dinged and she stepped off. The offices were extravagantly decorated with expensive oriental furnishings. Brenda didn't normally like oriental stuff, but these were superb.

The receptionist sat at a crescent-shaped desk that had a gorgeous dragon carved on the face of it. The phone rang and she answered, "Morgan Enterprises." She took down a message and hung up. There was an inlaid mother-of-pearl altar against one wall with an ancient dragon-shaped ship sitting atop it. It was made of elaborately carved ivory. On the opposite wall was thick frosted glass with an etching of a Japanese geisha. She was standing on a cliff; the wind was blowing her kimono and swirling her hair. It was beautiful.

"May I help you?" the young Asian woman behind the desk asked. She had straight, gleaming black hair and the most beautiful complexion Brenda had ever seen.

"Yes. I'm Brenda Brumbaugh from Associated Mutual. I have a nine o'clock appointment with Mr. Morgan," Brenda said.

"I'll let him know you're here," the receptionist said and with a smile motioned for Brenda to take a seat.

Brenda sniffed a bud vase on the reception desk containing white cymbidium orchids. They were beautiful, but the smell wasn't very strong or pleasing. Brenda sank into a soft leather sofa. She heard the young woman punch in the numbers on her switchboard and speak into her headset, "Your nine o'clock is here."

The receptionist walked over. "Mr. Morgan will see you now. I'll show you the way."

"I'd appreciate it."

Brenda peered at the young woman. *Odd, she looks like she should have those little, silver dangling things in her hair like the geisha dolls have, not a microphone headset.* She was lovely, but she'd obviously had plastic surgery on her eyes to make them look more Caucasian. *What a shame that she felt it was necessary to change her looks to "fit in," or to fit someone else's idea of "beautiful."*

Brenda stood up and began dragging her medical case behind her, but had trouble pulling the wheeled case on the thick carpet. Finally, exasperated with the effort, she picked it up and carried it the rest of the way. She followed the receptionist down a hall making a right turn at the end. Then the receptionist pointed and said, "Continue down this corridor. It's the third door on your left." Brenda thanked her and continued on her own to Mr. Morgan's office. Entering the room, she looked around.

His office was the complete opposite of the elegant outer office. It looked like it had been decorated by Andy Warhol. Everything was in primary colors. A red sofa in the shape of lips was framed by a canary yellow wall. The carpet throughout the room was royal blue. Brenda felt she'd been thrown back into a time warp of the seventies. From the ceiling, a giant Calder mobile twirled slowly, propelled only by the flow coming out of the air-conditioning vent.

"Mr. Morgan?" Brenda called. "I'm Brenda Brumbaugh from Associated Mutual. I'm here to do the medical exam for your new policy."

"Be right with you," said a male voice, coming from behind a cracked door. "Fix yourself a drink, if you want."

Brenda was startled by the offer—it was only nine in the morning. She snooped around a mirrored mini-bar. Suspended above the crystal decanters was a bright-yellow plastic cat holding a real fiddle and a cow jumping over a moon. The moon was lit up, of course.

This guy's got some weird art. I bet he paid a fortune for this stuff.

Brenda heard him clear his throat and she turned. Mr. Morgan stood there in nothing but his silk boxer shorts, holding a jar filled with urine. He was fiddling with his watch, mumbling something about Kuala Lumpur having an eleven-hour time difference. Brenda was glad there was a lid on it so he couldn't spill the specimen.

Mr. Morgan was fiftyish, tall, super skinny and surprisingly stylish. His black hair was slicked back and he had a good looking but oily quality about him. His sideburns were gray and his nose, she noticed, had the ruptured vessels frequently indicative of alcoholism. *Not a great bet to recommend for insurance.*

Brenda was a bit taken back by the sight of him. She'd never had anyone meet her in his underwear before. She told herself it was all part of her job, gritted her teeth and marched up to him.

He smiled at her. "Russell Morgan, at your service."

"I'll take that," she said, reaching for the urine sample. She unscrewed the lid and plopped a thermometer in it.

"Why'd you do that?" he asked.

"We register the temperature to make sure it's fresh from the body. Drug addicts like to try to fool us by giving us somebody else's urine."

"Was I supposed to be in the buff?" Mr. Morgan asked, smiling.

She shook her head, "No, you didn't even have to strip down to your underwear, but let's get started. I have a parking meter ticking away downstairs."

She unpacked the blood pressure cuff from her medical case and wrapped it around his arm. She squeezed the pump and noticed that with each squeeze he moaned.

"This isn't hurting is it?" she asked.

"No," he said, his voice strange.

Is he getting off on this? Brenda wondered as she wrote his blood pressure on the chart. She checked the temperature of the urine, wrote it on the chart, sealed the specimen jar and placed it in her medical kit. She took a measuring tape from her pocket and began measuring his chest.

Brenda started her regular spiel. "The insurance company pays me for the exam. You don't have to worry about getting a bill. They just want to make sure you're healthy before they issue the policy. Do you have any questions, Mr. Morgan?"

Mr. Morgan watched her measure his chest, "Yes. What're you doing that for?"

"It's just part of the exam," Brenda said frowning as she scribbled his measurement on the chart.

"That's not the part of me you ought to be measuring," he said. Brenda grimaced and turned away. She hated those kinds of comments. She punched the start button on her portable EKG machine.

"You're really cute," he said.

Oh damn, he's going to hit on me. She turned back to face him and took a deep breath. "Mr. Morgan, I'll need to draw some blood."

"Mine is sapphire blue just like my Jaguar, which is, by the way, right out front in case you'd like to join me for lunch."

Brenda shook her head, jabbed a needle in his arm and started drawing a blood sample. All the while, Morgan was staring at her. "Looks red to me, Mr. Mor—"

"Ah, ah, ah," he admonished, wagging his finger at her. "You can call me Russ."

She quickly labeled the vials of blood and stuck them in her medical case.

"You like sushi?" he asked.

"Can't say that I do, *Mr. Morgan*," she said, quietly. Brenda put away her tools and peeked over at the EKG printout of the peaking chart.

"I love it. I missed it bad in prison. They don't serve inmates sushi. It's such a shame. My favorite is eel. O-o-ow e-e-e-e! It's as good as sex and I'm extra hungry. But maybe not as good as you." Morgan smiled and reached for her. But she was quick and slipped away. *Oh great, not only is he a pervert, he's an ex-con pervert. Well, I'll fix him good.*

"Please put your hand up here and close your eyes," Brenda told him.

He obeyed her every command. Brenda switched the EKG machine to *CODE BLUE*. She lightly touched one of the paddles and Mr. Morgan's hand at the same time. The machine sent an electrical charge through her and into him. He jerked around, as if he were having a seizure. Brenda pressed the *STOP* button on the machine and removed her finger from the paddle. Mr. Morgan stood there.

"O-o-ow e-e-e-e-! That's pretty potent!" he said and collapsed onto the sofa. Grabbing a cigarette from the end table, he lit it and inhaled deeply. Without another word, Brenda finished packing her equipment, walked out and slammed the door.

When she strode out of the building, she saw a blue Jaguar parked in the loading zone and figured it had to be Morgan's. "Well, at least he was right about the color," she murmured. She walked around to the back to get the license plate number. "Oh, that'll be easy to remember," she laughed under her breath. The vanity plate read MORGAN.

She felt unnerved when she came home later that evening and told Glen about her unusual patient. His response was immediate. The vein in his temple began throbbing, and a diamond shaped patch on his brow turned white. She had never seen him so angry before. The rest of his face was bright red, except for the patch. "I think I'll go over there and teach that guy some manners right now," he said.

"Thank you for wanting to protect me, but it's alright, darling. I shouldn't be surprised by anything. Not everyone I deal with behaves professionally, but this guy was a bit of a nut." She winced. "Anyway, I make a lot of money even if some problems come with the territory."

His eyes had narrowed. "I don't like some jerk hitting on my wife."

"I don't like it either," she said, "but I have this house to pay off and all the rest of the stuff. Look, I'm sure you'll be getting a great position very soon and then maybe I can pick and choose my clients." She put her arms around him. "Let's forget my day and concentrate on us." He nodded and they walked arm and arm toward the bedroom.

But the next morning when she got into her car to drive to work, she didn't like what she saw in her rearview mirror. It was Mr. Morgan's Jaguar. He grinned and waved as he drove past. Brenda ignored him. *It's best not to react in any way to this sort of thing. If I act scared or angry it gives him power over me and will probably encourage him. If I ignore him, he might just go away. He's probably just infatuated with me. I think he'll give up pretty soon if I don't encourage him.*

When she saw Morgan's car had rounded the corner

and was out of sight, she began to slowly back out of the driveway. She thought of going back to tell Glen, but he had reacted so badly the night before she didn't want to upset him again. *Anyway, I've handled other guys who've tried to put the moves on me. I can handle this one.*

The rest of her workweek inched by. Late on Friday afternoon, she went to see her favorite client, Almeira Punchak, who had been in Florida with her cousin. She'd missed her. Brenda stared sadly at Mrs. P.'s green bedroom door. She knew her client was dying of cancer. They both knew it, but Brenda had grown to love the old lady over the past years. She couldn't bring herself to call her Mrs. Punchak anymore. It seemed too formal.

When they'd first met, Mrs. P. had been a strong, dynamic, single woman buying insurance. Though there'd been a huge age difference between them, they had bonded and become friends. Brenda had watched her weaken in the last year. She had given away most of her valuable jewelry, paintings, antique furniture and oriental carpets. Brenda had even called an attorney to come to Mrs. P.'s bedside to write her Last Will and Testament and she'd helped Mrs. P. make the arrangements for her funeral. Looking at her now, Brenda saw that she'd worsened. All that was left for Brenda to do was to make her friend comfortable, help her keep what dignity she had left and bring some human warmth to her otherwise drab days.

Brenda sucked in her breath. The place smelled of disinfectant and Brenda made a mental note to bring Mrs. P. some perfume. She prepared herself for what awaited her on the other side of the door and entered in a swirl of gaiety.

"Good morning, Mrs. P. How was your night? Close

your eyes," Brenda said. She threw back the wooden shutters and shafts of light streamed into the room.

As was her routine, she flipped on the coffeepot and radio, which were kept on the bedside table so Mrs. P. could easily reach them. Soft classical music spilled into the farthest corners of the bedroom. Brenda turned to face her patient. She took Mrs. P.'s bony wrist in her hand and began to take her pulse.

Mrs. P. was in her late seventies, although, when asked, Mrs. P. said she was sixty-nine and three-quarters. It was her way of letting people know it was none of their business. Of course, she'd been sixty-nine and three-quarters for almost a decade now.

Brenda looked at her friend today. Even though it was a familiar site, she was still a bit horrified. The woman had skin cancer, which had attacked her nose. The doctors had cut away as much of the disease as they could and sent her home. They'd mentioned getting a prosthesis, but Mrs. P. figured it was a useless expense if she was going to die soon anyway.

Brenda peered into the old lady's soft-brown eyes and smiled, "How are you feelin' today?"

Mrs. P. mustered a weak, "Okay."

It was a lie and Brenda knew it by looking at the dark circles under the old woman's eyes. She suspected Mrs. P. probably had gotten almost no sleep. The coffee maker began dripping. The smell was making Brenda hungry and her stomach growled.

"Skip lunch again?" Mrs. P. asked.

Brenda nodded and let her eyes travel down to the woman's wounded nose. The entire right nostril was gone. A bloody membrane outlined the groove that used to be covered by the outer nose. Yellowish mucous clogged the nasal passage where it went into the head and when the old lady exhaled, the mucous formed a gooey bubble. Then when she breathed in, it retracted. Brenda snatched a tissue from the bedside table and wiped the mucous away.

"Did you take your antibiotics last night?" Brenda asked.

Mrs. P. nodded that she had.

"You sure are quiet today."

"Got nothing new to say," Mrs. P. mumbled.

"Well, I've got good news. The Doctor's coming to visit around dinnertime."

"On a weekday?"

"Yep."

"Does he have bad news?" Mrs. P. asked. Brenda could tell she was trying to keep the worry out of her voice.

"Nope," Brenda laughed. "He told me he was taking the week off but wanted to see you first," Brenda said.

"Y'all know something I don't?"

"Don't ask me. Doc's the expert," Brenda teased.

As Brenda washed Mrs. P.'s face, she thought about the pictures she'd found in the old china cabinet in the dining room. One was of a string of girls dressed in old-fashioned pantaloon type swimsuits. Mrs. P. was in the center holding roses. The gold caption underneath read, Miss Missouri 1939. Mrs. P. had been a real beauty in her day, with strawberry blond hair and a full but lovely figure. Now, the old woman was almost bald from the chemotherapy and so thin Brenda could see all the veins and arteries through the tissue paper she called skin.

"We're going to fix you up real pretty today," Brenda said, as she dabbed at Mrs. P.'s nose with betadine solution and began applying makeup to her sunken cheeks. Brenda always tried to keep Mrs. P. in touch with the outside world. She knew Mrs. P. especially liked hearing the town gossip.

Brenda covered the old woman's liver spots with foundation as she talked.

"You hear the latest gossip yet?"

Mrs. P.'s eyes filled with mischief. "Is it more about Charlie Carson and that stripper?"

"No. It's better. Guess who rumor says is having an affair!"

"All I know is it isn't me," Mrs. P. teased.

"Judge Carson and the new female deputy. I heard it from Jane."

"I guess if it's true, that will put a stop to the rumor that she and the judge don't get along," Mrs. P. said.

"Yep. You're a pistol," Brenda laughed.

"Geez-Louise, who knows what to believe?" Mrs. P. went on, lifting her neck for Brenda to smooth on makeup. "Have you seen her yet?"

"No, but Jane has. Jane says she's attractive, fortiesh and redheaded. Apparently she says she's a *feminist* and wants to run for sheriff in the next election."

"She's got my vote. Any woman who's got the gall to stand up in these parts and say something like that—"

Brenda nodded her agreement and Mrs. P. continued. "A feminist! Can you believe it? That's as bold as admitting you're the one who left your panties hanging on the bull's horn on top of the Holden Meat Plant."

"You're too much," Brenda said and they laughed hysterically. Brenda wiped the tears of laughter from her eyes and Mrs. P. was holding her ribs.

When Brenda finally got control of herself, she said, "She plans to come down hard on wife beaters, too."

"That's might-near every man in the county," Mrs. P. frowned. "Say, isn't she the daughter of that woman Congressman?"

Brenda nodded. She took a step back and looked at her handiwork. "Mrs. P., you're lookin' good."

The coffee was ready and Brenda poured them both a cup. Brenda sniffed her own, as she handed Mrs. P. hers. It was a special blend that had a vanilla smell to it. "You want anything in that?"

"I'd love some Irish Cream," Mrs. P. said, sweetly.

"I meant cream or sugar." Brenda acted as if she was surprised by the request. She removed the bottle of Bailey's Irish Cream from under the bed. Mrs. P. held out the steaming cup and Brenda poured a little liquor in it.

"Why don't you pour yourself a little nip?" Mrs. P. suggested.

"You know I'm on duty," Brenda said, as she replaced the lid and slid the bottle back under the bed.

Mrs. P. covered the exposed nostril with one hand and used the other one to lift her coffee cup.

"Does it still hurt when the steam rises on your nose?"

"Like the dickens," Mrs. P. said, then took a sip of coffee.

"Let's put a bandage on. That'll help," Brenda said and made a bandage out of beige athletic tape. She attached it to Mrs. P.'s face and covered it with makeup. When she was done, the bandage was barely noticeable. Then Brenda reached into her handbag and pulled out a handful of nail polish bottles. "Which one do you like?"

Mrs. P. was fingering them all, turning them and shaking them to see their true colors. She seemed to get such enjoyment out of the decision making process. Brenda thought it was funny that such a small thing could bring her so much pleasure. Finally, a pretty pink having been chosen, she began to trim Mrs. P.'s toenails.

Brenda brushed the half-moon toenail clippings off

the sheet and into the trashcan then carefully applied the polish. Now, with her toes all pretty pink, Mrs. P.'s feet were neat and tidy looking. Brenda untied the apron from around her waist and folded it carefully.

Then she told Mrs. P. her own news.

"Mrs. P., I want you to know I've gotten married." Brenda pulled the clean sheet over Mrs. P.'s feet. It arced like a parachute and filled the air with the lemon scent of the fabric softener. "The ceremony was when you were in Florida, otherwise I would have invited you," Brenda said graciously.

Mrs. P. smiled. "That's wonderful, but, I guess you won't have time for me now." The old woman had a wistful look on her face.

"I'll always have time for you, Mrs. P."

Brenda told her all about Glen and the wedding.

"Brenda, you deserve happiness. But I know how hard you work, maybe too hard," Mrs. P. said. "Why don't you go home early today?"

"That's really nice of you." Brenda smiled, knowing her friend was giving her the ultimate gift, the little time Mrs P. still had left for companionship. "I believe I will."

At home, Brenda found Glen in the laundry room washing the clothes. He'd turned half their white socks, underwear and T-shirts pink and Brenda figured it was time to rescue him.

"You want to wash my uniform?" she asked.

"May as well," he said pouring soap into the washer.

She began to undress and handed him her clothes. The dryer had tennis shoes inside and they went *ker-plunk, ker-plunk, ker-plunk*...Brenda had on her new bra and panties.

"I read in *Cosmo* that lots of women achieve orgasm by sitting on a warm, hard...dryer," he said in a sexy voice. "Wanna try it?"

Blushing, she nodded. He helped her climb onto the dryer and began to kiss her neck and breasts. She thought it'd be more comfortable in the bed and started to hop down from the dryer.

"Stay there. I want to see if *Cosmo's* right."

"If you desire it I'm sure you'll make it come true," she smiled.

He laughed, scooted a step stool over and stepped up. It made him just the right height. He unfastened his pants and let them drop to the floor. Brenda felt the heat of the dryer on her butt and crotch. *Ker-plunk...ker-plunk...ker-plunk...ker-plunk...*The rhythmic vibration of the drying shoes sent ripples through her body. She wanted him and she could tell he wanted her. *Ker-plunk...ker-plunk...ker-plunk...*She was moist and ready and he was full and firm. *Ker-plunk...ker-plunk...ker-plunk...*They kept time to the rhythmic ker-plunk of the shoes and discovered that women really could reach orgasm on a dryer.

The only problem with sex on a dryer was there was nowhere for afterglowing. So they wound up on the floor on top of the dirty laundry, snuggling.

"That was wonderful," Brenda said. "I'm going to have those tennis shoes bronzed as a memento."

He laughed. "Think I should write *Cosmo* a thank-you letter?"

"I would," she laughed. "Whatever you want."

"I'm glad you said that. You need to lighten up and have some fun. There's someplace I want to take you," he said.

CHAPTER SIX

THE CARNIVAL

Brenda found herself with Glen at the Somerset Carnival. In an attempt to raise money for a new building, The Joy Fellowship Church had brought a carnival to town. It was set up on the vacant lot where the new facility would be built. Brenda had actually nailed the flyers on phone poles around town announcing the fund-raiser, but she hadn't planned on going.

She could hardly believe that *this* was where Glen wanted to go. Brenda hadn't been to a carnival since she was a teenager. Now she almost felt like that girl again. But this time she was there with the best looking guy in town instead of just watching others.

It was a delicious spring night. A cool breeze brushed their faces and any other body parts that were exposed, making them comfortable. Carousel music filled the air and lifted their spirits.

In the cloudless sky above them stars sparkled. It seemed to Brenda, as they moved upward on the Ferris wheel, she could reach up and grab a few. Between the shining stars and the dappled blue lights lining the Ferris wheel, it was very romantic. Their seat stopped at the very top and Glen gave her a long, lingering kiss. Brenda didn't catch her breath until they were on the ground.

Glen pulled her behind as he rushed to the roller coaster. "I love the excitement of careening down," he said. In fact, he wanted to ride all the scary rides, while Brenda's tastes leaned more toward the carousel. When she screamed loudly on the roller coaster, he covered her mouth with his own and then rained little kisses all over her face.

They ate corn-dogs, cotton candy, corn-on-the-cob and drank lemonade. And they rode the Zipper, the Hammer and the Death Trails before Brenda felt sick to her stomach and couldn't manage the rides any more.

"Come on, let's play some of the games," he said.

Brenda crossed her arms and stood at Glen's side as he played games. She was hoping that her mere presence would make him hurry and take her home. It didn't work. Her back was beginning to ache from all the bouncing on the rides, but she didn't want to spoil his fun. She watched him raise the basketball and pitch it toward the hoop. The ball spun around the rim and fell outside the net.

"Dammit to hell," Glen growled.

Brenda gasped in surprise. Glen rarely cursed and certainly not in public.

The old barker lowered his eyes, "Say Bud, we're here for the church. Watch your language."

Glen stiffened and the muscles in his neck bulged. He shrugged and said, "Sorry, I forgot."

He threw another basketball and it bounced off the rim. Glen slapped his leg in frustration and spun on his heels. That's when Brenda saw him staring at a rifle stand two booths down.

"Now that's something I'm good at," he said and started toward the booth.

Brenda grabbed his arm, "Maybe we should go, Glen. It's getting late." He shook her off and continued toward the booth.

"I don't like guns."

Glen stepped up to the counter. "These aren't even real," he said, grabbing a rifle.

The young barker who ran the rifles had been watching them with interest. His attitude said he knew a customer when he saw one. "You look pretty strong, Mister. How many rounds?"

Brenda figured the young guy with the rough complexion from teenage acne was probably seventeen or eighteen.

"Give me twenty dollars worth," Glen said, slapping a twenty-dollar bill in the boy's hand.

The barker shot a glance at Brenda and smirked. "Alright!"

Men are like children, she thought. She bit her lip, annoyed, but didn't say anything.

Glen aimed the rifle and shot. The pellet went into the target's second circle from the center.

"Your site's off. Is that how you bring in a little extra cash?" Glen asked the barker.

The boy kicked the dirt, hung his head and said, "I don't know nuthin' about it."

"Well, I'll just take care of it then." Glen made some adjustments to the site and shot again. Bull's-eye.

Brenda caught someone out of the corner of her eye. He was pointing his finger like a gun at Glen. She turned to see who it was and saw a tall, thin man with slicked back black hair disappear into the crowd. She hugged herself around the waist. An eerie feeling came over her. She feared the man was Mr. Morgan.

Glen kept shooting in rapid succession. Every pellet went into the bull's-eye. He turned to Brenda.

"I have one shot left. Come on up here, Darlin', and shoot this thing."

"Please, I don't want to shoot it, Glen," she said shuddering.

"Aw, come on. It won't hurt ya," he said and scooped his hand around the back of her neck to bring her to him.

"I really don't want to!" Brenda planted her feet, so he couldn't pull her to him.

Glen fired the rifle, while still glaring at her. It went into the center of the target.

"See," he said. "I don't even have to look at the target to get a bull's-eye." Glen turned to the barker, "Give me twenty dollars more."

"I can't, Mister. You done won enough. You're gonna get me in trouble with my boss as it is."

"I said twenty dollars!" He slammed down the rifle.

"No," the young man said, with a quiver in his voice.

"I don't see a sign saying there's a limit!" Glen said, angrily grabbing the barker by the collar. He was bringing back his fist to strike the boy when Brenda screamed.

"Let him go! Glen, let him go!"

Brenda grabbed Glen's arm and stopped the blow right before it touched the barker's face.

Glen gave an angry shove as he let him go and the barker stumbled backward. Glen pointed to a giant green dinosaur. "I want that one," he said.

The frightened teenager pulled the dinosaur from the line and handed it to Glen.

Glen turned around, handed the stuffed toy to Brenda, then sauntered off.

"I'm sorry," Brenda murmured to the barker, then she fell in line behind Glen.

"What's the matter? What's gotten into you? Why did you act like that?" she asked, confused.

"Shut up!" he screamed at her.

His eyes were glassy and full of rage. The white diamond on his temple was pulsing. He stomped off ahead of her. Brenda had never seen Glen like this before and she wasn't sure how to handle him. She wanted to talk out their problems, but she figured she'd better wait until he cooled down.

"I'm going home," he called over his shoulder. "You coming?"

She nodded and silently followed Glen out of the carnival grounds.

CHAPTER SEVEN

A HOUSE
IN THE COUNTRY

They drove home from the carnival without speaking and slept, for the first time, on separate edges of the bed.

But when she woke the next day to a gorgeous blue-sky morning and went out to the kitchen, she found a cooked breakfast plus a beautiful bouquet of red roses awaiting her. Next to them was a note, "Forgive me for acting like a child. Remember I'll never stop loving you. I have to go to yet another job interview."

She sat down at the table and took the top from the tureen. Under it was a delicious omelet with crisp bacon by its side. As she nibbled on the food, her mind darted about. She knew Glen was nervous and ashamed because he hadn't found a job yet. Perhaps all the frustration had built up, causing him to explode last night. Yes, that had to be it. Everything else had been going so well. Glen had just snapped under the pressure.

She mulled it over for the next few days and decided she had to help him. It was tough coming to a small town like this where strangers were tolerated, but not welcomed. Where people hired those they knew from childhood, not those they'd never seen before a few months ago.

Brenda sat pondering the problem. Suddenly she knew what she had to do. Her sister Suzy was managing Billy Gunn Motors, the car dealership their father owned. Sales would be a perfect job for Glen. She could call her dad direct. She knew he would do whatever she wanted, but that would put Suzy's nose out of joint. No, she had to go through her sister. Their parents were on vacation, so this would be the perfect time.

Brenda dressed quickly. She had a lot of physical exams to do. This was going to be another late day. Luckily, though, she didn't have an appointment until eleven, but after that they stretched into the evening. Anyway, she had time to go down to the dealership first.

It wasn't going to be easy for her. She hated asking anybody, even her own family, for help. She knew most people found it unpleasant because it made them look weak, but that wasn't it for her. Brenda just didn't want to impose. She figured people had their own agendas and didn't have time to help her.

"Hi, Sis," she said entering the huge showroom.

"What are you doing here?" Suzy asked, raising her eyebrows.

"Well, that's just it. It's just that, well..."

Suzy put her finger on her cheek. "Brenda, stop hem-hawin' and spit it out."

Brenda swallowed, "It's Glen."

Suzy motioned her into the cubicle she used for an office.

Brenda sighed. Suzy always got right to the point, and even though Brenda knew it was impossible for Suzy to understand why other people couldn't, it still irritated her.

"Do you think you could, uh, give Glen a job here at the dealership?"

"I don't know. I don't do the hiring—Dad does."

"Just forget I asked," Brenda said apologetically.

"Will you let me finish? I was going to say, I'd talk to Daddy and put in a good word for Glen," Suzy continued. "I swear, you're just like mama. She always feels guilty as sin just for asking somebody to pass the salt."

"Thanks for making it easy for me to ask," Brenda said, giving her sister an affectionate pat on the hand. "I'm hoping if he gets a job, he'll feel better about himself and he'll stop saying we should move."

Suzy shook her finger in Brenda's face as if she were a four-year-old child. "Don't you let him talk you into selling that house! It's paid for and every gal needs a little security, just in case life doesn't deal her a winning hand."

With those pearls of wisdom, Suzy jumped up from her desk. "Well, time to get back to keeping up my million sales a year image," she rolled her eyes. "Come on," she laughed, motioning to Brenda.

Brenda joined Suzy and they did their traditional hip bumping routine. Both women giggled like teenagers.

A week later her dad returned and a few days after that he called to offer Glen a job. Glen reluctantly accepted. Brenda thought now that Glen finally was working, even though it was for her father, and was making some money of his own, his depression would lift. However, it didn't. Over the next few weeks, his mood swings actually became worse. He was staying out late too many nights and began pestering her again to sell the house she had taken such pains to fix up and move to the country.

Finally, to make him feel better, she offered to call

Jane to show them some places. That Saturday, the three of them headed out. Jane was driving; Brenda sat in the passenger seat and Glen was in the back of the car looking at photos and descriptions of the house they were going to see. When they had been driving over an hour, Jane sighed. "According to these directions," she glanced at her notebook, "we're getting close. Keep your eyes peeled for a gravel road going back to the west. It's road 370. Maybe it's this one coming up."

"That's it," Glen called out. "I can see the sign. Turn right there," he pointed up ahead.

After the turn, they headed down a gravel road.

"Now it's on your right, approximately one mile."

Jane darted a glance at Brenda. "Are you sure you want to live this far out? You'll have quite a commute and your nearest neighbors are miles away."

Brenda was silent.

"Jane, don't start trouble," Glen broke in. "I grew up in the country. I can't stand the city. Besides, Brenda keeps coming home with more pets and they need to be out where they can run around."

"What did she bring home now?" Jane laughed.

"Another homeless dog. This one's a female Doberman pinscher. Brenda claims she brought this one for me."

"I did. Her name is Frances and she was born on Glen's birthday. And when she gets a little older, we can raise puppies."

Suddenly Glen called out, "There it is! It looks just like the picture!" Huge trees and a drive dotted with daffodils and flowering forsythias lead to a large, two-story Normandy style home.

"God, you have to have good eyes to see past all these trees," Brenda said.

Jane, an adroit sales associate, acted as if she already knew their decision. "If you buy this, what are you going to do with your house?"

"Brenda wants to rent it out in case she hates country living, but I want her to sell it and commit to our new secluded life."

"Well, if you decide to sell—" Jane said.

Glen cut her off, "I know," he said. "Let you make the commission."

"Well, somebody's got to make it. It might as well be me." Jane parked the car.

They got out and walked to the front door. Jane put her key in the lock box and they all went inside.

Gesturing expansively, Jane began to point out the house's features. Brenda thought she knew the place awfully well for someone who had seemed not to know how to get there. She shrugged. Of course, it was Jane's job to know all about a property before she showed it, even if she didn't have the chance to see it in person first.

"I like these patio doors going across the front of the house," Glen said excitedly.

Brenda's mood lifted. "I love this. Look at the size of this living room. It would really show off my collections and take in that clean wood smell."

Jane nodded, "That's because nobody's been smoking in it yet. Glen, don't you smoke?"

"I've been trying to quit. Brenda, I promise, if we move out here I'm gonna give it up."

"You ought to. There are twelve acres of wood behind this place," she said.

"Well, what do you think?" Jane asked as they walked into a huge bathroom with a dressing room area.

"I have to say I like it," Brenda said. "This is a real step up from our bathroom where you can hardly turn around and this tub here is big enough for two." She winked at Glen.

They walked toward the sunroom.

Glen was ecstatic. "And I'll build you a separate house out here for your big cats and an aviary. I'll build myself a workshop and I can make you a huge garden. Maybe we'll even get some chickens and—"

"Wait a minute, you haven't signed the papers yet," Jane said.

"Okay," Brenda took a deep breath. "So what would we have to do next?"

"First we have to make them an offer. I'll take care of that if you'll trust me."

"You're my best friend. Of course I trust you. I just need a little time to think about this. It's a big move and really expensive."

"What about you, Glen?" Jane said softly.

"I'm all for it." He looked back at Jane for a long moment. "I guess this is the first time you and I have agreed on something, but Brenda controls the purse strings," he said curtly. "We'll have to wait if that's what she wants," he said bitterly and walked out of the house without another word and got into the car.

"I'm sorry," Brenda said embarassedly to her friend. "We'd better go."

"Glen, I didn't say no." No one said anything. "I just said I needed some time," Brenda said on the way home. "I talked to Suzy about selling our house and she doesn't think I should."

Glen's temper flared. "That's the damn problem, Brenda. I'm your husband, not Suzy, and I want to get out of that house and that's all there is to it."

"But I—"

"Oh, shut up. We'll discuss it at home," he said.

For the rest of the trip no one said a word.

It was twilight when they arrived home and then, just as Glen and Brenda began to get out of Jane's car, a blue convertible which had been parked by the side of the road, the motor idling, came out like a shot, nearly knocking the two of them over. Russell Morgan leaned out the window and, as if he were a friend playing a practical joke, waved to them as the car sped by.

"Damn nut," Glen muttered to Brenda. "He's been doing that all week. I don't like being watched or teased. You'd better tell your boss to do something about that guy or I will."

CHAPTER EIGHT

A FIERY PLAN

He knew her habits from careful and stealthy observation. He knew how she usually drank a warm glass of milk before bed, sitting at the kitchen table and looking over her appointments for the next day in her blue book. He knew what time she usually woke, the time she allotted for dressing and a quick breakfast. He knew how she scheduled her first appointments for late morning. And he knew where she kept the spare key for the house.

Quietly letting himself in, he went straight into the kitchen and washed the milk glass in case there was residue from the sleeping pills he'd peppered the milk with the previous day. Then he went over to the refrigerator, took out the milk container, poured the remainder in the sink and rinsed it out as well, collapsing it to put it in the garbage. Next he dried the milk glass and placed it in the cabinet.

"Don't worry, sweet Brenda. I'm definitely not going to wake you up," he said to himself and started humming, "You Are So Beautiful To Me."

He looked under the sink and pulled out a bottle of rubbing alcohol. He'd placed it there several days before when no one was home. Afterward, he lay on the floor and stuck his upper body under the sink. It was a tight fit, but he made it. He'd done it before so he knew he could. He removed a trap door at the back of the sink. It was intended to be used by plumbers to reach pipes when they needed repair, but he had hidden something in the space between the trap door and the outside wall. He pushed aside the insulation, reached in and felt around. Finally, he snagged what he was feeling for and pulled out a box. The label read CALCIUM CARBIDE.

He replaced the trap door and climbed out from under the sink. He stood, picked up the box, happily tossed it in the air, turned around and caught it behind his back. He chuckled because the move reminded him of a majorette.

Stop fooling around and get on with it.

He quietly walked to the bathroom door and listened. Silence greeted him. He opened the box, pulled a mask over his nose and mouth and began to sling the calcium carbide into the air. The fine, gray powder with its acidic smell settled on the floor, furniture, everything. It left a ghostly dust throughout the house.

He went back to the kitchen, removed his mask and took a soda from the fridge. He swished it around in his mouth and spit it out in the sink. His mouth was dry and he wanted to wash any of the carbide residues out before he took a drink. He took a sip and swallowed.

Then he grabbed the rubbing alcohol, opened it and poked a rag in the top of the bottle. He could smell the astringent smell of the alcohol and wondered how much would evaporate before he set it on fire. He took it to the hallway leading to the bedroom. He stood there trying to decide the best placement of the alcohol bottle.

He wanted the fire to start near the bedroom, but it needed to spread just enough to the living room that the firemen would douse water on it. Once wet, the calcium carbide would burn like hell. The more water the firemen put on it, the more it would burn. When it was all over, there would be nothing left.

He decided to set the alcohol bottle in the middle of the hallway right outside the bedroom. He struck a match and lit the rag. The fire caught quickly. There was no doubt in his mind that the fire would continue to spread. He promptly walked out of the house.

Driving rapidly, he came to the corner, but didn't stop. Another vehicle came out of nowhere. He threw on his brakes and swerved. The other car screeched to a halt, barely missing him.

If I had the time, I'd stop and give that jerk a piece of my mind.

Instead, he kept on going. He looked at himself in his rearview mirror and smiled. *Perfect,* he thought. *A perfect alibi. You are one damned smart fellow.* He chuckled to himself.

As he drove on, he envisioned the flames that would come sprawling across the carpet, licking the draperies, expanding to other rooms and finally becoming a massive fireball. He could almost hear it crackling. He checked his watch. He was running late. He only had fifteen minutes to substantiate his alibi. He put his foot to the floor hoping he wouldn't pass any cops.

He rounded the corner, slowed and calmly pulled into the 7-Eleven parking lot. He checked his watch again. *Right on time.* Actually he'd driven the distance in less time than his practice runs.

He parked as far away from the phone booth as he

could, which was easy to do since morning commuters were coming and going like bees to a hive.

More people are hooked on coffee than booze. I sure am glad of that today.

It worked just as he had planned. He easily got lost in the crowd in the parking lot and didn't even go inside. He ambled over to the phone, pulled a quarter, a small piece of paper with a phone number on it and a handkerchief from his pocket. He inserted the quarter and dialed, placing the handkerchief over the mouthpiece.

While the phone was ringing, he got a strong whiff of the trashcan beside him. Someone had thrown a soiled diaper on top and it was rank. The flies buzzed and swarmed as if they were in heaven and he wondered if flies had a sense of smell.

A woman's voice at the other end of the phone said, "Energy One. How may I help you?"

He spoke in an exaggerated southern accent, "I's drivin' down Sunshine Street and I smelt somethin' strange. I'm not sure, but it might be gas. I thank you oughta check it out."

Before the woman could ask any questions, he hung up. He looked around to see if anyone was watching. They weren't. Using the handkerchief, he wiped his fingerprints off the phone and poked the kerchief back in his pocket.

Again, he waited for a couple of customers to come out of the store and slipped in amongst them. He slid into the car and slowly drove away.

Once he was out of sight of the 7-Eleven, he floored the gas pedal. He took out the small piece of paper that the gas company phone number was written on, wadded it up and started to throw it out the window, but he stopped himself. Instead, he popped it in his mouth and chewed it. It was dry and tasted like glue. He quickly swallowed it. *They aren't going to catch me because of something that stupid.*

He slowed to normal speed and pulled into the Piggly Wiggly parking lot. On his way into the supermarket he stopped a delivery boy.

"What time does the pharmacy open?" he asked.

"Nine o'clock."

"What time is it now?"

"One minute till," the delivery boy said, looking at the clock on the wall.

The inside of the store smelled like fresh baked cinnamon rolls and his stomach growled. He ignored it and yanked a quart of milk out of the cooler, then went to the pharmacy counter. The pharmacist's assistant was rolling up the metal partition in preparation for opening.

He placed the container of milk on the counter and rubbed his forehead as he said, "Ma'am, I have a migraine. What's the strongest thing I can get?"

"The pharmacist always recommends *Excedrin for Migraines*. Second row, on the left side," she said.

He walked to the shelf and pretended to look. He knew they'd be out of *Excedrin for Migraines* because he had been buying a bottle a day for several days—just to make sure there wouldn't be any.

"Ma'am, I don't see any."

He could tell the assistant was exasperated by his interruptions. She set down the pole that she'd been using to roll up the partition a little too hard and it clanged. She marched over to the area where the headache remedies were and looked. He smelled her cheap perfume and wanted to tell her she used too much. Instead, he watched her frown and lean closer.

"I guess we're out," she told him.

"Oh great! My head's about to explode and you're out!" he yelled.

She backed up. "I'll check the back and see if there are some more packages."

"You do that!" he said. He could tell she wasn't used to such volatile people. It delighted him that he could have such an impact on someone. He watched her run behind the counter and shut the safety door behind her. She quickly checked the shelves and returned.

"I'm sorry, sir, but we are out," her lip quivered and he thought she might cry.

"Oh God, my head is killing me," he said a little too loudly. As he put his hands to his forehead again, he intentionally swiped the quart of milk with his elbow. It fell off the counter and the carton burst open as it hit the floor. Milk went everywhere. He could barely contain his grin. He had no doubts that the pharmacist's assistant would remember him.

"Ah shit! I can't take this!" he yelled, turned around and stomped off to his car. As he drove through town, he went over everything he did that morning in his mind. When he recalled the pharmacist's assistant's reaction to his behavior, he howled with laughter.

A few minutes later, when he got to the right block, he hung back at the corner where he could see the house at the end of the street. Huge red flames shooting in the air already engulfed the west side of Brenda's house.

CHAPTER NINE

OF SUSPICIOUS ORIGIN

Dan Gilbert, the sheriff, and his deputy, Elizabeth Hanson, came to see Brenda twice at the hospital while she was recovering. Gilbert told her they'd deemed the fire "of suspicious origin" and he needed to question her further.

Though she was still kind of dazed because of the effects of the fire and the medicine the doctors were giving her, she tried to be as helpful as possible. Nevertheless, she kept slipping in and out of consciousness as they spoke.

Once, half-awake, she heard the sheriff and deputy conversing in hushed tones and was shocked.

"I just picked up the report. I brought it with me."

"What does it say?"

"That fire was started with calcium carbide. It's a chemical that burns worse than hell when it's mixed with water. Somebody wanted the house to burn to the ground," the sheriff said.

"You think she and the husband did it? But she almost died." Hanson ran her fingers through her auburn hair.

"Maybe they botched it. I'm not making premature decisions. Let's just say I quit trusting people long ago," the sheriff said.

After the sheriff and deputy had left, Brenda's dad arrived for a visit and saw tears falling down her cheeks.

"What's the matter, Sugar?" he asked, setting down his Stetson and pulling up a chair. "The doctors tell me you'll be fine and out of here very soon."

Unable to hold it in, Brenda told him about the sheriff's visit and the conversation she'd overheard. "My God, I don't know how he can think I had anything to do with it. Look at me."

Her father shook his head. "I don't either, but..." he paused for a moment, and then went on. "What about Glen?"

"What about Glen, Daddy? You can't possibly believe he had something to do with this! I know you'd rather I'd married someone from around here, but Glen's a good man. You told me yourself he's working real hard at the dealership and doing really well for someone who's never sold cars before."

"That's true," her dad mused. "He is. But we don't know much about him. Maybe I should make some inquiries."

"No Dad, please. You shouldn't. That will just make Glen think I don't trust him." Brenda wished she hadn't said anything about the sheriff's visit. Her father could be just as stubborn as she was and he didn't often let go of something. "Dad, it'll be alright. They'll find out the truth."

Her dad nodded, but she saw his chin set in that way they both shared when they'd made up their minds about something.

Then quickly, perhaps too quickly, he changed the subject. "How 'bout you two coming to our place until you figure out what do to next?"

"Oh, Dad, thanks for offering. We'd really appreciate it." She smiled.

"Your mama will be happy to spoil you until you get on your feet. And it will be real nice to have you home again," he said shyly. "So it's settled then, I'll pick you up as soon as the doctors give us the good word."

After two more days at the hospital, Brenda felt almost alive again. Her lungs still ached when she lay down, but other than that, she was okay. When Dr. Thomas released her, she went to her parent's house.

"I meant what I said about you staying here until you and Glen decide whether you're going to rebuild or buy a new house," her father said as he opened the front door to find her mom anxiously awaiting. She embraced Brenda.

Brenda thanked her parents again and told them, "We'll stay here but I need to check on my animals."

"Not until you spend a few days with us getting your health back." Brenda let her mom spoil her though Glen was mostly silent during their stay.

Jane, who came by the following week, offered to take Brenda to see the house and care for the animals.

Brenda stood in her backyard and looked at the charred remains of the whole west side of her house. There was water damage too, but some of the things she loved in the living room, dining room and kitchen were saved.

"I'll have to go through the wreckage sooner or later, but not now. I can't stand to do it right now." The place reeked of smoke and made her queasy. "We have to bathe the animals before we do anything else," she said, immediately busying herself with the task. "By the way, thanks for moving the animals upwind from the smoke. If you hadn't, they might have died. I care more about them than all the other things."

"You would've done the same for me."

As she began preparing Sniffer for his bath, Brenda purposely turned her back to Jane. That way she wouldn't have to see Jane's face when she told her friend about her fear, the one she hadn't confided to anyone else.

"Jane," she said, summoning up her courage. "I don't know how to say this, but I have to talk to someone other than my family." She told Jane about the sheriff's visit. "He said the fire was set purposely." Then she told her what her dad had said about their not knowing much about Glen, although she purposely left out her dad's words about investigating his past. "I'm starting to think really crazy thoughts, like maybe Glen might have, could have, set the fire," she blurted out. Keeping her back to Jane she began lathering Sniffer with his doggie shampoo. Thank goodness he had escaped the fire by exiting through the doggie door in the kitchen.

Sammy screeched and grunted in his monkey's voice.

"You don't believe that," Jane said in surprise.

"I don't know what I believe anymore. Glen's been bugging me to move away from here and now, because of the fire, we have to move."

"Yeah, but Glen would never set the house on fire with you in it," Jane said. "He loves you. You know I don't get along with Glen, but even I wouldn't think him capable of such an awful thing."

Brenda turned her back on the charred, skeletal remains of the house and looked at Jane. Sammy was playfully swinging on the bars in the holding cage. Jane was hosing out the monkey's cage, but she was watching Brenda. The stream of water was broken by the cage bars and tapped out an almost musical beat.

Brenda went back to bathing Sniffer. "Yeah, you're right," she said, relieved to be told that her suspicions were ridiculous. Her father was making her paranoid about Glen just because he wasn't a local man. She grasped the garden hose, held her thumb over the end of it and sprayed water on Sniffer's back. He wagged his tail and soapsuds slung across Brenda's face. She wiped her eyes with her forearm and sputtered. Some of the soap had gone in her mouth and tasted bitter.

"Sniffer, I've already had my bath," she said, giggling.

The adorable puppy liked his bath and yipped his delight. He put his paws on Brenda's shoulders and licked her face. His moist breath smelled of peppermint and she knew he'd been sampling her herb garden again.

Jane, who was bathing the uncooperative monkey, frowned. "How come you get Sniffer and I get Sammy?"

The wet monkey shrieked and slipped out of her hands. She attempted to catch him by the tail, but he was too slippery and escaped. He hid under the picnic table and chattered his disapproval. Jane reached under the table to pull him out and he hissed at her. She withdrew her hand when he showed her his sharp little teeth.

"Jane, don't be afraid. He won't bite you."

"Brenda, you better get him."

"He's all bluff. Just reach back there and get him."

Jane shook her head. "I'm not going through rabies shots."

Jane went to Brenda, took Sniffer out of her hands and began to dry him.

Brenda chuckled, jogged over to the picnic table and pulled the screeching monkey loose from his hold. She nuzzled his head under her chin and spoke softly to him in baby talk.

"You don't like your bath, do you Sammy? Even so, it's not nice to scare Miss Jane."

Jane gave her a side-glance. Brenda put the monkey in the dishpan and began to rinse him with the warm water. The monkey chattered but didn't resist.

"What'd you do, hypnotize him?" Jane asked.

Brenda smirked, "Something like that. He senses that you're afraid of him and he out-bluffs you."

"I never was any good at poker," Jane said.

The following week Glen convinced Brenda to take a ride in the country. "I have a wonderful surprise for you, so you have to wear this blindfold."

Brenda felt the car slow to a halt and heard the electric window lower. A rush of damp spring air entered the car. "I don't know if I can take anymore surprises," she said.

"This one you'll love," he said. "I promise. Now let me put this scarf on you and lead you to my chariot."

Brenda felt Glen fumbling with the knot at the back of her head. He'd insisted that she wear it and she had no choice but to go along.

It took nearly an hour to reach their destination. Glen chitchatted all the way and seemed happier than he'd been in a long time. Brenda felt foolish wearing the blindfold, but given Glen's good mood, she bit her tongue and went along with it all.

Finally he announced, "We're here."

As he untied it, the black silk cloth fell into her lap and she looked up. Brenda gasped. It was the house to which Jane had taken them. The lights shining inside the house refracted through the beveled, diamond-shaped windows and cast rainbows of light on the ground. Brenda saw a small nearby lake she hadn't noticed when they first looked at the house.

"It's beautiful," Brenda said admiringly.

"The neighbors call it Paradise Lake," Glen whispered in her ear.

He got out, went around the car and opened the door for Brenda. Glen took her by the hand and led her to the house. The faded smell of cedar gave the place an instant homey feeling. Brenda peered at the heavy cedar beams. There was no doubt where the smell came from. Despite the lovely scent, after what she'd just experienced, all that flammable wood made her nervous.

"Is anybody here?" Brenda asked.

"No one but Jane, and I'm not sure what I'd label her," Glen replied.

Jane came out and embraced Brenda. "Well, you're home," Jane said as she ushered them in.

Brenda thought Jane was being a little bit too encouraging. Though she hated pushy sales tactics, she also knew it was tough working on commission. Brenda shook the thought from her mind and looked around.

Seeing the house again, Brenda realized how beautiful it was. It had the old-world charm that she loved—arched doorways, leaded glass, built-in bookcases, built-in bar and china cabinet. She peered out the window at the grounds dotted with pecan trees, forsythia and tulips. This side of the house was landscaped with red and yellow tulips. The yard sloped down to a small lake. A family of white ducks was already paddling around in it. It was very secluded, but the place was right out of a fairytale. Brenda could see herself and Glen sitting on the back porch in rocking chairs. They'd be old and wrinkled, holding hands and watching the sunset together every day.

"Well," Glen announced, "it's ours. Or it will be soon.

I put a deposit on it while you were in the hospital. Now that the other house is gone, we need someplace to live. I would have told you sooner, but I wanted to surprise you."

"You know I love it, but can we afford it?"

"With the insurance, me working now and a little loan from an old friend, we'll be fine," he said. "I promise."

"Well, let's go past the old place and hammer a 'for sale as is' sign on our front yard," Brenda said.

He embraced her.

Jane smiled. "I already did that for you," she said.

"How thoughtful," Glen laughed.

CHAPTER TEN

INSURANCE

It was their first weekend in their new home. They had spent the last eight weeks buying new furniture and replacing the smoke and fire damaged bedding and other household articles. They wanted to start out fresh and organized in their new home. She sat on the arm of the new teal sofa, took a handful of cashews out of the dish Glen held and popped a few in her mouth. "What do you want to do tonight?" she asked and kissed Glen on the top of the head. She noticed his hair smelled like jasmine. She had smelled that exotic scent before but couldn't remember where.

"I don't know," he answered.

"It's Friday night. You mean there's no place you want to go?"

"Yeah, there is, but I made an appointment with some life insurance salesman that called."

"Glen, you don't need to do that. I work for insurance companies. I can get all the insurance we'll ever need." She fluffed his hair with her fingers and said, "Why are you interested in life insurance anyway?"

"If we're going to have a passel of kids, then we need to get insurance," he said.

Brenda smiled. She'd wanted to bring up the subject of children, but felt it was way too early for that. "How many is a passel?"

"Oh, more than five, but less than ten," he said.

"I was thinking more like two," she said meekly.

"Me, too. I'm just teasing you, but it doesn't matter how many we have if I die or if you die, we'll need insurance to take care of 'em." He held the cashew dish out to her again and she took a few more. He continued, "If I die, you'll need it to live so you can stay home and take care of the little rascals. And if you die, I'll need it to hire a nanny."

"Well, I already have a half-million."

"Don't you have it made out to Suzy?"

"Well, yeah, but now that we're married I'll change it."

"There's no rush." He kissed her on the shoulder and added, "I don't have *any* insurance and I'd sleep a whole lot better at night knowing that if anything happened to me, you'd be taken care of."

"How much do you think we need?" Brenda asked.

"How about a million?"

"Okay. Five-hundred-thousand for you and—"

"No. I meant a million a-piece," he said, casually flipping some cashews in his mouth.

Brenda pulled back and looked at him. "Why so much?"

He grinned, "Darlin', you're irreplaceable. But if I got to do it, half-a-mil will only get me an ugly nanny. I want a pretty one," he teased.

Brenda picked up a throw pillow and bonked him on the head. He grabbed one and threw it at her. She turned and the pillow hit her in the back of the head. "You challenging me?" she asked.

She gripped the pillow and threw it at his shoulder. It hit his leg.

"You're asking for it!" he said and commandeered the pillow. He held on as if it were a football and launched it. She dodged. He missed. He nabbed the pillow and chased her around the sofa. He'd go left. She'd go right. Back and forth until she took off running to the bedroom, laughing and screaming all the way. He hurled the pillow down the hallway and it landed square in Brenda's back. She pursed her lips together in mock anger and picked it up.

"You're in big trouble now, Buddy!" she said in a serious tone, then broke out laughing. She was laughing, but Brenda had a competitive spirit and she was determined to get him back.

The doorbell rang. Glen stopped. "See, you bothered the neighbors. That's probably the police coming to get us for disturbing the peace."

Brenda giggled and brushed her fingers through her mussed hair. "Get the door, silly."

When he turned to go to the door, she threw the pillow at him. It hit him squarely on the butt.

"That's cheating," he said and clutched the pillow.

"You didn't call *time out*," she said as she followed Glen to the living room.

He answered the door. Standing there was a bald, rotund man mopping the sweat off his forehead with his handkerchief.

"Unseasonably warm for May, don't you think?" he said, pocketing the kerchief and sticking out his hand. "Mr. Brumbaugh, I'm Jason Curtis with Universal Life. We spoke on the phone."

Glen moved the pillow into his left hand so he could shake Mr. Curtis's hand. "Come on in." Glen ushered the salesman into the foyer with a sweeping gesture.

Brenda sighed.

"This is Brenda, my wife. Darlin', this is Mr. Curtis. Let's all go to the living room," he said. When Brenda passed Glen, he swatted her on the rump with the pillow.

The salesman heard the thump and turned around. Brenda covered. "Mr. Curtis, would you like something to drink? I have peach iced tea or lemonade."

"Tea sounds good."

Brenda raised her eyebrows and looked at Glen. He nodded that he'd take a glass. She went to the kitchen and filled three glasses with ice.

She heard Sammy rattling his cage door. He could see her whenever she stood in front of the kitchen window and he jangled the cage door to remind her it was feeding time. She smiled, "I'll feed you a little later," she said to the monkey as she pulled a pitcher of tea out of the refrigerator. She didn't like having salesmen in her house. She'd have to tell Glen that.

She poured a little tea and took a sip. It needed more sugar. She reached into the canister and spooned a little sugar with the scoop she kept inside. *I'll have to tell Glen that once your name's on their lists, they bug you to death.*

She scooped out a bit more sugar and dropped it into the tea. *Why is Glen in such an all-fired hurry to get insurance, anyway? Course, it's sweet that he wants to take care of me, but I'll get a better rate through my job.* Absentmindedly, she got another scoop of sugar and sprinkled it into the pitcher and stirred. She'd have to think of a polite way to tell the salesman they wouldn't be needing his services.

Glen called from the other room, "Brenda, come in here. We need you."

She looked down at the tea; it was so thick with sugar it was almost syrup. She put in more water, gave it a stir and poured it into the glasses, returned the rest to the refrigerator and noticed her 'To-Do' List. She grabbed a pen and added "tea" to the list.

She placed the tea glasses on a silver tray and carried them into the living room. She stopped when she saw that Glen was signing papers.

"What are you doing, Glen?"

"Mr. Curtis already had these drawn up." He pointed to the other contract. "You need to sign here."

Brenda crossed to the coffee table and set the tray on top of the policy contract. She was buying time while she searched her mind for what to say. She handed the men their glasses of tea, took hers and sipped. The salesman carefully slid the contract out from underneath the tray.

She swallowed and turned to Glen, "I thought we were going to think about this for a little while."

"What's there to think about? We need insurance. Mr. Curtis has the forms filled out. All we have to do is sign them," Glen said.

Brenda didn't want to create a scene, but she didn't feel right about this. Mr. Curtis held the papers out to her, "There you are, little lady. Just sign at the X." He was a little too forceful for her taste. She took it, scanned the policy and began to read. She saw Glen look at Mr. Curtis and roll his eyes. Stubbornly, she continued to read.

They waited a few seconds, then Glen got impatient. "I've already read it, Brenda. Just sign it so that this nice man can be on his way."

Though Brenda normally would have dug-in her heels and protested, she was embarrassed to do so in front of Mr. Curtis. She was afraid she might see him again at some work-related function. And, she didn't want to have a fight with Glen in front of a total stranger. She exhaled, threw the document on the table and signed it.

The salesman, sensing her anxiety, said, "If anything ever happens, Mrs. Brumbaugh, you'll be glad you did this. And with you two being so young, if you die, it'll probably be an accident. Then it's double indemnity. Also, you should start looking into grave plots and headstones. We can recommend reputable companies." He handed them some business cards. He seemed uncomfortable and continued packing his stuff as he talked. "Mr. Brumbaugh said you're thinking about having kids. When you do, you just can't have too much insurance."

He chattered on about how the policies would be processed, the physicals they'd need and finally he left.

Brenda glared at Glen. "I don't like being pushed into things."

"What do you mean? I didn't push you," he defended.

"I came in here and the two of you practically grabbed my hand to make me sign."

"We did not!"

She stared at him and he fidgeted with his wrist-watch. He finally conceded. "Alright, I'm sorry if it felt like we were pressing you. He was pressuring me while you were in the kitchen and I just folded. I'm not good with guys like that."

She sighed. His admission made her feel better. The truth was she wasn't good with high-pressure salesmen either. She always heard her mother's voice saying, *Be nice, Brenda. Be nice.* She slowly walked to Glen. He took her hand and pulled her into his lap.

"Sorry, but at least now we're covered," he said.

"Yeah. Now we can go kill ourselves," she joked.

Glen laughed, then turned serious. "We should probably look into the cemetery plot and headstone at some point soon."

"Yeah, you're right," Brenda said with a sigh. She hated having to think about such morbid things. She changed the subject. "Let's do something fun today."

"Okay. Earlier you asked me if there was someplace I'd like to go today," he said.

"Uh-huh."

"Well, I know where it is. Go get your purse and come on," he said, giving her a helpful shove off his lap.

Brenda grabbed her purse and they headed for her car.

"Where are we going?" she asked, locking the back door.

"Shopping," he said.

They walked out to the car together.

"What are we shopping for?" she asked.

"I don't know. I thought we could just look around," he said while opening the passenger door for her.

She got in. Then Glen walked to the driver's side, opened the door and got into the driver's seat. She smiled, moved closer to him and pinched his cheek.

He drove them into Kansas City to the Plaza. To her it was just a typical shopping mall, but Glen seemed to love watching the shoppers, the hustle-bustle. He looked in every window and browsed at every kiosk. At the center of the mall where they usually have the Christmas tree or the Easter bunny, were two brand new cars being raffled off. Along with other shoppers, Glen climbed in to each car, trying out both the driver's and passenger's seats. When Brenda urged him to fill out an entry form he did but put her name instead of his own. "I want you to win, Honey," he told her.

Glen was also overwhelmed by the selection in every store. Things Brenda took for granted were fascinating to Glen. He was especially fascinated by the wares in electronics stores. It was as if he'd never seen computers, compact disks, cell phones and camcorders.

In one store, Glen held a CD in his hand and scratched his head. "It's amazing. How do they get the music on there, Brenda? There's no grooves on it like a record."

"I don't know. Maybe they'll have an explanation on the Discovery Channel."

"What's the Discovery Channel?" Glen asked.

"It's a cable channel on science and nature." Brenda saw the confusion in his eyes. "I guess you haven't watched a lot of cable television. Don't worry, we'll get the cable hooked up real soon."

They continued on their shopping adventure and when he found the Dust Busters, he playfully chased Brenda around the store vacuuming her shirt. In some ways, living with Glen was like living with a child. He saw things with new eyes. But Glen had a dark side and those same eyes also saw people in terms of predators and victims. She wondered why. Brenda hoped she could help him make the transition into her gentler world without losing her own sense of self.

When they arrived home with their purchases, she was surprised to see the red message light flashing on the phone. Walking over and pressing the button she heard an angry Morgan berating her for sending in a failing exam on his one-million-dollar insurance policy.

"You've ruined my new business venture," he said. "And I won't forget it."

"Who was it?" Glen asked.

"Oh, that guy Morgan. He's mad he didn't get the million-dollar insurance he wanted and blames my report."

"He sure is a creep," Glen said. "How did he get our new unlisted number?"

"Who knows? Let's not let it spoil our night," Brenda said trying to shrug off Morgan's threat. But she couldn't take her mind off of Morgan's message. *I wonder when he first learned of the bad report?* Suddenly, the thought struck her, *Suppose he found out before the fire. Could he have been the one who tried to burn our house down? Losing a million dollar policy would upset anyone, but for someone like Morgan, could it push him to commit such an insane act?*

CHAPTER ELEVEN

BAD BUSINESS

Glen stared at the calendar hung on the refrigerator and marked an X on June 15th. He wondered why he still had the obsession to mark off the days. Was he still just marking time? Was this a habit he would have until the day he died?

A kitchen timer buzzed and Glen flipped it to *off*. He peeked in the oven at the frothy cheese and basil soufflé he'd made as a surprise for Brenda when she came home. He was proud of his efforts. It was rising perfectly and smelled great. He eased the oven door closed so the soufflé wouldn't fall. The phone in the other room began to ring. Glen quickly reset the kitchen timer then raced to get the phone. He caught it on the third ring.

"Hello?" he said into the mouthpiece. There was silence on the other end. "Hello?"

A gruff voice on the other end finally spoke, "Man, I need that money."

Glen recognized the voice. It was Manfred, his old friend. He tried to make his own voice sound friendly, "Manny, how's it going?"

"Cut the crap. The deal was you'd make a deposit into my account and I need that cash."

"I've only been working a few months. Give me some time."

"Oh man, you're making me bleed," Manfred said, then added, "If I don't get the money I'm calling your little wifey. I'm coming over there right now to talk to you about it."

Glen stared angrily at the phone. That was all he needed. He'd have to explain to Brenda that part of the deposit for their house came from Manny, who was calling the loan in already. His temple throbbed.

"Look, you don't have to come over. You'll get it," Glen said angrily. "There's no need for threats."

He slammed down the phone. His oven timer went off. *Buzz-zz-zzz.* He ran back to the kitchen. He put on an oven mitt and looked in the oven. His soufflé was flat. He poked a finger into the squishy soufflé. *I must have bounced the floor too much when I ran to get that damned call. Why does everybody always squeeze me just when things are going better?* "Damn this world and the people in it," he muttered.

Frustrated, he seized the hot casserole dish and threw it against the wall. Bits of china, cheese and egg peppered the wall like a cafeteria food fight. When he turned around, Brenda, who had just arrived home, was standing in the doorway staring at him.

"What are you doing?" she asked incredulous.

"The bowl was too hot and it was burning me."

"So you smashed it against the wall?"

"I guess I taught *it* a lesson. It won't do that to me anymore," Glen joked.

"Glen, I don't know why you're suddenly in such a bad mood, but you have to learn to control your temper." She glanced at the shattered dish. "That casserole dish cost me over fifty dollars," she said and grabbed a juice box from the fridge. Wearily she added *new casserole dish* to her 'To-Do' list taped to the refrigerator door.

Not wanting to say something she'd be sorry for, she spun around and walked out. Glen followed her. When they got to the living room, Brenda kept going and disappeared into their bedroom. Glen went back in to the kitchen to clean up the mess. A short while later he heard the doorbell and knew it had to be Manny. He considered not opening it, but decided he had to. Brenda might hear it or Manny could get even madder and God knew what he'd do.

Opening the door, Glen saw his friend standing there. "Well, aren't you going to ask me in?" Manny asked in a querulous tone.

"Would it matter if I said no?"

"Hell, no."

"Well, just be quiet. Brenda is bushed and she's gone back to our bedroom." He ushered Manfred into the living room. "I'll be right back."

"Where are you going, Glen?"

"I was just going to get us some iced tea," Glen lied.

"I don't need any tea," Manny said dryly. "Come on over here and sit down." He emphasized the last two words.

Glen trudged over to his favorite chair and sat. Sniffer, who'd wandered in, heard the word *sit* and scampered over and sat at attention near Glen.

"Now look," Manny said. "I ain't your wife and I'm not your mother. I'm just an old friend who was foolish enough to loan you some money and I expect you to keep your word about paying it back pronto."

Glen looked away. He got the message. Manny walked around the room, looking between the cushions on the couch, opening decorative boxes, looking behind picture frames and generally giving the place a good search as he talked. Sniffer cocked his head and watched with curious interest.

Manny eyeballed the wisteria planter. "Nice tree. You're getting real domesticated," he said. "You know if you don't get it, my friends and I could get real nasty."

"I know," Glen said. "But I can't put a gun to somebody's head to get the cash."

Manfred stopped his search and shook his finger in Glen's face. "That's not funny unless I say it."

Sniffer barked at him.

"Sorry," Glen said.

"I don't make the rules, Glen. If you can't abide by them, we'll have to make some other arrangements," Manny said in a menacing tone. He took a piece of butterscotch candy out of the candy dish and ate it. He peeled another one for Sniffer and held it out. The puppy lapped it up, moved closer and whined for more. Manny patted the shaggy dog.

Walking out, Brenda felt like an intruder in her own home. She needed to get her purse from the table so she could empty it into the one she'd set out for the next day, but when she came in the room to get it, Glen and Manny clammed up. They watched her in silence and she wondered what she was interrupting. She saw Manny slip Sniffer a piece of butterscotch candy on the side, but didn't say anything.

Finally, Glen broke the silence. "You know my wife, Brenda. By the way, she has three jobs. Maybe she can give me one of hers."

Manny stuck up his hand, "Hi again."

"Could you excuse me for a minute," Glen asked nervously. "I need to use the bathroom."

"One minute and counting," Manny said.

Brenda didn't know from the tone of his voice whether he was joking or not.

"How do you think he's doing?" Manny asked Brenda after Glen left. His voice had a confidential tone.

Brenda shook her head. "He hates the long hours I keep, he has made no friends, has to work for my dad and resents it. Other than that, I guess he's fine."

Brenda took a package of breath mints out of her pocket and offered Manny one. He shook his head. She popped one in her mouth. It tasted minty cool and immediately opened her sinuses. Sniffer came over and begged for a candy. Now that her sinuses were open, she could smell his bad breath and gave him a piece. She put it on the slick coffee table so he'd have to lick it—and hopefully clean his breath.

"Do you have a joint checking account?" Manny asked.

"What kind of question is that? You're sure nosey, aren't you?" Brenda said. "Well, the answer is no, and he doesn't have a charge card or beat his wife either," Brenda said. "And he promised me he'd never drink again and he hasn't."

There was a tense pause and Brenda watched Sniffer continue to lick at the breath mint. It was a game to him.

Manny nodded. "So, how about you? How are you holding up since the wedding?" This time there was something genuine in his voice.

It took Brenda by surprise and she softened. "I can't solve all his problems. All I can do is try to make our lives as happy as possible," she mused. "I think if he could get a really good job on his own he'd be fine."

"Employers are reluctant to hire people with Glen's record," Manny said.

"Record?" she gasped. "You mean a prison record?"

"Yeah, he was in Algoa for quite a stretch. He floated more checks than anyone else in the history of Missouri.

People are reluctant to hire someone who might help themselves to their checkbook."

Suddenly Glen came back into the living room. "Well, were you two getting acquainted?" he asked with forced conviviality. He flashed a warning look at Manny who turned away from him, a small smile on his lips.

"Not really, just passing the time," Manny said. He looked at his watch. "Speaking of time, I better be going. See you again real soon, Glen."

Numb, Brenda sat in the chair gripping the armrest as her knuckles whitened. Manny nodded farewell to her, patted Sniffer goodbye and strode past Glen. In an instant, he was gone.

Glen walked to the window and peered out as Manny climbed into his car and drove away. "There's a blue Jag parked on the street opposite the house. That damn nut Morgan is out there again. I need to take a walk," he said, "and chase that loser away."

Although the thought of Morgan outside made her shiver, Brenda couldn't think about that right now. The shocking revelation of Glen's past was all she could focus on. Once he left the house, she turned out the lights and sat down, trying to calm herself and think.

Now it all makes sense. That is the reason Glen had such a hard time getting a job. The reason he looks at things like CD's and computers like he's never seen them before. Brenda had some tough questions to ask herself. Could she let Glen go? Did this change the feelings she had for him? Brenda wondered if she should divorce Glen. *After all, isn't a good marriage founded on truth and trust? Though he told me right before the wedding he'd passed some bad checks, he didn't trust me enough to tell me he'd been in jail. He was a convicted felon.*

She shuddered at the thought that she had married an ex-con, but when she searched her heart through, she came up with the same answer. The truth was she loved him. She was still sitting there waiting for him hours later when he returned. She thought he looked like he'd been drinking, but she couldn't be sure.

"We have to talk," she said and blurted out what Manny had said, desperately hoping it was a lie, knowing all the time it was the truth. "Is it true?" she asked. "Have the decency to be honest with me."

"I told you earlier," he said defensively. "I wrote some hot checks."

"You didn't say you were in prison," she retorted. She thought she might be in shock; her head pounded and her hands and feet were numb. She never would have guessed this mild-mannered man had a record. She had thought it was just a minor thing, a bad check or two. Prison had never occurred to her.

"Twelve years," he said. "You don't have to worry, Brenda. I'm never going back."

She heard herself say again, "You didn't say anything about prison. Twelve years, Glen! What did you do to get twelve years?"

"I thought you knew. They lock you up if you write *hot* checks."

"People bounce checks all the time without being sent to prison! I thought it was just a couple of hundred dollars."

"No," he said meekly. "It was a lot more than that. I was young and thought the world owed me a living, so I spent more money in a year than a lot of people make in a lifetime."

Glen cupped her face in his hands. "I'll understand if you want to break it off right now. We can get our marriage annulled, but I want you to know, I'll love you till the day I die."

Brenda gazed into his eyes, but he looked away, ashamed of the tears forming in them. She'd never seen a man cry before and it moved her. She took a deep breath and prayed for control of her emotions.

"Why didn't you tell me sooner?" she asked quietly.

"I thought you might leave me." His voice cracked and he cleared his throat. "Are you going to leave me?"

Brenda felt dazed. The silence between them grew to a minute, then two.

"Are you going to leave me, Brenda?" he asked again, sounding desperate.

She shook her head no. *He's paid for the bad things he's done and he's a good man now. It's not like he murdered somebody,* she told herself. She studied his face, then said, "I didn't marry the man that you *were*. I married the man that you are today."

He bent down and kissed her passionately, but this time she pulled away.

"I thought you loved me," he said, a hurt tone in his voice.

"I just need a little time to adjust to this," she said quietly, hoping the disappointment she felt didn't show.

"Take all the time you need, Brenda," he said walking away.

Brenda had a fitful night. She kept waking every few hours from nightmares about Glen. Though she was certain her nightmares were due to anxiety, knowing the cause didn't make her feel any better. Now, she bolted straight up in the bed trying to shake off the last dream...

The police broke down the front door, shoved her

aside and took Glen away. When she begged them to tell her why they were taking him, they had just laughed at her. She pleaded with them to leave him with her, but in an instant they were gone and she was alone.

What a dream! She rubbed her eyes gently. She lay back on the bed, making sure not to wake Glen. She could hear the dogs barking in the backyard and wondered if it was that creep Morgan that the dogs were trying to get at out there. *No*, she told herself, *it's probably the neighborhood raccoon snitching their food. Relax. You've got to get some sleep. You have to work tomorrow. Close your eyes and try to relax*, she told herself. *Stop thinking.* She yawned and tried to clear her mind. *Relax...Relax...Relax...* she repeated her mantra until the first light of dawn shone in the bedroom window.

CHAPTER TWELVE

THE HONEYMOON IS OVER

Mrs. P. had become Brenda's sounding board. Sometimes Mrs. P. was her only lifeline to keeping her sense of self. She could tell the old lady anything and never fear criticism. They'd discussed her financial problems, her sex life, her sibling rivalry, her fears, her hopes and her insecurities. Now they were discussing her marital problems.

Brenda smoothed a thick layer of velvety foam onto Mrs. P.'s skinny leg, took a pink disposable razor and ran it toward the knee. Brenda thought it was sweet that as old as Mrs. P. was, she still wanted her legs shaved and hoped she'd feel the same way when she got old.

"The honeymoon is definitely over. I got the shock of my life last night," Brenda said.

Mrs. P. was propped against the headboard eating Cheetos. "That sounds ominous," Mrs. P. said as she took another Cheeto out of the bright orange bag and ate it.

Brenda could hear her crunching and smiled. Finally, she'd found a food that Mrs. P. liked and Brenda would have bought anything to fatten her up.

"He was in jail and he never told me," she said quietly. "His friend Manny was over last night and told me. I asked Glen about it. He not only admitted being in prison, but it was for quite a long time—twelve years, in fact." Brenda finished shaving one leg, lathered the other and started shaving it.

Mrs. P. stopped munching and looked at her. "What a shock! It must have been an awful revelation for you. Was there a scene?"

"Worse than you can imagine," Brenda said. "Right after his friend left, Glen left and didn't come back for hours and then when he did, he looked like he'd been drinking, which didn't make me happy." She swished the razor through the bowl of water to take off the excess shaving cream. "We talked about it and in the end I said I wouldn't leave him." She sighed. "I do still love him, even though he lied to me."

Brenda finished shaving the second leg, dropped the razor into the bowl of water, grasped a washrag and began washing Mrs. P.'s legs. "Afterward, he wanted to make love and..."

"And you wouldn't?"

Brenda nodded. "I just couldn't and now we're hardly speaking."

"He'll get over it," Mrs. P. assured her. "The question is, will you?"

"I don't know. I'm trying, but I feel like our marriage started out based on a huge lie."

"What was he in for?" Mrs. P. asked, interrupting.

Brenda gave a mirthless chuckled. "He was financially impaired—hot checks—a lot of them. He got a long sentence."

Mrs. P.'s face was serious. "Brenda, maybe you should take some time off and get to know your husband better."

"I just can't, Mrs. P. Glen's working for my dad and he's not happy there. I'm keeping my fingers crossed he doesn't quit and with the fire and the new house and all, we've got a lot of bills not covered by insurance. I guess the honeymoon is literally over."

Brenda sighed. She had to work at all three of her jobs even though Glen was left alone a lot. Her typical day started with a forty-minute drive into Kansas City to perform physicals for Associated Mutual Insurance Company. Later, during rush hour, she'd wait for traffic to die down by studying and doing homework at Denny's. After that she'd drive to the homes of people that couldn't see her during the day because of their jobs. With Mrs. P.'s condition getting worse, when she finished those physicals, she'd try to stop by and only then could she go home.

Once home, Brenda's third job kicked in. She bred a variety of dogs, Chinese dwarf deer and exotic cats to sell and she was the quasi-animal shelter for the small community of Kingsville. Any time animals were abused or abandoned they were brought to her and she cared for them until she could adopt them out to new families.

This afternoon she had a late appointment and had sandwiched a visit to Mrs. P. in-between. The thick, damp air felt muggy as Brenda opened her car door to do her last exam of the day. Swinging her legs out she caught her panty hose on the edge of the door and ripped a hole in them. *Dammit it. I can't go change them now. Maybe the lady won't notice.*

"Darn, it's going to rain," she murmured. The sky was pretty slate-colored blue, but in the far distance gray clouds were forming. *I'll make this quick. This will be an early evening,* she told herself as she walked up the old stone sidewalk. Because of the uneven stepping stones, she had to carry her bag of medical equipment rather than wheel it. *Maybe I'll surprise Glen and fix him a special dinner tonight. His favorite—roast beef with mashed potatoes and gravy.*

She stopped and stared at the prettiest wooden door she'd ever seen. It had carvings of women's faces. Their long flowing hair extended from one end of the door to the other. The cut glass doorknob with beveled edges must have been at least a hundred years old and sparkled like a huge diamond. Her thoughts were interrupted by the door opening.

"Are you Brenda?" asked a frail, little lady.

"Yes, I'm Brenda. You must be Mrs. Topper," she said. The older woman was skinny, had sunken cheeks and wore her gray hair extremely short.

"Honey, come on in and have a seat," she said to Brenda.

Brenda stepped inside and looked around. The parlor was fabulous; it was like stepping back in time. The room was a stylish mixture of 1930 Art Deco and Victorian furnishings. Brenda recognized a Louis Icart painting of a willowy woman in a fantastic garden. On the Art Deco frame was embossed "Orchids." Brenda scanned the rest of the room. There were marble pedestals, bronze busts, an antique baby bed that held an old fashioned ceramic-faced doll and a fainting couch.

"O-o-oh, a fainting couch," Brenda hadn't meant to say it out loud and found herself a little embarrassed.

"Have a seat," Mrs. Topper motioned for her to sit on it. Brenda did and rubbed the thick velvet material. It was a rich purple and Brenda was sure it looked as perfect today as it did the day it was made.

"This is beautiful!" she said.

The delicious smell of fresh baked chocolate chip cookies wafted in from the kitchen.

"Can I get you something to drink?" Mrs. Topper asked.

"No, thanks. I'm fine." Brenda couldn't help but stare at all the lovely antiques that decorated the room as she pulled the medical history papers out of her bag. There was a four-foot wide picture of a nude lady lying beside a blue pool of water. The ornate frame looked as if it were made for an antique mirror.

This house is incredible. Brenda checked her forms and saw that Mrs. Topper was applying for a ten thousand-dollar policy. *This lady is loaded. Surely she doesn't need a small insurance policy. Either some fast-talking salesman has sweet-talked her into buying this policy or she is just lonely and this is her way of getting someone to come and visit.*

Brenda soon realized it was the latter. Before Brenda knew it, Mrs. Topper had related almost her whole life story. She could tell that the sweet little lady enjoyed the company and conversation very much. Brenda gave her the physical examination as they chatted. Afterward, Mrs. Topper brought in an ornate silver plate full of homemade cookies. They ate some and drank half a pitcher of freshly brewed iced tea before Brenda realized that over two hours had passed.

Suddenly, lightning flashed and the lights dimmed for a second.

"Oh boy, I meant to get home before this storm started," Brenda said. "I got married a short while ago and my husband will be worried."

"My goodness, sweetie, I guess we have literally talked up a storm," Mrs. Topper said jokingly. "I didn't mean to take up so much of your time."

"It was my pleasure and the chocolate chip cookies were superb. They were just sweet enough to be addictive," Brenda smiled.

"Oh, honey, I've enjoyed having you here so much.

You are such a breath of fresh air. Please stop by and see me anytime. I'm always home."

"I've really had a good time, too."

"Now you wait just a minute. I want you to take some of these cookies home to your husband. If you chose him, he must be as sweet as you are." Mrs. Topper disappeared into the kitchen and returned a few moments later with a brightly colored bag full of her cookies.

"Thank you. Chocolate chip is Glen's favorite," Brenda said. "Bye!" she yelled back over her shoulder as she walked out the front door, held her medical bag over her head and ran to the car. *I wish I'd brought an umbrella, but this wind would have torn it right out of my hand.* By the time Brenda unlocked her door and made it into the car, she and her bag were sopping wet.

Brenda put the car in gear and left Pleasant Hill. She drove down Highway 58. It was the quickest way to get home because the old one-lane blacktop had less traffic.

As she drove on, she shivered in her cold, wet clothes. Little streams of water ran down her forehead. She turned on the heater, but the warm air blowing on her actually made her feel colder. *I hope there's no traffic.*

As she drove along the narrow highway, the sheets of rain grew thicker until she could barely see twenty feet in front of her. *Wow, it's getting hard to see. I shouldn't have stayed and visited with her so long,* she scolded herself. *If I had left on time, I could have been home before this storm hit.*

The sky had turned to a thick charcoal gray and she thought there were the makings of tornado clouds. *It's a lot darker than it should be for this time of day.*

Brenda began to speed up when she noticed a car coming up behind her. It was traveling entirely too fast. The headlights glaring through the back window were getting closer and closer. She could barely make out the figures of a man and a woman. The woman was driving. All Brenda could see of her was blond or silver hair glistening in the flashing lightning.

"You'll just have to go around me," Brenda said.

Brenda knew there was a narrow bridge just ahead and she could see what looked like a big tractor-trailer rig coming toward her from the opposite direction. She checked her rearview mirror. The car behind her wasn't slowing. Frightened, Brenda decided to pull off to the side of the road. She didn't want to be on that bridge at the same time as the truck. *I'll let that stupid idiot pass me.* She quickly pulled over.

The headlights behind her were still coming faster and faster. They didn't seem to be slowing down. At the same time, the big truck passed her, drenching Brenda's car with pooled water from the road. The roaring engine of the big truck drowned out the faint sound of the squealing tires behind her. There was the loud crunch of metal, then a crash! Brenda was suddenly thrown forward, then instantly slammed back against the seat and felt her car tumbling over.

The car behind had rammed the back of her car while going about sixty-five miles per hour. The force of the impact catapulted Brenda's car to the edge of the embankment and flipped it on its side.

She realized her car was dangling on the edge of the ridge and if it toppled, it would fall into the river. Brenda was afraid to move. The car jostled slightly. *What was that? Did the car move? I don't like this. I've got to get the hell out of here.*

She braced herself so that when she unstrapped her seat belt she wouldn't fall over. Opening the belt, the slight shift in her body weight made the car move again. *Creak!* She had to get out of there before the car went sliding down the embankment and into the river. Brenda pushed open the car door. It came flying back on top of her and closed with a bang! The car teetered. She tried opening it again, but it did the same thing. This time, she put her feet on the side of the console between the two seats and stood up, forcing the car door to stay open.

Rain was pelting her face so she couldn't see. Lowering her head, she planted her hands on the edge of the opening. Struggling, she pushed herself up. Then she hopped on the seat back to give herself a little boost and crawled out onto the side of the car. It made another creaking sound as Brenda jumped down.

"Ow!" She fell on the gravel, scraping her hands. Brushing her wet hair from her face, Brenda could see that more than half her car was hanging over the edge of the embankment. Both tires on the left side were blown.

Brenda looked into the heavens and whispered a silent prayer of thanks for being alive. She looked around. The other car was gone.

A beat-up old pickup truck pulled alongside Brenda and the driver yelled, "Do you need some help?"

Brenda looked through the truck window at the driver. He was middle-aged, completely baldheaded and had a thick goatee. It was odd how he could be so bald and yet have such a good crop of hair on his face. Before she could answer, he added, "I just passed a car up the road, they said they're calling the highway patrol. Is anyone on their way to help you?"

"No," she said. "I was just about to see if I could reach my car phone. It's in the floor board."

"I don't think that looks very safe. I've got one," he said and sniffed the air. "Besides, I can smell gas."

Brenda hadn't noticed the slight smell of gas lingering even in the rain, but she looked down. She was standing in a puddle shimmering with a thin layer of gasoline.

"Do you think it'll be washed away in the rain?" she asked.

He scratched his bald head and answered, "Probably. You'd better climb in and get out of the rain."

Brenda was soaked all the way down to her panties. She was tempted to strip and ring out her clothes, but of course, didn't. She didn't even want to climb into the truck with a complete stranger, but she was wet, cold and her hands were beginning to burn a little where she'd skinned them on the gravel. The adrenaline was wearing off and she was shaking.

"Thanks." Brenda opened the door, hiked her leg and got in.

"What happened?" the driver asked, rubbing a bead of Sprite off his goatee.

She told him and he was incensed. "Those assholes. I'd say they're probably on something."

Brenda noticed he had a chaw of chewing tobacco in his cheek. He rolled down the truck window and spit. "Here," he said handing her his cell phone.

Brenda dialed home. *If Glen's not there, I don't know what I'll do, though he's gonna be mad as hell at me for wrecking the car.*

"Can't you get anybody?" the driver asked.

"It's ringing but there's a lot of static. No, there doesn't seem to be anyone home," she said, upset.

She noticed the flashing lights coming over the hill. "Oh, thank goodness, here comes the highway patrol!" She could hear the relief in her own voice and hoped the driver didn't take it the wrong way.

The patrol car pulled to a stop behind them. Brenda slid out of the tall truck and her feet landed in the puddle again. *Damn!*

"Thank you for the shelter," she said to the driver.

"I'm gonna stay and put in my two-cents worth. You

can come back here when you're finished if you want to," he said. "And I'll take you home."

"Thanks," she smiled appreciatively.

The young, red haired patrolman was already igniting flares and tossing them on the road. He looked up, "That your car?"

"Yes, sir."

"You can go ahead and sit in the backseat of my car. I'll be done with this in a minute."

A few minutes later, the patrolman returned to the car and she told him her story. "Are you alright? Should I call an ambulance?" he asked, scrutinizing her.

She shook her head. "I was shaken up and I'm bruised, but okay."

"Did you get the license plate of the other car?" he asked.

She shook her head.

"Can you describe the people?"

"It was so dark and it all happened so fast. All I saw was a man and a woman, and the woman was driving," she paused, trying to think. "Oh, and she seemed to have blond or silver hair, but it may have been the light."

"The light?" he asked, confused.

"Lightning," Brenda said. "It was lightning."

"Well, you may remember more later. You don't have any enemies, do you?"

"Why would you ask that?"

"We have to check out everything," he said. "Do you have a way home?"

"I tried to call my husband, but there's no answer. The truck driver said he'd give me a ride if I needed one, but—"

"It's alright," the young officer gave her a friendly smile. "I'll drop you off if you'll feel more secure."

"Will you just wait a minute so I can thank him?"

The patrolman nodded.

When she got to the house, Glen was still out. She showered and changed into a nightgown, longing to see him, to be comforted by him.

It was after midnight when she heard the door. She jumped out of bed, ran to greet him, but he looked more startled than glad to see her. "Brenda, what are you doing?" He stopped and stared at her as she embraced him.

"I didn't mean to startle you," she said. Never had she been so glad to see him.

He held her apart. "I had to go to a late sales meeting. I thought you'd be asleep. When you jumped out at me, I thought you were a prowler." He seemed rattled.

Still shaken by the night's events, she poured out her story.

"Did you see the driver?"

"It happened so fast, but I think it was a woman with silvery hair and there was a guy sitting close to her. I couldn't really see them."

"But the guy—did you see his face or hair?"

"Just that it was dark."

He pursed his lips. "I just hope it wasn't that moron, Morgan, and some crazy girlfriend of his."

"Oh, my God," she shuddered, afraid. Could it have been Morgan? Between losing the insurance policy and having his advances rebuffed, he certainly seemed to have plenty of reasons to want to get back at her. But she couldn't positively identify either person in the car so even if it was him, what could she do about it? She pushed any thoughts of Morgan out of her mind. All she wanted at that moment was to be in the loving and safe arms of her husband. "Glen, let's go to bed," she said suddenly. "I want to be close to you."

"Is that all you ever think about?" he said gruffly.

She put her arms around him. "Yes," she said, planting a kiss on his forehead. She unfastened the top several buttons of her nightgown and let it drop to the ground.

He tensed. "Brenda, for goodness sake, I have a customer coming in at eight tomorrow morning. Your father's a slave driver!" He shoved past her.

Tears came to her eyes. She stood there transfixed. Finally, she snatched her nightgown from the floor, put it back on and followed him to the bedroom. His rejection stung. She stood silhouetted by the moonlight as she watched him come out of the bathroom and silently get into bed without even looking in her direction. *How could he treat her this way after her ordeal earlier? Didn't he find her attractive anymore? Was he upset the car had been wrecked? Was he paying her back for not wanting him when she'd found out he'd been in jail? That must be it. I'll have to make peace with him.*

She lay down beside Glen. His back was to her and she kissed him on the nape of the neck. "Just to say I'm sorry," she whispered.

Glen groaned and pushed her away. "Dammit, Brenda, I'm tired. Let me sleep."

Her feelings were badly hurt and she moved to the other side of the bed. When she woke the next morning, he was already gone.

CHAPTER THIRTEEN

SUSPICIONS

Brenda recovered from being bruised and sore from the hit and run accident, but she could not seem to resuscitate her relationship with Glen. He was getting more moody by the day. Sometimes she wondered if he was manic-depressive. One evening she would come home from work and he'd have prepared a candlelight dinner for the two of them. The next he'd be ranting that she didn't love him. He even began to accuse her of cheating on him though he knew her late nights were caused by clients and stopping by to see Mrs. P., who was getting closer and closer to the end. *It doesn't make sense,* she thought, *unless he is feeling guilty and he's the one cheating on me. Could that be it?* She prayed it wasn't but couldn't stop thinking of it. Her nerves frazzled almost to the breaking point. She kept telling herself it was her imagination and worked harder trying to forget her suspicions. Yet they remained sharp thoughts, like pinpricks in the back of her mind.

On Saturday, it was grooming day for the animals. Brenda was glad that Glen was working. Jane had come to help her. It made the job go faster and was a lot more fun.

They used the time to catch up on what the other one was doing and to share town gossip.

Jane turned on the blow dryer and began fluffing Sniffer's thick, black hair. "I like Sniffer. Think I'll adopt him when he's old enough. I'd like a dog to keep me company since I've had it with men!"

Brenda leaned over and kissed Sniffer on the nose and patted him. "Don't try to con me," Brenda said joking. "You can't date a man without skydiving into love."

"Hey, I just parachuted out of my marriage. I've changed. I swear. I'm only having casual affairs from now on."

"Jane, you think you have to have a man to take care of you, when the truth is *you* usually wind up supporting them," Brenda said.

"Well, you should talk. Anyway, not this time. I'm going to change my life."

"Uh-huh." Brenda wasn't convinced.

"I read in the Classifieds that there's some factory in Alaska that'll pay your way up there, give you room and board and pay you twenty-five dollars an hour plus overtime."

"What's the catch?"

"You have to sign a six-month contract." Jane turned the hair-dryer off and began brushing Sniffer, who rolled over on his back so she could scratch his tummy. Jane obliged and continued to explain. "If you leave before six months, they charge you for the airfare, room and board and the hourly wage is dropped to minimum wage. Hell, I could live with the devil himself for six months."

"It's probably a fish cannery," Brenda said. "Pugh! I can smell it just thinking about it." She wrinkled her nose and covered it with her hand. She saw Jane give her a side-glance and said, "I guess it never crossed your mind that the men outnumber the women five-to-one in Alaska?" Brenda could tell by Jane's expression that she'd nailed her motives.

Jane grinned at Brenda and nodded. "Does that mean I get five *dicks* all to myself?" Jane teased.

"Oh, you're bad," Brenda said as she wrapped the monkey in a towel and placed him in his clean cage.

She wanted to talk to Jane about her problems with Glen, but she didn't know how to broach the subject. How could she say, "Speaking of men's bodies, I think Glen's having an affair." *No, that would make Jane laugh because she'd say "Brenda, you're a prude. Say dick if that's what you mean."* "I have something to tell you. Promise not to tell?" *No, that sounded like an eight-year old.*

She surprised herself by blurting out, "I'm afraid Glen's having an affair."

"What?" Jane asked and stopped rubbing Sniffer's tummy. "You can't be serious."

"I am," Brenda said. She rubbed her neck, trying to relax the muscles, then she continued, "I've noticed that Glen takes off at odd times. He yells at me for nothing and seems a lot less romantic."

"Brenda, I think you're becoming paranoid." Jane came over to her and rubbed her shoulders. "You don't really believe that, do you?"

Brenda sighed. She did and she didn't. Maybe Jane was right. Maybe, she was blowing everything out of proportion.

"You know I've never liked Glen very much, but he acts like he's crazy about you," Jane said.

"Think so?" Brenda asked, hoping for reassurance.

"Well, let's put it this way: he's the only guy in the county that's never made a pass at me," Jane said.

Brenda laughed. *Leave it to Jane to use herself as a barometer.*

"You're just depressed," Jane added. "My God, look at all that's happened to you in the past several months. You fell in love, planned a wedding in three days that would've taken most people a year. Then Glen had all those job problems, the fire plus that car accident...It's no wonder you're a nervous wreck."

"You're right. I can't believe I'm even thinking this," she said as she turned around and gave Jane a hug. "Thanks for listening."

"Hey, what are friends for?" Jane said. She broke the hug, walked back to Sniffer and continued grooming him.

Brenda noticed Sammy reaching for her pocket, but his little arm wasn't quite long enough. She smiled and pulled a small banana out of her pocket, peeled it, sniffed the fresh fragrance and pretended to take a bite. Sammy went wild. He was screeching and jumping around his cage. Brenda laughed and handed him the banana.

"Is that one of those bananas that tastes like an apple?"

"Yeah. They fly 'em in from Jamaica," Brenda said. "Sammy loves 'em, as you can see."

Katula growled. It was her turn. Brenda went to the lion's cage and unlocked it.

"You hear from the Detroit zoo yet?" Jane asked.

Brenda nodded. "I got a letter from them. They're going to pick Katula up, either next month or the one after, depending on when she's in heat. They'll have her back in three weeks, pregnant, hopefully. When she delivers, they'll pay me a couple of grand for the cubs." The lion grumbled again and Brenda spoke in baby talk to it. "Does that sound like fun to you? You'll like being a mommy, won't ya?"

Jane rolled her eyes. Brenda saw her and asked, "What?"

"I like animals, Brenda, but I don't believe in treating them like humans," Jane said.

Jane gave Sniffer a kiss on the forehead and put the fuzzy bundle back in his cage. All fluffed out, he resembled a baby bear more than he did a dog. With her back still to Brenda, she asked hesitantly, "You give any more thought to the shortage of white mice?"

"What?" Brenda said absentmindedly as she brushed the lion's coat. She went deep enough to massage the skin and the lion was purring like a finely tuned motor.

"You know, I told you about it a few weeks ago—colleges, pet stores and research labs buy thousands of them. If we start a mouse farm and get in on the bottom floor, we can make a fortune."

Brenda frowned. She didn't know how to get out of it without hurting her friend's feelings. Jane was always thinking up get-rich-quick schemes and asking Brenda to finance them. Brenda hesitated, then said, "Thanks for thinking of me, but I'd never get into anything where animals are misused—"

Before she could finish, Jane interrupted her. "My friend's making a killing. You put up the money and I'll do all the work."

"Mouse farming just isn't for me," Brenda said and intentionally bent over to attach a chain to Katula's collar. She didn't want to have to face her friend, but Jane bent down to look her in the eye.

"Brenda, you know me. I'd never take advantage of our friendship," Jane said. Her cigarettes fell out of her pocket to the ground.

Brenda grabbed the package and stood up. "I know, but—I have a problem bringing life into the world just so it can be killed."

Jane released a disappointed, "Oh."

Brenda handed the cigarette package back to Jane, who snatched it abruptly out of Brenda's hand. She knew Jane was angry with her and nervously changed the subject. "Did I tell you? Glen's quit smoking cold turkey. Said he did it by telling himself that tobacco wasn't in them, it was cow manure. Once he sets his mind to something, he'll do it or die."

"Can't you talk about anything besides Glen?" Jane said harshly.

Rather than fight with her, Brenda said, "Yes, I got a raise this week and an additional $10,000 insurance."

"Good grief, Brenda, how much life insurance do you need?"

"Well, they just keep giving me more with every bonus," Brenda answered.

"With the insurance, the new house, the retirement nest-egg and the house you're renting to me, sounds like you're set," Jane said.

Brenda could tell Jane's temper was beginning to cool. She was glad. "Yeah, Glen and I are—"

"We aren't going to use the 'G' word," Jane interjected. "I got this really great sample of nail polish today." She pulled a bottle of pearly plum-colored polish out of her pocket and held it up for Brenda to inspect. "You want to play beauty shop tonight and do our nails?"

Brenda noticed the small mole right below the smile line at the edge of Jane's mouth. On anyone else it would have been ugly, but on Jane it was sexy—like the classic movie stars of the '40s. She thought of it as a punctuation mark to Jane's smile. She was happy that her friend wasn't angry at her anymore. Jane was like that. One minute she was mad or sarcastic and the next she would give you the moon. A pale blond tuft of hair fell out of Jane's ponytail and Brenda pushed it behind her ear. "I'll do yours if you do mine," she said.

They heard a car pull into the driveway, gun its motor and turn around.

"Who's that?"

Brenda looked toward the drive. Mr. Morgan was driving slowly past the front of the house. "Darn, it's that guy who made a move on me," she frowned. "And then I gave the company a bad medical report on him he didn't like. He's been following me around and making threats. I think he might have been the one who ran me off the road. And the fire..."

"You think he had something to do with the fire?" Jane asked, shocked.

"Well, maybe. I don't really know. I've got no proof that he has done anything. All I know is that first, I rejected him, and later, he lost out on a million dollar insurance policy because of me. He left a threatening message and during my exam on him, he casually mentioned that he had been in prison—who knows what for. Let's just say he has plenty of reasons for wishing harm on me."

"He gives me the creeps," Jane said, rubbing the chill bumps on her arms. She ran toward the driveway angrily screaming, "Stop following her! Damn you!"

When Morgan saw her coming, he goosed the car and sped away.

It took Brenda and Jane two hours to finish feeding all the animals and to clean their cages. When they were done, they shampooed and curled each other's hair. Then they sat at the kitchen table to do their nails.

Somewhere in between their activities, Glen came home

and made them a late lunch of grilled cheese sandwiches, but served them with a cool attitude.

It was clear to Brenda that Glen didn't like Jane one bit. She figured it must be Jane's confrontative personality and the way she treated him when he fixed her fence.

Brenda had to agree that Jane could be bossy at times and she almost always demanded she get her way, but they'd been friends so long that Brenda overlooked a lot of it. That was just Jane. She hoped that with time, Glen would grow to like Jane, too.

Brenda had put off making their dinner to get Jane's fingernails finished and she knew Glen wouldn't be pleased. She wanted to hurry so Jane could go home because—like Mt. Vesuvius—she never knew when Glen was going to erupt.

Brenda snapped out of her thoughts when she realized *Waterfalls* was on the radio. It was her favorite song and she sang along as she glued a tiny rhinestone onto Jane's pinkie nail.

...she'll be by his side
But he doesn't realize he hurts her so much
But all the praying just ain't helping
At all 'cause he can't seem to keep
His self out of trouble...

"What did you do with the money I gave you for singing lessons?" Jane teased.

"You never gave me any money."

"Even if I had, you woulda spent it on poetry books," Jane said.

Jane shifted in her chair and it tilted. Her handbag which was hooked around the post of the chair, fell to the floor. A letter in a money-green envelope plummeted out. Jane used two fingers of her free hand to pick up the letter. She was determined not to smudge her wet polish. Jane waved the letter at Brenda. "My friend sent me this chain letter. You send ten people ten dollars and they send it to ten people. Before you know it, you've got checks coming in from all over the country."

"*That stuff* is what prison bars are made for, Jane. It's a pyramid scheme, and it's illegal." Brenda set down the finished finger and started on the next. She stroked on a smooth, even coat of plum polish.

"It may be illegal, but my friend is driving a Mercedes—bought and paid for by *that stuff.*"

"Well, I'll come and visit you in jail and bring a present on your birthday."

"Will you bring me a cake with a file inside?" Jane joked.

"No, I'm gonna put a guy inside the package."

The women cracked up laughing. Suddenly, Glen came into the room.

"You two giggle-boxes hold it down! I can't even hear the news!" he scolded.

"There's no good news on TV anyway," Jane shot back.

"Well, Miss Know-it-all, why don't you go home and paint your own damned fingernails," he said, picking up her handbag from the floor and tossing it to her. Brenda jumped out of her chair and pulled on Glen's arm. She was hoping to get him out of the kitchen before he exploded.

"You can't kick me out! This isn't your house. It's Brenda's," Jane yelled.

"Hey, what's going on here? You two sound like a divorced couple," Brenda joked, trying to extinguish the heat. She tried to pull Glen into the other room so they could talk.

"If you don't get that witch out of here, there really might be a divorce!" Glen shouted at Brenda.

"Brenda and I have known each other longer than she's known you. We're practically sisters."

"Stop it!" Brenda shouted at both of them. "Glen, we'll try to keep it down. I only have three more fingernails to do and we'll be through."

Glen stomped away like a child who just lost his turn on the swing. Brenda turned to Jane and whispered, "He's *so* impossible these days."

"I can understand being jealous over a man, but I'm no threat."

"Will you do me a favor?" Brenda asked.

"Maybe," Jane said hesitantly.

"Please try to get along with him," Brenda begged.

Begrudgingly Jane nodded her agreement. "I'll try, but it ain't easy."

Brenda plopped back down in her chair. She wanted to say she was coming to the same conclusion, but bit her lip and said, "Thanks," with a sigh.

CHAPTER FOURTEEN

THE HUNT

Because of the scene with Jane or something else—Brenda couldn't be sure what—Glen was in a foul mood all that week. Whatever it was seemed, she thought, to be directed toward her; that was all Brenda could figure out. Glen was out late almost every night and when he was there he said he had to help the neighbors and would stay out in the woods for hours.

"You were the one who wanted me to have friends."

"Yes, but Glen, we have so little time together," she finally said, trying to reach him. "And when you're here, you're out mending some neighbor's fence or helping build a barn. I wanted you to have friends, but you seem to use them to get away from me...from us. What's wrong?"

"Brenda, who are you to talk? How much are you here? If you're not working one of your three jobs or visiting Mrs. P.," he said sullenly, "you're studying. Look, just give me some space. Can't you stop nagging me?"

"Okay, Glen," she said quietly, "but just remember I love you."

"Sure, I'll remember," he said heading out the door.

The conversation seemed to have done no good. *Our relationship is going nowhere,* she thought sadly.

The next week inched by with the two of them barely speaking. But on Saturday morning, Glen's bad mood seemed to lift. He got up early and she could hear him whistling as he got dressed. Not wanting to say anything to agitate him, Brenda pretended to be asleep and heard Glen go outside. Then she got dressed and went into the library to do some work. An hour or so later, she heard the front door open.

"Brenda, are you here?" Glen called. "Come here."

She got up and went to meet him in the front hall.

"Come on," he said. "It's a beautiful morning. Come on out with Dave and me. I want to take you hunting."

"Hunting?" she said aghast. "With my brother and you?" She shuddered. "I can't believe you two want to do that. You know I don't believe in killing things. Besides, I need to pay our bills; with the new house and furniture, we seem to be spending more than we make. We just can't get ahead."

"Brenda, will you stop worrying. We're doing fine. I've even been thinking of going into business for myself. I hate working for your dad and Suzy. They just gave me this job because of you."

"Glen, you haven't quit or anything, have you?" Brenda said anxiously.

"Now would I do that without asking your permission, Baby?" he said sarcastically.

"Glen, don't joke with me. If we don't have both our incomes, we can't afford this house. I'll have to cash in my life insurance policies."

"You'd better not do that," he said hollering. "I told you, you're going to need that someday. Don't cash it in, I mean it. Now come on and go hunting with Dave and me. Just for a little while."

"Glen, I'm not going hunting with you. No way."

"You're a bitch," he walked to the door and opened it. "You never want to do anything with me." He slammed the door and left.

Brenda walked back to the library and sat down at her desk. "Anything but hunting. Couldn't you have asked me to do anything but hunt?" Tears ran down her cheeks and fell on the papers in front of her.

Nothing excited him more than the kill. Glen looked down the barrel of his rifle at his victim. She was lovely, with big brown eyes, perfect form and standing still. He held his breath and fired. *BLAM!* She fell in her tracks in the clearing.

"Good shot!" Dave said, patting him on the back. "We'll have venison tonight."

Glen grinned and tried to look calm when in fact his heart was racing. It was the ultimate control—to take another living thing's life. He loved being judge, jury and executioner. There was no other high like it.

When they arrived at the clearing, Glen looked down. The deer was quivering and blood was pumping out of her chest.

"Oh, God," Dave said and turned away.

This was more than Glen could have hoped for. It was still alive. He could shoot it again. He slid a cartridge into the chamber of his rifle, took aim at the deer's chest and squeezed the trigger. The bullet exploded out of the rifle barrel and he felt his own excitement mount.

Glen's moan made Dave turn back and look at the carcass.

"You couldn't help it," Dave tried to say something comforting.

Glen looked down at the bloody mass on the deer's chest and he knew Dave thought he'd moaned at the mess. *What a jerk Dave is,* Glen thought.

Glen began preparing the deer for the trip home. Dave was useless until Glen got the deer in the bag. Once he didn't have to see the blood, Dave was okay. They loaded the doe into the back of Dave's truck and drove it back to the house. Once at Glen and Brenda's property, they looped a rope over a tree branch, attached a pulley and hoisted the deer.

It was one of those wonderful early summer days that Glen had dreamed about in prison. The leaves on the maples surrounding him were a silvery green. The air was crisp and clean. He breathed it in greedily, feeling like one of the pioneers bringing home the night's dinner for his family.

Glen tightened the rope and tied it to the trunk of the tree. The dead deer hung by it's back legs, twisting and turning with its eyes wide open. The rope whined under the strain and Glen lowered himself to the ground to sit next to Dave, who was spitting on both palms and rubbing them together to lessen the sting of the rope burn.

Glen pulled a vicious looking hunting knife from the scabbard on his belt and began sharpening it with a whetstone.

Glen paused a moment, laughed and took a Coors out of the cooler beside him. He popped the top and beer bubbled over his hand. The cold beer foamed in his mouth and felt good flowing down his throat. He handed it to Dave. They passed the beer back and forth. "This way, if Brenda catches us, we can truthfully tell her it's your beer, Dave."

His brother-in-law laughed weakly.

Glen wiped the knife on his camouflage pants and looked at the deer. This was his second favorite part of hunting. He was in complete control again. Glen knew Dave had a weak stomach and he looked forward to taunting his brother-in-law. It made him feel powerful when he manipulated people. He liked to see just how far they could go. What he could make them do.

Glen stood and stabbed the knife into the doe's abdomen. Blood oozed out of the wound. He held the knife tight with both hands and pulled it downward. He sliced it all the way from the hind legs to the neck. It made the sound of a dull zipper as it sliced through muscle and hide. When he got to the bottom, the entrails fell to the ground.

"Look at that. We got plenty of intestines for making sausages," Glen said and glanced over at Dave.

Dave looked at the innards and the blood streaming through the dirt and promptly threw-up. Glen, pleased with his success, smirked and tossed Dave his handkerchief.

"Ooh, that smells like week-old eggs," Glen teased, then set to work skinning the deer.

After dinner that evening, Glen said he was taking some of the venison to their neighbors. "Take the truck, Glen, so you'll be back soon," Brenda urged.

"No. I like the walk," Glen replied and headed out.

Glen walked about a mile down the road until he reached his destination. He didn't see Morgan, who was watching him through binoculars hidden behind a grove of bushes. Glen stood on the side of the road for a few minutes. *What is he waiting for?* Morgan wondered. Then a car pulled to the side of the road. A woman stepped out and ran to Glen. With night settling in, Morgan couldn't see too well, but he could tell that after Glen and the woman talked, they came together in a passionate embrace. Finally, he saw the woman blow Glen a kiss and prance back to her car. *What does Glen see in that cheap tramp when he has Brenda? Even though I could have killed her when I found out about the medical report, I still think she's sexy. If she knew about her husband's infidelity, that marriage would fall apart.* He smiled. *Maybe I should tell her about her husband's escapades.*

He heard the woman's car door slam and the motor start. Her headlight swiped across the nearby brush as she turned her car around. He lay down flat until the car disappeared and Glen continued down the street to his neighbor's. Then Morgan got up, dusted himself off and moved further into the woods.

CHAPTER FIFTEEN

SOUR MELODY

Mrs. P. was almost at the end of her long road of suffering, Brenda thought, looking sadly at the old woman. She had insisted on giving Brenda her ruby ring and the piano that had given her so much pleasure, back when she was not too weak to play.

"I want to see your enjoyment," she said. "Not have some dumb lawyer tell you after I'm gone. Anyway, consider the piano a belated housewarming present."

Brenda hugged her friend. "I love them both," she said. "Always." But she couldn't stop her tears.

"Don't fret about me, Brenda. I'm going to be with God. I'll be fine. It's you I worry about."

Mrs. P. wanted them to take the piano that weekend and Brenda agreed.

The portable radio was playing a medley of patriotic songs in honor of the Fourth of July. She, Glen and Jane were sitting on the patio. It was a hot, muggy day, but around two o'clock a few clouds had rolled in from the west and now it was getting bearable.

Brenda wiped the beads of sweat from her upper lip and licked her lips. They were salty. She looked where the beautiful tulips had been just a couple of months earlier. The tulip stems hung limply as if sadly surveying the dead flower petals that lay scattered about on the ground. Something squeaked and moved under the dead foliage. Brenda moved her head sideways to get a better look. It was a cute little chipmunk. He peered out at her with his black shining eyes. "Hi there," she said in a calm voice. "Are we going to be friends?" He chattered at her, then as fast as a roadrunner he was gone.

Brenda wore old jeans and a red gingham shirt knotted at the waist. Though she hated the peasant look and Glen called her *Heidi*, the cotton scarf she had tied around her head did keep her hair out of her face.

Jane had come over to lend a hand.

"Well, let's unload the piano," Brenda announced. She wrote down in her notebook 'To-Do' List: *food for chipmunk*. They all got up and headed to the rental truck.

Jane laughed. "I thought we'd get triple hernias getting that sucker in the truck."

"It should be easier getting it out. We won't be pushing it uphill," Glen said, wiping the sweat from his brow with his forearm.

"Why do you want that old thing anyway, Brenda?" Jane asked.

"After I get really good on the saxophone, I'm going to take piano lessons," Brenda said, getting herself a drink of water from the outdoor tap. It was well water and it tasted sweet, not at all like the bitter, acidic water of her last house.

"Don't lie to me," Jane said. "It's because it belonged to Mrs. P., isn't it?"

"Yes," Brenda admitted. "She knows I like it because I've played 'Chopsticks' for her. I think it's her way of encouraging me to follow my dreams, but she said it was a housewarming present."

"Yeah, like Glen's going to learn to play it," Jane teased.

Glen checked his watch. "Alright. Enough with the chitchat. Y'all ready to tackle it?"

"I guess so," Brenda answered.

"The last people who used this truck must have loaded it with mothballs. It stinks," Jane said, holding her nose.

The Beckwith piano loomed like a giant at the far back wall of the rental truck. It was covered with padded blankets that were held in place by ropes.

"Thank goodness it's on rollers," Brenda remarked. "How are we going to do this, Glen?"

"Let's move it out from the wall so we can get to it on all sides," he said. Glen scratched his head and continued. "I think I'll wrap a safety rope around it and tie it to the railing in the truck—just in case it gets away from us."

"How are we going to keep it from flying down the ramp?" Brenda asked.

"Let's tie two ropes around it with pulleys on them, then we'll lower it slowly by walking our hands down the rope."

"That sounds good," Brenda said.

Glen picked up two pulleys. "You two wrap the end of these ropes around the piano."

Brenda stood at one end of the piano and threw the rope to Jane on the other end. When Jane tossed the rope back to Brenda, she missed it. They tried again. Again she missed. Brenda wasn't tall enough. She looked for something to stand on and she noticed there was a small lip on the bottom of the piano. She grabbed the top to hold on to and stepped up on the lip. The four-inch rise was just enough to enable her to reach the rope. Brenda leaned across the top. The moving pads had a greasy smell that made her want to take them to the laundromat, but she resisted the urge. Brenda and Jane wrapped the ropes around the piano twice.

Glen took the ends of the rope and began attaching them to the pulley. The pulley squealed as the rope turned the roller.

"Those pulleys look awfully small, Glen," Brenda said.

"They don't need to be big, Brenda. Didn't you study physics in high school? That's what pulleys do. They disperse the weight so—"

Jane interrupted, "He's right, Brenda. I watched this guy on TV lift a Mack truck with a pulley about that size."

Brenda still wasn't sure, but they made her feel so dumb she just shrugged and said, "Okay."

Glen finished knotting and testing the ropes, "Alright. We're ready. Brenda, you get on one side and Jane, you get on the other. I'll push it from this end. We need to shove it to the ramp, but we don't want it to go down the ramp—not just yet."

The women did as they were told.

"On the count of three, push," Glen said. "One, two, three."

They pushed and shoved. Finally, the piano groaned a melodious sound and crept forward. It seemed to Brenda that, once it was rolling, the pushing got easier. They got it to the edge of the ramp and Glen yelled, "Stop!"

Brenda gladly fell back. She leaned against the wall of the truck. Her back was really hurting.

"Are you okay, Baby?" Glen asked.

"My back aches like hell."

"Why don't you lie down for a minute? I have to look this thing over anyway," he said.

Brenda slid to the floor of the truck. It was nasty with

ground-in dirt, but she didn't care. She would have lain on a bed of nails if it would have helped her back. She lay back. The mothball smell was stronger on the floor and it occurred to her that it wasn't mothballs at all. It was some sort of disinfectant the trucking company used. The metal floor was cool and she sighed with relief.

Jane pulled a package of Juicy Fruit Gum from her pocket and offered a slice to Brenda. She took it, unwrapped the silver foil and put it in her mouth. It tasted sweet, almost too sweet.

"You want me to get you anything?" Jane asked.

Brenda moved the gum to the side of her mouth with her tongue, so she could talk. "A new back would be nice," she joked.

"Girls, we've got a problem," Glen said. "This thing is angled. One of you needs to get at the bottom and tell me which rope needs loosening so it goes down the ramp straight."

Jane looked at Brenda. "Why don't you do it, since your back hurts. I can help Glen handle the ropes."

"Are you sure?" Brenda asked. She hated for her friend to do more work than she. Especially since she knew Jane was tired too.

"Of course. Don't be silly. You can buy me a steak dinner when we're done."

"I hate to break up this little tea party, but it's getting late," Glen reminded them.

Jane gave Brenda her hand and helped her to her feet. Again, Brenda groaned. She crossed over in front of the piano and walked down the ramp.

Glen got on one side of the truck and Jane got on the other. They held their pulleys.

"Think you can hold it while I push the piano onto the ramp—just to get it started?" Glen asked Jane.

"I think so," Jane said.

Glen walked to the piano, "Ready?"

"Yeah," Jane said.

Brenda watched from the side as Glen put his shoulder to the piano and pushed. He groaned as if he were using all his might. The piano lurched forward. The wheels rolled like thunder onto the sloping platform.

The rope snapped taut and Brenda wondered if Jane would be able to hold it. Jane tugged on it, gripped it tight and was able to stop the piano from rolling. Glen ran back to his pulley and he helped her hold the piano steady.

"Okay, Brenda. Which way does it need to go?" Glen yelled.

Brenda moved in front of the ramp and looked. "To the left," she called back.

"Our left or your left?" Jane asked. She kept the rope taut, but moved forward to the opening of the truck.

"Your left," Brenda said.

Glen loosened his rope and the piano slid into place in the middle of the ramp.

"It's centered," Jane yelled, extending her upper body out the back of the truck to see the position of the piano. As she straightened up, she seemed to overextend her body and wobbled at the edge of the ramp.

An instant later, Jane gave a yelp and toppled off the truck, dropping the pulley. The piano came hurling down the ramp toward Brenda.

Brenda heard clacking sounds of the rollers on the ramp and looked up to see the piano descending toward her. The rollers were bumping along the treads of the ramp, which made the mallets inside the piano plunk and ping the chords. The piano was almost on top of her.

She didn't have time to get out of the way, so she

jumped up, grabbed the top of the piano and put her feet on the bottom lip as she'd done earlier. She was whizzing along, riding the piano. The rushing wind in her face blew her bandana off her hair. Brenda saw that she was headed straight for her car.

Her only chance was to jump off the piano. If she didn't, she'd be mashed between the piano and the car. At this rate of speed, that could do as much damage as falling from a three-story building!

Her heart was rushing to keep up with the adrenaline surging through her body. Brenda had no time to think—just act. She held her breath and lunged away from the piano just as it hit a rock, turned sideways and smashed into the car—broadside. A cloud of dust from the gravel driveway was kicked up around it.

The sound was horrible. It was a mixture of splintering wood, crunching metal, snapping piano strings and Glen and Brenda's screaming.

"Oh, my God!" Brenda yelled.

"Brenda, are you okay?" Glen screamed.

"What happened?" Jane cried.

"Brenda?" he called, in a concerned voice.

Where am I? She blinked her eyes, but her mind didn't register. She was dazed, but the smell of axle grease finally jogged her memory. Realizing she was under the car, she raised herself onto her elbows so she could crawl out, bumping her head in the process. Now it hurt along with the rest of her body. Using her elbows, she dragged herself to the edge of the car.

"Brenda, where are you?" she heard Glen say, as she crawled out from under the car.

Brenda was less stunned now and anger overtook her. "What happened to the safety rope?"

"It broke," Glen said and ran to help her to her feet.

"I'll say," Brenda added, coughing a cloud of dust out of her lungs. Her mouth had grit in it and her elbows stung. She looked down. Her pants were ripped at the knee and both elbows were scraped and bloody.

"Are you okay? Do we need to take you to the ER?" Jane asked.

Brenda shook her head. Between her back, her elbows and knees, she ached all over and could barely walk, but she knew nothing was broken. Jane hovered over her.

"You need some ice for that. Come on. I'll get you some out of the cooler," Jane said, wrapping her arm around Brenda's waist.

Glen went to the cab of the moving van, removed the first-aid kit from under the seat and gave it to Jane. "You'll need this." He turned his attention to Brenda. "Are you sure you're okay?" he asked.

"Yeah. Check the car for damage," Brenda said.

Jane led Brenda toward the house.

"You're just about crippled and you're worried about the damned car?" Glen said.

"Yeah!" she yelled over her shoulder. "It's leased, remember?"

"It's going to need a whole new fender and door," he answered, wiping his brow. "Thank goodness you're okay, Brenda. Why don't you help her inside, Jane and I'll return the truck."

They made their way to the kitchen. Jane helped Brenda into a chair and opened the first-aid kit.

Brenda watched Jane cut away her torn pants and pour hydrogen peroxide onto her cuts. It foamed and burned. She winced. Brenda could see the tiny chunks of gravel embedded in her wounds.

"Brenda, I'm so-o-o sorry. I lost my footing and fell. I feel like this is all my fault," Jane said.

"Don't feel bad. It was an accident," Brenda told her.

"I know, but if you were really hurt—I'd never forgive myself."

Jane tore open a bandage and taped it on. Brenda tensed and groaned. Every time she tensed her muscles it made her back hurt.

"You need to relax," Jane said.

"I know, but I can't."

Jane pulled a Chimay Ale out of the cooler. "Here, drink this. It'll relax your muscles and help your back." Jane removed the wire covering and the cork, then held it out to Brenda, but she didn't take it. "Go on. One beer's not going to hurt you."

"That's a beer?" Brenda asked.

"Yeah, it's wonderful. It's made by monks in Belgium."

Brenda took the beer and sipped. She frowned. She didn't like the yeasty taste of the barley, but didn't say so. "It's bittersweet."

"That's the Rolls Royce of beers, I'll have you know," Jane said with a chuckle. "Let me help you into the living room. You can lie down on the couch and ease your back pain." She supported Brenda, Jane's arm around Brenda's waist, as they slowly made their way to the other room.

Brenda lowered herself to the sofa, stretched out and rolled onto her side. The movement plus the beer made her burp and she tasted the chili dog she'd had for lunch. She covered her mouth and hoped Jane couldn't smell the onions. There was a small piece of paper on the arm of the couch. Brenda swept it away and it leafed its way to the floor.

Sniffer was lying in the corner and he perked up when he saw the paper float to the floor. Brenda watched him scamper over and begin wrestling with the paper, which was probably one of her many 'To-Do' lists. She and Jane laughed at the playful pup.

"He's really brave with a piece of paper," Brenda said, taking another sip of the beer and grimacing. "This stuff is beginning to work." She felt a warm rush and a little light-headed. Since she didn't normally drink, it didn't take much to make her tipsy. Brenda took another swallow and put her hand to her flushed face.

"Are you alright?" Jane asked, walking over. She looked down. "Oh, nice ring."

"Mrs. P. gave it to me. It has a necklace to match. She said she *willed* it to me, but she wanted me to take it now—just like the piano, so she could see me enjoy it," Brenda said. "I hate to tell her about what happened to the piano."

"Don't tell her. She'll never know," Jane said.

"I'm not good at lying. I think I better tell her the truth."

"Look at it this way, if you tell her, she'll feel bad. You know she'll be gone soon. Why not let her die thinking you're enjoying her gift. What's the harm?"

"You have a point. You know me though, I hate to lie. But if it makes her happy..."

"Well, the ring is beautiful. Will you will it to me when you die?" Jane asked in a joking tone.

"Sure, if you will me your topaz earrings," Brenda shot back.

"I don't have a will. Do you?"

"Oh, Glen and I made one just after we took out all that insurance," Brenda said.

"Well, you tell Glen *I* get it," Jane said. "I need something for this," she said, pointing to her unadorned ring finger.

CHAPTER SIXTEEN

SPOILED

Standing in the shadows of a clump of evergreens, he watched the rosy sunset and drank Johnny Walker Red straight from the bottle. Even without the liquor, it would have been his favorite time of day in his favorite month, September. The sun bounced off the underside of the clouds and looked to him like yellow cotton candy on a pink background. His prison cell had been on the wrong side of the compound to ever watch the sunset. As he thought about it now, it seemed like a lifetime ago. Now the only thing he feared more than prison was losing the woman he loved although he still liked variety.

He was attracted to Brenda, but in a different way. Brenda was more of a friend, a companion, a mother...Did he really think of her as a mother figure? He shook his head, bit his lip. He couldn't. He hated his mother...*I can't think about that. It's way too heavy.*

Even if he discovered that he loved Brenda most, it was too late, he was trapped. He couldn't pick her. He had to go through with the plan.

As the sun dipped behind the horizon, he took a final gulp of whiskey. He needed his "liquid courage." He hid the Johnny Walker bottle in the rain gutter. "I can't put it off any longer," he murmured.

He picked up the rake handle he'd bought and went to the lion's cage. The vicious lion growled at him. He poked the handle through the cage and stabbed at the lion, taunting him. The lion shrieked and swiped at the handle. He gave it another jab and the lion went wild, bearing its teeth and hissing. The foul breath of the lion slapped him in the face and he hit Katula on the head to make her even angrier. The lion could barely catch its breath it was snarling so hard.

He jumped back, then inched forward. He carefully opened the lock and took off running. The lion sprang out of the cage and chased him. He was barely able to stay head of the animal and felt it clawing at his heels.

Suddenly, an excruciating pain shot through his calf. He knew instantly that the lion had forced her sharp fangs into his leg. All he could do was hope the lion hadn't taken a huge chunk out of it. He was almost to the fence gate. Almost to safety. He leapt for the gate. The cat was still on him. He gave it a kick as he grabbed the handle; barely making it outside, he slammed the gate just in the nick of time.

His heart was pounding and the lion was jumping up and clawing on the gate, still determined to get at him. He looked at his pant leg. It was ripped and bloody. He tore the material away from the wound. There were seven holes where the teeth had pierced the skin. He was relieved to see it wasn't more serious. *What made that lion let go?* He wondered, but he didn't linger on the thought. He was just glad it had.

He kicked the gate just to agitate the lion. The lion snarled and he smiled as get in his car and he pulled away. Now the accident he had engineered was just waiting to happen.

The lion released a terrifying roar that sent Brenda's little dog Sniffer running for cover. He had somehow gotten out. Now he whimpered, then peeked out from the safety of a tree and mustered a defensive growl.

The house was dark when Brenda came dragging in from work. Her day had started at 6:00 A.M. She went to a staff meeting at Associated Mutual Insurance Company. After a grueling hour of stats and business policies, she'd left for her first appointment. She'd done six physical exams, studied for her Biology exam during lunch and then had gone to take care of Mrs. P. Now all she had to do was feed the animals and then she could go to bed. It was days like this that made her question whether she could continue to work at this pace.

Brenda flipped on the kitchen light and washed her hands. She couldn't afford to pass along any diseases her patients might have to her *babies*. She dried her hands and tiptoed to the bedroom door. She peered in but the room was empty. Glen wasn't home yet. She wondered where he was at this hour.

Brenda heard Katula growling. She smiled and murmured, "Okay girl, I'm coming."

She slipped a smock over her white uniform and went to the refrigerator. Taking out some soup bones the butcher had given her, she placed them on the table then filled a bucket full of dried dog food. She grabbed her flashlight, stuck it in her pocket and gathered up the food. Her hands were full with the bones and the bucket and she had trouble turning the door handle. Finally, she was able to turn it with the inside of her elbow and slipped out the open door.

Drinking in the cool night air, she turned back to shut the door. Suddenly, Katula pounced on her from out of the darkness. Startled, Brenda screamed.

She fell on her back and the dog food flew up in the air, scattering everywhere. Katula was on top of her and had her pinned to the ground. "Katula!" she yelled.

The lion let out a mighty roar. Then, she could hear Katula chewing. She turned her head to the side and saw that the lion was gnawing on one of the soup bones.

"What are you doing out of your cage?" Brenda said, using baby talk and stroking the lion's back. The giant cat rolled over and began to purr. Brenda sat up and scratched Katula behind the ears. She noticed a deep cut on its head. "What happened here?" Undisturbed, the lion rotated his head and began to lick Brenda's fingertips.

"Jane didn't shut the cage securely when she last fed you, did she?" Brenda said to the lion. "We'll have to scold her for that." She got to her feet and gave a gentle tug on Katula's collar. "Come on with mama," she said, and led the lion back to its cage. Katula obediently hopped inside and Brenda locked the cage, making sure it was safely latched.

Although she would never be afraid of Katula, the shock of the animal coming at her in the darkness kept Brenda awake long into the night. She was anxious for Glen to get home so she could tell him what happened, but she finally drifted off to sleep before he quietly slipped into bed beside her.

At about three in the morning, she awakened with a start, dreaming of Katula's big paws pinning her shoulders to the ground. She felt Glen's body next to hers and gently nudged him.

"Glen? Glen," she whispered, "are you awake?"

When he opened one eye, she began to relate her experience with Katula. Halfway through her story, Glen grunted, mumbling something incoherent to Brenda and turned over on his side, his back to her.

"Glen?" she whispered again, in a pleading tone. She slipped her hand beneath his undershirt and began stroking his bare back, but he shrugged her off.

With hot tears pricking at her eyelids, Brenda sighed and turned away from her husband.

Early the next morning, with Glen still lightly snoring, Brenda left for Mrs. P.'s house. The old woman had not looked well and she wanted to get some breakfast into her. Brenda stared at the mint green paint outside Mrs. P.'s bedroom door. It was guts-up time again. She sucked in a breath and prepared herself for what awaited her on the other side of the door. As usual, she entered in a swirl of gaiety.

"Hi, Mrs. P. How was your night? Close your eyes," Brenda said as she threw back the wooden shutters and shafts of light streamed into the room.

As was her routine, she flipped on the coffeepot and radio. She felt for Mrs. P.'s pulse and said, "We're going to make you beautiful again today."

Mrs. P. didn't answer.

Brenda's stomach growled, "Sorry. I skipped breakfast again, Mrs. P."

Brenda reached into her bag and brought out a makeup case. She began stroking the foundation on Mrs. P.'s face.

"Can you believe this? Last night I had another near accident," she said, and relayed the frightening story of what had happened with Katula. "It really unnerved me. I'm going to call the Detroit zoo today. Katula is about ready to conceive. They should come and get her now. Did I tell you that on the delivery of her cubs I'll get paid two thousand dollars? I can't wait to raise the little rascals."

Brenda had something she'd been wanting to talk to Mrs. P. about, so she just plowed ahead, "You've always been a good friend to me...I'm so confused these days. I don't know what to do," Brenda swallowed and fought back the tears. "It's like he has two personalities, Mrs. P. One minute Glen's picking me wild flowers and writing me little love notes. The next minute, he's somebody I don't even know."

She finished the foundation and started applying a soft pink lipstick to Mrs. P.'s lips as she rambled.

"Last night when I told him what had happened with Katula and tried to get him to hold me, he didn't want me to touch him. I thought *women* were supposed to be the ones that got a *headache*. Something tells me he's cheating on me." She looked at Mrs. P.'s lipstick and wiped a smudge.

"How about we put on a little rouge today?" Expertly, she brushed a rosy pink on her cheeks.

Brenda reached back in the bag and pulled out a bottle of cologne. She lightly sprayed Mrs. P.'s neck. She looked at the label on the bottom of the perfume bottle.

"Ahh, Mrs. P., you smell like *Country Bouquets* in the springtime." She set down the perfume bottle. "I don't know what do to." She snatched a hairbrush from the bedside table and continued, "I know you can't tell me what to do. And another thing...all of a sudden, he's chewing breath mints every time he's around me."

Brenda brushed Mrs. P.'s thin curls. She feathered them into a soft style around her face.

"Does he have garlic breath or a girlfriend? Go figure. Financially, he's got me in such a position that I can't afford to slow down." Brenda laid down the brush. "Now, look at you."

Brenda stood back and looked at Mrs. P. "You look beautiful."

She picked up the phone and dialed a number she knew all too well. Tears filled her eyes when she heard the man at the other end answer, "Windham's Mortuary."

"Mr. Windham, Mrs. P. is dead. Please come pick her up."

"What happened?" he asked.

"I found her when I came to work this morning. I pray to God she went peacefully in her sleep."

Brenda felt her lips contort and the tears come streaming down her cheeks. She couldn't talk anymore, so she dropped the phone in its cradle. She reached under the mattress and pulled out the bottle of Bailey's Irish Cream. "Here's to you, Mrs. P.," she said. She twisted off the top and took a deep swallow. It hit her empty stomach and gave her a burning sensation. She wiped her mouth, sat on the bed and clutched Mrs. P.'s hand. It was cool. She noticed the right index finger had an orange stain from eating Cheetos. She smiled and held Mrs. P.'s hand tight, as if by doing so she could somehow bring her back to life.

"You do look beautiful. I'm glad you're not hurting anymore."

Brenda broke down. She lay her head on Mrs. P.'s chest and sobbed uncontrollably.

Shortly after their wedding, Glen and Brenda proudly display their marriage certificate.

Brenda and Glen cut a cake at a small party with family and friends to celebrate their marriage.

Heartbroken over Glen's death, Brenda made a wreath for his grave.

In the early part of their marriage, both Brenda and Glen seemed happy and very much in love.

Glen and Brenda shared this cozy house after they married.

Glen and Brenda's home was destroyed in a suspicious blaze that almost killed Brenda.

After the fire, Brenda and Glen moved out to the country to a home which included several buildings to house her animals.

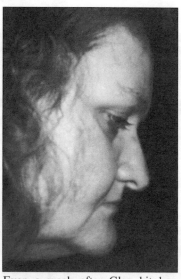

Even a week after Glen hit her, Brenda's black eye and cut nose are still visible.

Brenda's brother Dave, who had hunted with Glen, was supportive of Brenda through her ordeal.

Brenda's older sister, Suzy, whom Brenda confided in, enjoys a moment with the toy parrot Brenda gave Glen at their anniversary party.

Fearful for his daughter's safety, Brenda's father tried to protect her from Glen.

An animal lover at heart, Brenda cares for and raises a variety of strays, exotic animals and housepets including monkeys, wildcats, deer, rabbits and goats.

The tombstone Brenda had ordered for their family plot shows the depth of her love for Glen. Despite all that happened, Brenda continues to grieve for the man she fell in love with.

CHAPTER SEVENTEEN

RED LIGHT SPECIAL

On Tuesday, his day off, Glen had meant to call his girl-friend and tell her not to come over. They had been meeting in shadowy places for too long and lately she had been insisting on meeting him in his home, but he didn't like it. First, he was going to call her right after Brenda left for work, then he was going to do it after he read the paper. But while he sat on the sofa reading the newspaper and listening to the television, he got interested in *The New Detectives.* He began watching it. It was about some bozo who had drowned his mistress in the bathtub, then moved her body to the lake, only to have someone fish it up.

Before Glen knew it, his girlfriend was standing in the doorway in a flimsy red nightie, holding a bowl of strawberries in one hand and a bowl of whipped cream in the other.

One thing led to another. Soon he was pumping away on top of her and savoring every stroke. They'd reached their climax and were cuddling.

"You're a wild lover," he said. *Brenda's so gentle,* he thought.

He watched his girlfriend pick up a plump red strawberry, dip it in to the bowl of whipped cream and lick the
cream from it. She dipped the strawberry again and held up
the swirl-capped fruit. Glen opened his mouth. She licked
the very tip of the swirl, then stuck it along with two fingers
into his mouth. He sucked on her fingers and she slowly
pulled them out. "You're driving me wild and you know it,"
he moaned.

Glen chewed the strawberry. It was good. Just the right
flavor of tartness and sweet cream. He watched her seductively lick remnants of whipped cream from her fingers.

Suddenly, Sniffer jumped onto the bed and headed
for the cream. Glen pushed him off with his foot.

"Glen, don't hurt him," she reprimanded.

"I hate this damn dog!" he said.

"Well, it's time to say farewell to your wife *and* the dog
then."

"How can it be? She'll never let me go. She says I'm
her first, last and only love," he grimaced.

"Well, I'm tired of sneaking around. You have to get
away from her."

"Hold on. I didn't say—"

Sniffer barked and ran to the door. Glen bolted out of
bed and peaked out of the window.

"Holy shit! It's Brenda!" Glen yelped.

His girlfriend grabbed her clothes, the strawberries
and bowl of whipped cream and hid them and herself under
the bed.

Glen threw on his pants and shirt, straightened the
bed, ran his fingers through his hair, slipped down the hall
and into the bathroom.

Brenda entered the bedroom looking for Glen. She
heard the toilet flush. She walked across the hall and started

into the bathroom. The door was locked. "That's odd," she murmured. She knocked on the bathroom door and called to Glen through the door.

"Honey, my four o'clock canceled. I picked up some chilled oysters. Remember last time we had them? You..."

"You want to do *that* in the middle of the day?"

Brenda giggled and blushed.

"I don't think I can do it in broad daylight," Glen said, opening the bathroom door.

Glen feigned disinterest, but Brenda was sure he wanted her. She saw him glance toward the bed.

"What's the matter, you got your girlfriend under the bed?" Brenda teased and moved toward the bedroom.

Glen grabbed Brenda and shoved her onto the bed. She giggled as he plastered her with kisses.

"Wait a minute. Wait a minute," Brenda said. She climbed off the bed and flipped on the radio. "Red Light Special" was playing.

> Took a good look at it.
> Look at it now.
> Might be the last time you'll
> Have a go around ...

Turning her back to Glen, she pulled off her uniform and unsnapped the hook on her bra. She crossed her chest with her arms and turned around and he took her in his arms.

Brenda noticed Glen was more attentive than he'd been in a long time. *Why can't he be this way all the time? What is it that makes Glen so moody?* This afternoon was different. He smelled like jasmine again. Where had she smelled that scent before? She reached over and gently kissed him.

Under the bed, Glen's girlfriend had to listen to them. She hated Brenda. Never mind that Glen was Brenda's husband. She clenched her fist. She wanted to jump out from under the bed and strangle his wife, but she couldn't. It would ruin everything. She had to be patient.

Take a deep breath and calm down. Think, she told herself. *How are you going to get out of here?*

Sniffer crawled under the bed and tried to snuggle with her. He smelled of flea spray and it made her nose itch. She pushed him away and he whined. *Damn,* she thought. She didn't want Brenda to hear something and look under the bed, so she poked her finger in the whipped cream and let the dog lick it off. *That's one way to keep him quiet.*

She wondered how long she'd have to stay under the bed. She had a business appointment. Suddenly she smiled and thought, *I guess I have the perfect excuse. "I'm sorry but I was trapped under my lover's bed when his wife came home."*

She felt the springs above her tense and groan and she heard Brenda's moans of passion. *God, I'll be glad when that bitch is out of our lives.*

CHAPTER EIGHTEEN

LOVESICK

Glen poured cocktail sauce into a bowl. He sliced a lemon and squeezed the juice into the sauce, added a teaspoon of horseradish and a sprinkle of oregano. He stuck a finger in the sauce, stirred and poked his finger in his mouth. *M-m-m.*

It needed just one more ingredient to make it perfect. From the back of the cupboard, he pulled a jar so small it fit into the palm of his hand. Unscrewing the cap, he sprinkled the contents liberally into the sauce. His secret ingredient—Brenda would love this! She was always calling him a gourmet.

He placed the lid back on the jar then thought, *What the hell!* and poured the rest of the powder into the blood-red sauce. Carefully, he rinsed out the tiny jar and tossed it into the recycling bin under the sink. Then he picked up the wooden spoon and blended the secret ingredient into the thick cocktail sauce.

Glen scrubbed his hands with an extra dab of soap and rinsed them in the sink. He pulled a sprig of peppermint from a plant sitting on the windowsill. He sniffed its pungent odor and placed the sauce on the table next to the oysters-on-the-half-shell. The table looked great. He lit the candles, poured wine for Brenda and club soda for himself and flipped on the radio. Nat King Cole's "Unforgettable" lingered in the room.

The stage was set for a romantic dinner. Glen went to the bedroom to collect his wife, who was napping.

Brenda looked like an angel. She was sleeping on her side; her dark hair swirled around her breasts and across the pink satin pillow. Glen smiled, to himself.

"Wake up, sleepyhead. I have your dinner ready," he said, then kissed her on the neck.

"Um-m. Do I have to get up?" she asked sleepily.

"No. I can put the oysters back in the fridge. You want me to bring your wine in here?"

"No, I'll be up in a second. Let me grab a robe," she said, yawning and stretching.

Glen kissed her cheek. "Don't be long," he said sweetly and went back to the kitchen.

Brenda got out of bed, went to her dresser and, pulling out a nightie, slipped it on. Then she went to her closet and pulled out her silk kimono. It was pink with red and yellow chrysanthemums embroidered on it. The smooth fabric felt like clouds caressing her skin. She only wore it on special occasions because it was so delicate. She slid her feet into the silk slippers that matched and went to the mirror, where she twisted her long hair on top of her head and formed it into a bun. Then she picked up a ruby chopstick inlaid with mother-of-pearl from her vanity and thrust it into the bun. When she let go, the chopstick kept the bun in place. She sprayed perfume onto her hair and the fragrance of gardenias infused the air.

Pleased with her appearance, she went to the kitchen. Glen met her at the door with a glass of white wine and she took a sip. After she swallowed, she yawned.

"Thanks, am I that boring?" Glen teased.

"You're not boring. You just know how to push all my *relax* buttons," she said and nibbled on his ear.

"I can tell you're hungry. I better feed you before you devour my ear," he said and ushered her over to the table. "You look great in that outfit, my little geisha."

"Domo arigato," she said.

"What does that mean?" he asked, as he pulled hot croissants from the oven.

"It's *thank you* in Japanese."

Glen dished some oysters and noodles Alfredo onto their plates. Brenda sniffed the croissants. They were delicate and buttery. Glen lifted his glass of club soda to make a toast.

"I know I haven't been very good to you recently...," he said.

She sighed, "I love you anyway."

Glen took a deep breath. "Starting today, I'm going to make it up to you."

She sipped the wine and they began to eat their meal. Brenda picked up a croissant and began to butter it. "What do you have planned for this weekend?" she asked.

"Nothing," he said. "Thought I'd change the oil in the car. Why?"

"I'd like to go up to Lake Jericho—to spread Mrs. P.'s ashes. We could make a day of it. Maybe we could ride the paddle boats, have a picnic and watch the sunset."

"Sounds good to me," he said agreeably.

Brenda set down her butter knife, picked up her fork and took a bite of the creamy noodles Alfredo. "This is great," she said and took another sip of wine. *Glen's really a good cook. Who would have thought?* She giggled. The wine was going to her head.

"You want to let me in on the joke?" Glen asked, downing an oyster.

She nibbled on the croissant. "I know I've said it before, but I was just thinking again how you've become a gourmet cook."

"So?" he asked.

"What if you had your own cooking show on television? You know, all the chefs have their own gimmick and the thought suddenly came to me that we could call yours *The Galloping Ex-convict.*"

Glen burst into laughter. Brenda took another bite of the noodles, but swallowed it quickly so she could talk. She was encouraged by Glen's enjoyment and continued her silliness.

"And everything you make could have prison stripes on it—broiled chicken with mole stripes, cheesecake with licorice stripes, lasagna with cheese stripes..." Brenda picked up an oyster.

"And each week an inmate can call in and be the special guest," Glen said, "and give his or her favorite recipe."

Brenda was about to eat the oyster when she began imagining another funny idea. She set the oyster shell down so she could tell it to Glen. "And you could have a concealed weapon segment on each show—'How to Hide a Saw in Your Jell-O Ring' or 'Finding Files in Your Frankfurters.'" She was tipsy, she thought, or she'd never say such silly things, not with her law-and-order upbringing. She picked up the oyster, spooned some cocktail sauce on it and swallowed. It slid down her throat like it was coated in velvet. *M-m-m.*

"Or, 'Hiding Hacksaws in Your Hash,'" Glen said. He was getting into the silliness of it all.

Brenda picked up another oyster and poured sauce onto it. "Now you're the Glen I fell in love with. We used to laugh and have a great time playing charades, telling ghost stories or just acting silly," she said laughing, then downed the oyster.

Glen was still laughing. "Please don't mention this idea to Suzy. She'll think it's a great way to advertise your dad's cars and really want me to do it."

"I think we ought to do it on Public Access and see if we can sell it to *Saturday Night Live*."

"You aren't getting me within ten miles of a camera," Glen joked.

Suddenly, a sharp pain shot through Brenda's stomach. It felt like she'd swallowed a razor blade. The pain was so bad it took her breath away. She instinctively reached for her water glass, but knocked it over. Her sight was blurring and it was weird, but she could actually hear the blood rushing through her veins. Another stabbing pain ripped through her and she screamed!

Glen rushed to her side. She could see his lips move, but she couldn't hear what he was saying. She threw back her head and grabbed her stomach. As if she were doing the Heimlich maneuver, she forced her forearms into her abdomen in hopes it would make her vomit. It didn't work. Her head was spinning and she put it between her knees to keep from passing out.

Another pain gripped her and she thought that if she had a spear she'd use it to slit herself open to get out whatever was causing the pain. She wanted to throw-up and knew she needed to, but nothing was happening. She rammed her finger down her throat as far as she could get it. Brenda felt the warm mucous, the reflex action and finally the food came up her throat and spewed out onto the floor. Now that her stomach was expelling its contents, she couldn't stop throwing up. The smell was putrid.

"I feel like I'm going to die," she gasped. When she thought there couldn't possibly be anything left in her stomach, the sharp pains were replaced with gnawing deeper ones. Glen kept trying to give her Pepto-Bismol tablets, but she knew they weren't strong enough for this type of pain. Brenda feared she had an ulcer or stomach cancer, because once the bulk of food was out of her stomach, the sharp stabbing pains turned to severe stomach cramps.

She longed for the comfort of the toilet but didn't think she could make it. Her legs were trembling too much. Glen offered to help her to the bathroom, but she waved him off. "I can't move. Don't move me," she managed to sputter. Glen sat next to her and stroked her back, but was powerless to do anymore for her than that.

After about an hour, the pain began to subside. Brenda looked at her beautiful kimono. It was splattered with food and specks of blood. She was heartbroken and it took all of her strength to merely slip out of it.

"Glen, soak this in cold water for me," she said, letting it fall to the floor.

"You're sick as a horse and you're worried about some stupid robe?" he asked incredulously.

"Please?" was all she could muster.

She stood in her nightie watching him draw water in the kitchen sink and toss the grimy kimono in it.

"What do you think is making me so sick?" Brenda asked Glen.

"Maybe the oysters were bad. Where'd you get them?" he asked.

"The Red Snapper Market," she told him.

"I don't feel so hot myself," he said, holding his stomach.

"Food poisoning?"

"I think so," he said, dumping the tray of oysters in the trash.

Suddenly, the pain became intense again. Brenda doubled over, grabbing the table for support.

"Can you drive me to the emergency room?" she asked.

"Sure, but do you really feel up to a four-hour wait just to have them tell you it's food poisoning and there's nothing they can do?"

She knew he was right. She hated the emergency room. She'd probably catch some other dreadful disease from the person sitting next to her. She shook her head to indicate that she didn't want to go. "It's pretty bad when you don't feel well enough to go to the emergency room."

Brenda heaved again. She didn't want to make a further mess, so she stayed in the kitchen with her head resting on the edge of a trashcan. She watched Glen seal all the other food and place it in the refrigerator. He washed the dishes, cleaned the floor and even hung the kimono out to dry. Then he carried the wastebasket filled with paper towels and vomit outside to the trash barrel.

"Glen," she said. "I feel like I'm going to pass out" As she drifted into oblivion Brenda felt Glen pick her up and carry her to their bed.

She was grateful that she'd taken to parking her car behind the barn. If his wife had seen her, it would've been all over. Instead, she'd waited throughout the sex, Brenda's nap and her primping. When she heard them laughing in the kitchen, she dragged herself out from under the bed. She had to get out of there pronto, but she also had to be quiet about it.

She slid the latch on the window lock back and carefully raised the window an inch at a time. Sniffer watched her with curious eyes. When the window was finally open, she hiked her leg and stuck it out the window into the darkness. She bent over and straddled the window ledge. The stone wall scratched her leg. She winced and tossed her clothes out the window. She tried to inspect her leg, but it was too dark to see anything.

Shit, I hope there are no snakes out there waiting to bite me. She lowered her outside foot to the ground and pulled the rest of her body out the window. Sniffer barked. "Sh-h-h-h," she told him putting her index finger to her lips. He seemed to understand and wagged his tail. She carefully pulled down the bedroom window.

Well, at least she was finally out of the house. She picked up her clothes and took off running. She ran crouched over through the rows of Brenda's vegetable garden. She heard Sniffer barking inside the house and hoped he wouldn't blow it for her. The other animals heard Sniffer too and they joined the alarm. She looked back over her shoulder at the house to see if anyone was at the window. They weren't.

Suddenly, she went flying and landed face down in the dirt. Her red nightie snagged on a tomato stake and ripped. *Damn. It's ruined.* She picked herself up and started gathering her clothes. When she tripped and fell, they'd flown everywhere. She looked back to see what had tripped her. It was a big pumpkin lying in the middle of the row. She hadn't seen it before, but now it shone in the moonlight like a huge amber stone.

She took off running again. This time she did not look back. She ran to the back of the barn to her car. Now she'd have to wait for his signal before she started the car and went home.

She slipped into her jeans and replaced the nightie with her blouse. She looked out at the huge harvest moon. It was big and had an orange tinge to it. *How romantic.* She sighed and tried to doze off. She tried to get comfortable, but the plastic seats were cold.

Suddenly, the car door popped open. She tried to scream, but a man's hand pressed hard against her mouth. He was silhouetted against the full moon and she couldn't see his face. He softly whispered, "Sh-h-h. It's me."

She stopped struggling and kissed the hand against her mouth. He released his hold on her and climbed in the car. "She's sick and she passed out. I think you can safely go."

She nodded. "I'll be thinking of you."

"Me too."

He went back into the house. Some time later the telephone rang. He spoke only a few minutes. Then he got a blanket, lay down on the sofa and fell asleep.

The next morning, Brenda had a headache and her whole body ached. She'd never had food poisoning before, but she felt too awful for that to be all that was wrong. But she'd heard patients say that they thought they were going to die when they had food poisoning.

She came out to the living room and heard Glen snoring as he lay on the couch. "Glen," she called.

Awake now, he jumped up and stared at Brenda as if he'd seen a ghost.

"I'm sorry, I didn't mean to startle you. Could you bring me a cold compress. I still feel so dizzy."

"Right away. Just go back to bed," he said sputtering.

She made her way back to the bedroom and laid back down, her head spinning. She heard the phone ring and tried to focus but she must have dropped off to sleep again.

She woke some time later when she heard the front door open and close. "Knock, knock," Brenda heard Jane call out. Jane stuck her head around the bedroom door.

"Everybody decent?" Jane asked.

"Yeah, I'm a mess but come on in," Brenda answered.

Brenda flashed Glen, who was now sitting beside the

bed, a questioning look but he averted his eyes. Jane came in carrying a big bowl.

"I called early this morning and Glen told me you ate something and were sick. I brought you a bowl of chicken soup." Jane set the bowl on the dresser and turned to look at Brenda. "You do look awfully pale. Do you have a fever?"

"No. Thanks for bringing the soup, but I don't feel like eating anything right now. Glen, could you put it in the refrigerator for later?" Brenda asked.

He nodded and took the bowl to the kitchen. Jane sat down in the chair beside the bed. "Are you really okay?" Jane asked.

Brenda told Jane about the previous night. "I'm worried. It couldn't be food poisoning if Glen ate the same thing and he didn't have the same reaction I did."

"Maybe you're allergic to oysters."

"No, I don't think so. I've never had a problem before."

"What do you think it is?"

"I don't know." Brenda shook her head weakly. "But I'm going for a physical as soon as I can set up an appointment."

"Well, you know Brenda, every *body* is different. Maybe Glen has a cast iron stomach. It'd have to be after twelve years of prison food."

Brenda sighed. She was sorry she had confided in Jane that Glen had been in jail. At the time, Brenda needed to get the news off her chest and she had rationalized that with Jane's ex-husband having been incarcerated, Jane would be sympathetic. But she almost immediately regretted telling her. She felt slightly guilty telling Glen's secret to someone who obviously already had something against him.

Brenda shrugged off her annoyance. "Yeah, but Glen's been acting very strangely lately. I've been afraid he was having an affair and then last night he was his old romantic self again and now this."

"Look, this is no time to think about these things. Just concentrate on getting better."

As Jane visited with Brenda, Brenda began looking more and more tired. "You need some rest, Brenda," Jane said. "I'll call later." She walked out of the bedroom and left the door ajar. Then she went to the kitchen.

Glen was sitting at the kitchen table looking out the window, staring off into the distance. Jane took the seat across from him.

"You've got a problem. Brenda is sick and miserable, and she's doubting you! As her best friend it's my duty to tell you, you better treat her right and show her you love her."

Glen gave her an irritated scowl. "What am I supposed to do?"

"Don't look at me like that. You have to make Brenda feel loved and protected. Try to be a good husband. No, try to be a perfect husband! No matter what happens, don't squabble. Pamper her. Why don't you take her on a vacation?"

"Brenda won't go on a vacation. She'd never take the time off work," Glen said.

"Well, shoot, you're right about that. She's a workaholic. Hmm...Your anniversary must be coming up, right?"

"Yeah, next month."

"Well, there you go. You should give her a wonderful gift and a party. Make it romantic, Glen. You have to prove to her you really love her."

Jane caught a flicker of movement out of the corner of her eye and turned her head to see Brenda walking into the bathroom.

Turning back to Glen, she asked, "You do love her, don't you?"

"Of course, just sometimes I let my temper get the better of me."

Jane glanced at her watch. "Oh, damn. I gotta go. I've got a gazillion appointments today. Think about what I said. And if you need help planning something, call me," she said and scurried out the door.

CHAPTER NINETEEN

ANNIVERSARY WALTZ

Brenda came home early. She wanted to clean the house just in case any of the guests at the anniversary party decided to come back there afterward for drinks. She looked at the kitchen clock. It was 3:06. The anniversary dinner wasn't until 7:30 at the Muehlebach Hotel. She had plenty of time to clean the house, shampoo her hair and get dressed.

Glen's being so sweet these days. I think seeing me so sick with food poisoning scared him, too. Oh, that reminds me.

She ripped her 'To-Do' list off the refrigerator, took it to the phone and dialed. As it rang, she took out a pen and put a line through "get a physical."

The receptionist answered. "Doctor Thomas' office."

"Danielle, this is Brenda Brumbaugh. I have an appointment on Monday and I'm going to have to cancel. I have got to work."

"Do you want to reschedule?"

"Yes, but I can't right now. I'll call you later when things slow down," Brenda replied and hung up.

She went back to the kitchen and stuck the to-do list back on the fridge. Then she picked up the dirty dishes from the table and washed them. Afterward, she tackled the junk mail. It amazed Brenda how the stuff took over the house. When she was finished, she had two big dog food sacks full of advertisements and catalogs. She checked the kitchen garbage; it was full. She hadn't done much housework since being sick and she figured that Glen must have forgotten to take out the trash this week. She went around the house collecting trash from all the wastebaskets and, with the bags full of junk mail, carried it all outside to the trash barrels.

As Brenda went to throw a trash bag in the first barrel, she saw it was full. She walked over to the next barrel. It too was full. *If I don't take care of the garbage, it never gets done! I'll have to remind Glen what day the trash pick-up is,* she told herself. *We can't have all this garbage piling up.* The next one seemed only half-full, but on top of the heap was the cute little chipmunk she usually fed. He was dead.

"Aaah...What killed you?" she said sadly. She looked more carefully. "Gosh, that looks like the mess from me being sick. That's strange," she murmured, and promptly forgot about the garbage having accumulated.

When she returned to the house, Glen was raiding the refrigerator for something to drink.

"What were you doing out there?"

"Taking out the trash. That little chipmunk was dead inside the trash barrel. He was lying on my pukey paper towels. Do you think he got into some of the fertilizer we put out or poison or something?" she asked

She noticed Glen had a shocked look on his face and it surprised her because she didn't think he cared anything about the chipmunk. She was the one that was always feeding it.

"He probably got in there and couldn't get out. I bet he had a heart attack," Glen added and kissed her on the forehead. "We better go take our showers. Don't want to be late to our own party."

Brenda carefully poked the delicate porcelain butterfly encrusted with rubies on a tortoise comb into her hair. She wore her hair in a french twist and the butterfly nested perfectly in the top of the swirl. She looked in the visor mirror. The wine-colored velvet dress draped across her shoulders in a sexy V. She picked up the string of rubies resting in her lap. They were a simple strand with an old-fashioned clasp. Mrs. P. had insisted she give them to her and that made them special, like having Mrs. P along with her for the evening. Brenda fastened the clasp around her neck; she was surprised at how heavy they were.

"How do they look?" she asked Glen.

"Nice. What do you think those are worth?"

"I don't know. Mrs. P said she got them in 1952 in Thailand. They're probably worth several thousand dollars."

Glen whistled in amazement. "You sure you want to wear them out?"

"Yeah, I won't let anything happen to 'em."

"Okay, it's your neck," Glen said.

"So to speak." She smiled at the pun and thought about how far Glen had come since their wedding day. He'd evolved from a man who couldn't accept a simple wedding party to a man who'd planned a sit-down dinner for eighteen people. It was their first anniversary and they were going to celebrate in style.

She glanced over at Glen. He looked stunning in his black tuxedo and gold bow tie. The stark white collar made her realize he'd lost some of his usual year-round tan. She supposed it was from his job which required him to be inside most of the time. In prison, he'd told her, he'd been the caretaker of the grounds and the Warden's yard. He was outside all the time then.

Still, it was odd that a prisoner would have a tan and a free man wouldn't. She smiled at him and he grinned back. He was still a man who could turn women's heads. His hair was swept back in natural waves and he'd gotten a manicure for the occasion. He looked even more handsome than at their wedding. She loved him more now than she ever had back then.

The car slowed to a stop in front of the Muehlebach Hotel and the doorman opened her door. She stepped out of the car and sucked in a breath. She'd never seen such a beautiful place. Huge planters containing full-sized shrubs and trees lined the front and were bordered by deep purple and yellow chrysanthemums. Behind the greenery stood the lovely old hotel. Its face was of red brick and at ground level huge arched windows looked out on the hotel front. Above those were rows of smaller windows and each one was dotted with a decorative keystone.

Walking through the wide front doors, Brenda looked at the deep burgundy carpet runner leading into the foyer and thought how serendipitous that it matched her dress perfectly. She waited for Glen and wondered how much this soiree was setting them back. *It doesn't matter*, she told herself. *He's done this for me*.

Glen finally joined her. She tucked her arm in his and they strolled inside.

The foyer walls were a smoky, pink marble with gray streaks and all the woodwork was a dark cherry. Extravagant chandeliers hung from the ceiling and huge artworks of smiling cherubs graced the walls. Brenda knew she was out of her element. This must have been how Cinderella felt going to the King's ball. She squeezed Glen's arm. He gave her a confident smile. "We have our own private reception room," he said leading the way.

The plush carpet under her feet sank luxuriously with each step she took. Brenda felt like she was gliding and everyone they passed was jealous. What were they thinking? *What a fine couple?* Or, *What is she doing with that handsome guy?* Then her thoughts turned to her classmates' voices. "You're homely, Brenda. Nobody but your daddy is every gonna love you."

Brenda willed their voices to go away. *This is stupid. It doesn't matter what they said or what other people in this hotel are thinking. You're married now and he thinks you're beautiful.* She pushed away her past doubts about Glen's loyalty. *Stop putting yourself down.* She straightened her shoulders, stood tall and kept on walking.

Soon they came to a sign which read, Private Party by Invitation Only. She hesitated, but Glen kept her moving as he whispered, "We're the guests of honor."

She laughed. *Of course we are.*

As Glen swung open the door, Brenda was taken aback. The overall effect of the reception room was dazzling. It was decorated as an old-fashioned parlor, with a Victorian settee, elaborate swags and drapes and fern stands. To the back of the room were three round tables laid out with crystal and gold-rimmed china and in the center of each was a crystal bud vase filled with baby green orchids.

When Brenda stepped into the room and Glen joined her, everyone applauded. As she looked around the room, she saw all the people that she loved. The first two people her eyes landed on were her siblings, Dave and Suzy. They were wearing matching western cut tuxedos made out of forest green silk. The only difference between them was Suzy's had silver and black beaded fringe around the shoulders and she wore a coordinated beaded cummerbund. Next to them were her parents looking proud and happy.

Brenda searched the room and found her best friend. Jane was wearing a flesh-tone, strapless dress that conformed to her body like a second layer of skin. It was covered with opaque silver sequins and when the light caught it just right it looked like she was nude. She looked great as usual and Brenda wished that just once she could be prettier than Jane. No sooner did she have the thought than she was scolding herself for thinking such a thing.

You should never think ill of someone, Brenda. God will turn those thoughts on you, she heard her Daddy's voice say. She wouldn't let the past ruin tonight and she blanked the memory from her head.

Brenda looked around at all her friends and her eyes swelled with tears of joy. Glen kissed her on the cheek and said, "This is all for you Brenda."

"This is so sweet. I can't believe you did all this," Brenda said to Glen and then kissed him on the cheek.

"That's because you don't know how special you are to me," he replied.

Glen nodded to the wine steward and the tuxedo-clad gentleman brought in three bottles of champagne, popped the corks and poured Glen a glass. He sipped and nodded his approval like a pro. "I'm suspending my alcohol-free state for the evening," he whispered to Brenda while the wine steward and his staff poured everyone a glass. She was so happy tonight, that she decided she shouldn't spoil the evening by reprimanding him. It was a special occasion, after all.

Dave raised his glass to make a toast. "To Brenda and Glen, the best friends I've ever had."

"Thanks a lot!" Suzy said, jabbing him in the ribs.

"You're the oldest. You're too bossy to be my friend," Dave responded.

"Then sit down and keep quiet," Suzy teased and everyone laughed. Then Suzy raised her glass and turned toward Brenda and Glen. "Happy anniversary!"

"To long and happy marriages," her dad added.

There were a few "Here, here's" and everybody took a sip in honor of the couple. Glen nodded to his mother-in-law who disappeared through the double doors leading into the kitchen. She came out followed by a waiter pushing a cart that held a gorgeous wedding cake. It was four tiers tall, mounted on filigree columns and laced with peach-colored roses.

"This is even more beautiful than the one at our wedding—the happiest day of my life," Glen said and pecked Brenda on the lips.

The awe-struck guests *ooh-ed* and *ahh-ed*.

"That must have cost a friggin' fortune," Jane blurted out.

Everyone turned to look at her. She reddened and said, "Glen, you're pretty loose with Brenda's money."

"What's it to you, bitch?" Glen immediately retorted.

Brenda's smile melted. She couldn't believe this was happening. *How could they be so insensitive?* She wanted to grab them both by their ears like naughty children and lead them out of the room. Weren't they embarrassed by their bratty, childish behavior?

Brenda knew Jane was only trying to protect her interests, but couldn't she do it privately? And Glen, how could he call Jane a bitch in public? What was he thinking? Didn't he realize the impossible predicament he was putting her in? Was Glen so jealous that he would force her to choose between her husband and her best friend? Didn't he know she'd always choose him? What was she going to do?

Just as she was about to speak, her brother Dave stepped between Glen and Jane trying to be the peacemaker. "Calm down. We're all just trying to have a good time here."

"Can you two try to get along for just two hours?" Brenda asked.

"I don't think so. This *bitch* is going home," Jane snarled and stormed out of the room. There was an intense silence. No one knew what to say.

Finally Glen said, "I'm sorry, Brenda."

Brenda sighed. "Glen, don't apologize to me, apologize to Jane. Go see if you can talk her into staying."

Glen nodded and walked out of the room. Brenda noticed her father watching him with a troubled frown.

Brenda turned back to the guests. She knew everyone was looking to her to set the tone. Whatever her reaction was would dictate their mood. She painted on a smile. "It's time to celebrate. Please have a cocktail before dinner is served," she called out cheerfully.

Glen found Jane in front of the building crying as she hailed a taxi. When she saw him coming, she wiped her eyes with the back of her hand. "Do you have some other nasty wisecrack you want to make? Should I gather a group of people so you have an audience to insult me in front of?" she asked angrily.

Glen bit his lip. "No," he stammered. "I just wanted to say I'm sorry for losing my temper. Brenda really wants you to come back to the party."

Jane shook her head and sighed. "No, I look like hell from crying. Just tell her we made up, but I was too embarrassed to come back."

Glen was annoyed and angry with Jane, but at this moment, seeing her tears, he felt badly about his behavior. After all, it was she who had given him the idea of having an anniversary party to begin with. He put a hand on her shoulder and pleaded, "Jane, please come back in."

Just then a taxi pulled up. "No, my ride's here. I'll be okay. Go back in and have fun."

Impulsively, Glen gave her a quick hug. Jane stiffened in his embrace and when he let go, she stared at him, mouth agape. She was about to say something when she saw a dark look in Glen's eyes and realized he was staring at something behind her. She turned to see what had gotten his attention.

There was a man across the parking lot watching them. As the man walked toward them he passed under a light and Glen, realizing who it was, muttered, "Damn, it's that nut Morgan."

He opened the taxi door and pushed Jane inside. "Geez, thanks for the royal treatment," she said.

"Aaw, shut up Jane." He slammed the door and the taxi pulled away.

As the cab drove off, Jane saw Glen stride over to Morgan and sensed there was going to be trouble between the two men.

When he reached Morgan, Glen quickly lunged at him, grabbing the other man's arm and wrenching it behind his back. "What the hell are you doing here?"

Morgan twisted free and turned to face Glen. "I could ask you the same question after what I just saw." Morgan smirked. "Maybe I should go inside and tell you wife about your lady friend."

"That was nothin'. And you won't go anywhere near my wife unless you want to get hurt."

"Is that the same girlfriend I saw you with last week?"

"What are you doin,' following me around? Are you watching me? Maybe I should break your neck. Why are you spying on us all the time?"

"Let's just say I have a score to settle. What's your excuse?"

"I don't have to make excuses to you," Glen said. "Just stay out of our lives."

"What if I don't?"

"If you don't, I'll take care of you permanently," Glen shot back and headed inside so swiftly he didn't hear Morgan's reply.

"Not if I get you first."

By the time Glen returned to the reception room, Brenda was already opening their presents. He decided to stay at the back of the room until she finished unwrapping the silver paper of the gift she was on.

"I wanted to buy an infant swing," Suzy said, "as a really strong hint, but I didn't want you to spray me with champagne. So, I decided to give you great-grandma's vase—the one you always wanted."

Brenda held up the vase for the rest of the guests to see and then putting it down, went over to embrace her sister.

"Suzy, I love you. Thank you." She placed the gift next to a Lenox picture frame, satin sheets, embroidered towels and a crystal bowl.

Brenda hadn't really wanted to start opening the gifts without Glen, but it had been the only way she could think of to break the tension that had settled over the party. The lack of his presence made everyone nervous.

Glen walked over and took his seat next to Brenda. She was grateful that he was finally back. She was dying to know what happened with Jane, but she didn't dare ask. The guests were completely silent again. Brenda figured they were curious, too. She nervously tried to fill the void.

"Look at the beautiful things we've accumulated, Glen. This is like our wedding," she said cheerfully.

She opened the card attached to the next box. She read it aloud. "To Glen and Brenda. Love, Jane." Everyone looked at each other. Brenda tore open the box and peered inside. Swaddled in tissue paper was a collector's knife with an ivory jeweled handle. It was obviously an expensive antique, but the deep, sharp beveled edge of the blade made her wince.

"Well, I knew she didn't like me but..." Glen laughed and the others followed.

Then her brother Dave tossed Brenda a penny.

"What's that for?" she asked him.

"For good luck. It's the custom when you receive something sharp."

Brenda smiled, but her mind was on Jane's gift. It wasn't like Jane to give such an odd present. Whatever possessed her to... Brenda's train of thought was interrupted when Glen placed a long floral box in her lap.

"This is from me," he said. She gave him a quick kiss and opened the box. Inside was an expensive hunting rifle. Brenda frowned at Glen. *Is he crazy? I hate guns.*

He laughed. "I wish you could see the expression on your face. It's really my present to me." He leaned over to her and whispered, "Of course, I couldn't register it in my name." Then he took a small box out of his pocket and handed it to her. Inside was a diamond and ruby heart on a gold chain. Brenda gave him a big kiss and the rest of the room cheered.

Suzy handed Brenda a colorful package. It was wrapped in a manly paper that had an African motif. Brenda held it out to Glen, "I got this for you."

Glen ran his hand over the satiny paper and gently peeled back the tape on the ends of the package making sure not to tear it. When he finally slid the box out, scrolled across the lid were the words Pete the Repeat Parrot. Glen opened the box and peered inside. A colorful stuffed parrot, mounted on a perch, stared back at him.

"What in blue blazes is this?" he asked.

"What in blue blazes is this? What in blue blazes is this?" repeated the toy parrot.

All the guests laughed at the silly toy, but Glen's eyes twinkled like a child's on Christmas morning. As he took the velvety bird out of the box, he saw on the parrot's neck a gold chain with a number one encrusted with diamonds.

Glen looked at Brenda. "I don't know which gift I like best," he said and brushed his lips across her cheek. "You are wonderful."

"You are wonderful. You are wonderful," the parrot repeated.

Glen laughed. Then he leaned over to Brenda and said quietly, "I'll be right back. I gotta go pee."

"I gotta go pee. I gotta go pee," the parrot said.

Glen handed the parrot to Brenda for safekeeping and she watched Glen head toward the door.

Brenda was delighted that Glen enjoyed her gifts. She hadn't been sure what to get him. He wasn't into tools, sports, gardening or any kind of hobby. Hunting was the only thing he did like and she certainly wasn't about to buy him a gun. She was sure his lack of interests was due to the long time he had spent incarcerated. What do you give to someone who's been caged like an animal for so long and is so insecure? She bought the talking parrot because it made her laugh and she'd hoped it would do the same for Glen. Then she put the necklace she'd chosen for him around its neck so he would know what he meant to her.

The maitre'd announced, "Dinner is served."

The guests started gravitating toward the dinner tables.

Dave went to move the rifle out of Brenda's lap. When he touched the rifle, sparks flew. He quickly withdrew his hand.

"Static electricity," Suzy told him.

Brenda saw her dad staring at the rifle with a very troubled expression and wondered why.

After the sumptuous meal, a three-piece trio played "The Anniversary Waltz" as Glen whirled Brenda around the dance floor.

CHAPTER TWENTY

A BAD OMEN

The warm sun streamed through the kitchen window onto Brenda. She sat at the table with yesterday's newspaper spread out before her. She took a piece of the bumpy old milk-glass vase Suzy had given her and tried to fit it to several other pieces. The vase had slipped out of her hands as she was washing it. Repairing the vase was like putting together a three dimensional puzzle. She wouldn't have even bothered except it had belonged to her great-grandmother and she had to try and save it.

She found two pieces that fit and smeared super-glue on their edges. The glue stuck to Brenda's fingers and she couldn't let go of the vase. The tube of glue was also sticking to the newspaper. *What I need is four more hands. Why did it have to break?* She wished Suzy hadn't given it to her then immediately felt guilty for thinking such a thing. *Family's all that counts, Brenda!* her daddy's voice scolded in her mind.

The vase was the only thing she owned—besides her wedding dress—that had belonged to her great-grandmother. Well, there *was* a one-hundred-year-old, hand-painted egg from Russia that would be hers someday, but right now it belonged to her father.

Brenda thought she heard a door open and a chilling draft hit her. She looked toward the front door, but no one was there. "Glen?" she called. No answer. She wanted to get up and take a look around, but if she let go of the vase it would be ruined.

She tried to concentrate on the vase, but the dogs out back began barking and howling. She had a strong sense of dread. Her instincts told her something wasn't right. She shrugged it off and started looking at the other pieces of the vase, trying to figure out which one she could glue next when this one was dried.

Suddenly, there were hands around Brenda's neck. She screamed and jumped so high that she left the seat of the chair.

"Gotcha!" Jane said, laughing.

"Jane, you just about gave me a heart attack. Now wouldn't that have been nice?"

"Sorry. I didn't know you had a weak heart," Jane said in a tone that was a statement and a question rolled into one.

"I don't," Brenda said, turning her attention back to the vase. She couldn't believe her hands were still attached to the vase and she started ripping her sticky fingers away from the slick surface. She watched Jane flop into the chair.

"What are you doing to that old thing?" Jane asked.

"It belonged to my great-granny. I always wanted it and my sister gave it to us at the anniversary party last month. I tried to get the old residue off it and as I washed it, it slipped out of my hands."

"Here. Let me help you hold it," Jane said.

Brenda picked up the super-glue. The page of newspaper was stuck to the tube and it came up too. She tore off the newspaper, but it stuck to her finger. She pulled it off with one hand and it stuck to that hand. She finally pulled it off with another piece of clean newspaper and went back to her task. Brenda applied the glue on the edges of the broken pieces of the vase. She motioned for Jane to help her hold it together and she did.

"I think I need some nail polish remover," Brenda said as she picked at the glue on her fingers. "It makes me crazy having this stuff on my fingertips."

"Speaking of fingers, can I borrow your ruby ring?" Jane asked.

"No. Mrs. P. gave it to me. Anyway, you'll get it when I die. I already told Glen."

"Please?" Jane begged and lowered her head. She stuck out her lip in a pouty manner and looked up.

Brenda almost laughed, "That *poor, pitiful me* routine isn't going to work with me."

Taking a new tact, Jane said, "Come on. I have a new man in my life."

Brenda was peeling the flaking pieces of glue off her fingers. She looked up, "Tell me you haven't fallen in love again."

"I think you'd like this guy. He's not like the others," Jane said, trying to convince Brenda.

"How'd you meet him?"

"Through a friend."

"I knew you'd do this again," Brenda said, but she was thinking, *There's no use trying to tell Jane anything. When it comes to men she's deaf, dumb, blind and always looking for Easy Street.* "So when's the wedding?" Brenda asked, resigned.

"He's already married. We have to wait until he gets rid of his wife," Jane said.

Brenda gave Jane a wary look.

"What?" Jane asked innocently.

"I think I'll go to law school just so I can handle your divorces," Brenda teased. "It'd be a great paying sideline."

They laughed.

Brenda heard the front door open and looked up. Glen was coming in from work. His clothes were greasy. In one hand he held a small gift. He sat the lunchbox on the floor and began to remove his work overalls.

"Hi, honey. You're home early," Brenda said, smiling from ear to ear. She jumped out of her chair in the kitchen and ran to greet him at the front door.

"We were shortstaffed in the maintenance department today so I was helping out with oil changes, but the hydraulic lift broke down," he explained, embracing her. He smelled of motor oil, but Brenda didn't care.

"What's in the package?" Jane called from the kitchen.

Their moment was broken and Glen released Brenda. It was obvious he didn't know Jane was there until that moment. He glared at Jane, but handed Brenda the present. It was wrapped in her favorite color—peach. The afternoon sun streaming through the side window lit up the pretty foil paper. It glistened in contrast to the floppy bow that was a darker shade of peach.

"It's payday and I spent it on a little somethin' for you," he said to Brenda.

Brenda took the gift and went back to the kitchen table to open it. It was an unexpected surprise. She savored the moment and opened it slowly. Underneath the wrapping was a blue velvet jewelry case. She flipped up the brass clasp and opened the case. Inside was a lovely gold and diamond bracelet which spelled out *I Love You*. Brenda gasped.

"It's beautiful, Glen, but you shouldn't have spent your whole paycheck," Brenda said. When she looked at Glen, she could tell he was hurt.

"What's the matter? It's not good enough for you?" he asked in a snippy tone.

Brenda was sorry she'd even said anything. "It's not that...I didn't mean to insult you..." she said, reaching for his hand. He pulled away and she continued, "It's just that with the new house, we could've used the money to pay some bills."

"I wish I had a man who'd buy me something that nice," Jane said.

"See," Glen said angrily. "Even Jane appreciates me more than you." He opened the refrigerator and stared inside. "Where's my Dr. Pepper?"

"We're out Glen. I'll pick up some tomorrow. Have a Coke." Brenda said.

"I hate plain old cola drinks," he complained. "Tastes like your drinking nothing."

"Can I let go of this vase? I need something to drink," Jane said.

"Sure. I'm sorry Jane, I forgot you were holding it," Brenda said. Jane let go of the vase. It was as good as new. Brenda smiled. "There's peach tea in the fridge," she told Jane.

Jane walked to the mini-bar, "I'm making a rum and Coke, either of you want one?"

Brenda said, "No" at the same time Glen said, "Yes." Brenda glared at Glen.

"Glen, you're not supposed to be drinking," Brenda said.

"One drink isn't going to hurt," he said.

Jane went to the bar and started mixing Coke with triple shots of rum. She filled two glasses and placed them on a silver tray. Coming over, she handed one drink to Glen. Brenda noticed his hand quivered as he took the glass.

Surprised, she watched him down the drink. She thought of saying something to him but told herself to keep quiet. When he was in one of his stubborn moods, Brenda knew she was wasting her time trying to talk to him. It would just make him worse. At times like these, he reminded her of a rebellious teenager hell-bent on showing everybody he could do what he damned well pleased.

"That was quick," Jane said. She took his empty glass and handed hers to him. She shrugged at Brenda and went to the bar to make herself another drink. She took a clean glass, plopped in two ice-cubes and rubbed another ice-cube on her neck as she poured rum and Coke into the glass. "I'm hot," she said, "and the ice feels cool on my neck."

"Jane has a new boyfriend," Brenda said in a too cheerful manner, trying to change the subject.

"Who?" Glen asked.

"He's married," Jane said.

Glen sipped his drink and said nothing.

"Tell her she's crazy for dating a married man," Brenda said to Glen. "Ten-to-one, he'll never leave his wife."

"Brenda's right. You're playing with fire," he said, glaring at Jane.

"I don't look at it that way. I see it as having the guts to go after what I want," Jane said.

Glen downed his drink, stood and paused. Brenda could tell he was dizzy by the way he swayed. He regained his balance, walked to the bar and made himself another.

"Glen, slow down. You promised!" Brenda pleaded.

"I'm just being sociable. Aren't I, Jane?" he said.

"I think you're getting drunk," Jane replied.

"To hell with you two. I'll show you...drunk." He picked up the decanter and drank straight out of it. Lowering the decanter from his lips he said, "Aaah...Jamaican liquid gold—one hundred fifty proof."

Jane turned to Brenda, who had a horror-stricken look on her face. "I think I better leave."

"I think that might be a good idea," Brenda said, not blinking an eye.

Jane picked up her handbag and dashed out the door.

Brenda was glad Jane had gone home. She didn't understand why Jane had enticed Glen to drink in the first place. She knew he was a sober alcoholic. *That's like giving a suicidal man a gun. Of course, Glen's a grown man and should have known better than to accept the drinks.* It was his fault. Brenda watched him guzzling from the decanter and it sickened her.

"Glen, why did you do that?" she asked.

He lowered the decanter and spoke. "Because I don't like it when women tell me what to do!"

"But we agreed..." she said.

"But we agreed!" he said, mocking her in a hateful way. "Just shut the fuck up or I'm liable to break your damned neck!" he yelled.

"Then drink yourself into a coma, but I'm getting out of here!" she cried.

"There won't be any fucking divorce. The only way you're getting out of this marriage is in a pine box," he bellowed.

"Don't you ever use foul language with me again!" Brenda was hurt that he'd broken his promise and more than a little scared. His threat seemed genuine. She saw the vein in his temple pulsing. Suddenly, Brenda felt him grab her shoulder and strike a blow to her face. She twisted away, kicking him hard in the groin. She watched as he slipped, fell to the floor and hit his head. Running into their bedroom, she locked the door with trembling fingers.

Glen was roused to consciousness by Sniffer, who was affectionately licking him in the face. Glen grimaced and shoved the dog away. "Get away from me, sewer breath."

Sniffer cocked his head to one side as if to say *I'm sorry.*

Glen touched the goose egg at the back of his head and wondered what he was doing on the floor. He remembered drinking, grabbing Brenda and socking her before she kicked him and stomped off to the bedroom. He struggled to his feet and staggered to the bedroom door. He was still drunk and he was livid.

When he tried to turn the door handle, he found that Brenda had locked him out. He pounded on the door and angrily yelled, "Open the door, dammit! I want to go to bed!"

He waited, but she didn't answer. This time he knocked politely. "Brenda, please open up. I just want to go to bed." She didn't answer or unlock the door. "Damn you to hell."

Glen stumbled to the kitchen and prowled through the cabinets. He pulled out a can of dog food and opened it. Sniffer heard the can-opener motor and he came running like he always did. Glen looked down at him and grinned at the fuzzy creature. He held the can over a bowl marked *Sniffer* and poured the dog food into it. Sniffer sniffed the air and wagged his tail.

Glen thought he could almost see a smile on the dog's face. *You're hungry, aren't ya? You little shit.* He set the bowl down on the counter and Sniffer hungrily jumped to get at it.

Glen went to the cabinet below the sink and reached for a container of rat poison. He grabbed Sniffer's bowl again. Sniffer growled. He was still hungry.

Glen poured the contents of the box into the dog's food and mixed the two together. Glen was feeling dizzy and held onto the counter until the spell subsided. Then he took the bowl and held it down just low enough to use as bait to get Sniffer to follow him into the backyard.

Brenda lay on the bed. She wiped the tears from her cheeks with her fingertips. For the first time she noticed the blood from her cut lip on the bedspread, got up and went into the bathroom. She looked at the clock. It was already 1:08 A.M. *I can't think about this tonight. I have animals to feed.*

She marched to her closet, grabbed her jacket and a flashlight and walked out. On her way to the backdoor she called, "Sniffer, here boy. Sniffer?"

Where are you? You usually come when I call.

When he didn't come, Brenda went to the pantry. She shoveled dried food out of a barrel and placed it in a five-gallon bucket. She went outside and walked along the animals' cages filling their bowls. She felt bad about waiting so late to feed them. *How would I feel if I didn't get my supper until one o'clock in the morning?*

In the deer barn, a baby Chinese dwarf deer came to her. "I don't have anything," she said, feeling in her pocket. "Wait a minute. Yes, I do." She pulled out a piece of a carrot left over from the day before. The baby deer took the carrot from her. Afterward, he licked her fingers.

"I love you, little deer. You're so precious. That's what I'm going to call you. *Precious!*"

Now that the other animals were fed, Brenda searched the perimeter of the property looking for Sniffer, "Come on, Sniffer. Come to mama." She whistled and waited for a response, but none came.

It was so dark that even walking was difficult. Brenda tripped over stones more than once. She looked at the remnants of wispy white clouds sailing in front of the moon. "I hope you're okay, Sniffer." With that, Brenda walked around the outside of the house one more time.

Maybe he was hiding in the house?

She went back inside the house. The smell of microwave popcorn intercepted her the moment she opened the door. It made her hungry. *As soon as I find Sniffer, I'll make myself some popcorn.*

Brenda searched the house—the bedrooms, under the beds, in the laundry basket...She shined her flashlight around the inside of closets. *I can't imagine where he could have gone.* Brenda was on her way to the kitchen when she saw Glen watching the *Late-Late Show* and munching on popcorn. She didn't want another confrontation so she went to the kitchen for a drink of water.

Glen crept into the kitchen. He was holding his forehead and Brenda knew he had a hangover. When he saw her face, he turned away.

"Do we have any Alka-Seltzer?" he asked.

Brenda nodded and pulled some out of a drawer. "You sit down. I'll fix it for you." She plopped them into a glass of water and they began to fizz. She could feel the little sprinkles of water shooting out of the glass on her hand. She handed the concoction to Glen.

"Thanks," he said.

She wiped the tiny beads of water onto her jeans and took her flashlight to the pantry. She opened the door and looked around.

"What are you doing?" Glen asked.

"I can't find Sniffer. I've looked everywhere," Brenda explained. "'Somebody must have left the door open. Will you help me look for him?"

"Sure," Glen answered, getting up from his chair.

Brenda waited for him while he grabbed his coat from the hall rack and a flashlight from a drawer in the kitchen. Then they both went out the door. It slammed closed with a bang and the other animals barked and growled at the noise.

"Sorry about earlier. It was the rum talking," Glen said. "Now I know I still can't drink. I poured it all down the sink."

"Glen, you scared me tonight and I refuse to live my life in fear," she said.

"It scares me too. I'm like another person. Tonight has made me realize I don't like being out of control. Forgive me?" Glen asked.

"You promised me, Glen!" she cried.

"I made a mistake and I've learned my lesson. I promise, I'll never do it again."

"You promised me before. Why should I believe you'll keep your promise this time?" Brenda asked, ignoring his plea.

"I give you my word. I'll never drink again and I'll never touch you in anger. Just please forgive me," he begged.

She looked into his eyes. She wanted to believe him and have a long, happy life with this man. But how many chances should a woman give a man? How many are too few? How many are too many?

"I'll forgive you this time, Glen, but I will not live with an abusive drunk," she told him.

He reached over and hugged Brenda. He kissed her softly on the lips, then released her. "I bet Sniffer's out here kicking up his heels with those big dogs. I'll go this-a-way." He pointed toward the barn. "You go that-a-way," he said pointing in the opposite direction.

They set out to look for Sniffer with nothing to guide them but their flashlights and the silvery moon.

Down the path, he stopped to enjoy the full moon, then moseyed along toward the woods. He checked to see if Brenda was watching him. She wasn't. He veered off the path and made his way to a spot surrounded by tall straw-like grass. For a few moments, he looked down at Sniffer's dead body. He chuckled to himself, happy to be rid of the smelly hairball. He waited for what seemed to him like the right amount of time to have spent searching for a missing pet, then he turned and walked back to the house.

Later, Brenda sat on her bed, sniffing back tears. In the kitchen, Glen brewed a pot of tea. He brought it back to the bedroom and handed it to her. She took a swallow and tasted the sweet honey Glen had mixed in it. It was soothing.

"Maybe this will calm your nerves," Glen said.

She nodded and took another sip. She couldn't talk right now and hoped he understood.

"Don't worry Brenda. We'll find him tomorrow," Glen said. He placed his hand on her back and rubbed it up and down. It was soothing and she drank some more tea. "You've had a hard day. Come to bed," he said, running his hand across her back, over her shoulder and onto her breast. "I know just the thing to take your mind off of Sniffer."

She wanted to be taken away into the land of ecstasy, where little dogs didn't disappear and nothing mattered but love. She allowed him to take the teacup from her and place it on the nightstand.

He laid her back on the bed and ran his fingers through her long brown hair. Kissing her passionately, he stroked her inner thighs, allowing his hand to return again and again to the hot moistness between her legs. Brenda allowed herself to empty her mind of everything but the smell of his cologne and the feel of his touch—his glorious touch.

She took him in hungrily, without reservation. Their lovemaking worked. It transported her out of the present, up to the cliffs of ecstasy and shoved her off into the hazy depths of deep, soothing sleep.

But when she woke the next morning, the fears, which had faded for a few hours, returned.

CHAPTER TWENTY-ONE

CONFESSIONS

Brenda looked at the winter sky. To the west it was a peri-winkle blue, and the fading light of the setting sun felt warm on her face. Overhead and to the east, the sky sagged with low hanging gray clouds. *Looks like snow*, she thought absentmindly. She took another bite of the tuna sandwich Suzy had brought and poured them each a cup of hot tea from her thermos. The happy chatter of her nephews caught Brenda's attention and she turned to watch them play. *I'd like to have children someday*, she thought wistfully.

She hadn't been completely honest when she'd asked Suzy to meet her at the park. It was true she hadn't seen her nephews in a while, but that wasn't the real reason she'd asked Suzy to come. She needed to talk about Glen. She loved Glen, but last night had been frightening.

"Hey, come over here," Suzy said, snapping her fingers in Brenda's direction. "It's your turn. You said you were get-ting a drink and you've been daydreaming ever since. What's the matter? Afraid your old sister will clean you out?" She laughed and shook her head in mock exasperation. They'd been playing poker when Brenda had gotten up to get the tea and then drifted off into her own thoughts.

"Sorry." Brenda gave her head a shake as if to wake up, walked back, sat down at the table and re-evaluated her hand. She picked out a three-of-hearts and a five-of-spades and threw them down on the rough wooden picnic table. "I'll take two," she said decisively.

Suzy dealt out the two cards then stuffed a potato chip in her mouth. As Brenda studied her cards, Suzy watched her quietly then asked, "You want to tell me about it?"

"What are you talking about?" Brenda responded, swiping one of Suzy's potato chips. She stuck the salty chip in her mouth and let it melt. She liked this method of eating them better than just chomping away at them. She ate fewer this way.

"I don't know, but I'm sure you do. Miss Workaholic takes off a whole hour to watch her nephews in the park? It doesn't compute," Suzy said. "So tell your big sister what's wrong."

Brenda wanted to burst into tears, cry on Suzy's shoulder and let all her problems spew out like champagne from a bottle. But that wasn't her style. She'd always pretty much handled things on her own and she knew Suzy had her hands full, single-parenting two boys. She didn't need to worry about Brenda's problems, too. Brenda sat there trying to find the right words.

When Brenda didn't answer her, Suzy changed the subject. "I'm glad you called. It's been a long time since I went on a picnic."

There was a screech of delight from the boys. They were racing around the playground playing tag. Brenda and Suzy laughed at them.

"God, it feels like I haven't laughed in a long time." Brenda hadn't intended on saying it. It just came out.

For the first time, Suzy studied her younger sister and saw the artfully concealed cut on her lip, the dark circles under her eyes. "You look like hell."

"Thanks."

"I only say it because it's true. Now what's the story?"

Brenda began to pour out her feelings about Glen's staying out and his moods. "I don't know where he is a lot of the time. I've been afraid he's having an affair. Then last night he broke his promise to me about staying away from alcohol when Jane offered him a drink."

Suzy frowned. "She knows he's not supposed to drink. She's a bitch."

"Please don't start on Jane. She didn't force it down his throat." Brenda paused and wiped away a tear. "And then after she left, we had an awful fight. He grabbed me and hit me, but I kicked him and when he fell, I ran away."

"Good for you."

"No, there wasn't anything good about it," Brenda sighed. "And afterward, Sniffer disappeared."

"Disappeared?"

"Yes." Brenda nodded brokenheartedly. "I'm afraid Glen let him out and either he ran away or something happened to him or...or..." Brenda's voice cracked and she couldn't finish.

Suzy leaned back on the bench and was uncharacteristically silent for a few minutes. Then she said, "Brenda, I don't like the sound of this."

"Just forget what I said," Brenda said apologetically. "Don't worry about it. I guess everyone has problems in their marriage."

"The heck I'll forget it. If he was having an affair, you might be able to work through it to save your marriage. But drinking and becoming abusive? That's too much. You ought to get out."

"But I love him," Brenda whispered.

Suzy shook her finger in front of Brenda's face as if she were a four-year-old child. "If he's abusive, what's there to love?" With those pearls of wisdom, Suzy tossed down her cards. It was a five-heart-flush.

"Look, I have to get the boys to their karate lesson." Suzy jumped up from the table and gave Brenda a hug. "I have to go. Now Sis, you think about doing the same thing."

After Suzy had gone, Brenda remained on the bench thinking. She took a sip of her tea. The drink warmed her and for some reason she began thinking about her wedding day—the happiest day of her life. Tears welled in her eyes and she blinked hard to prevent them from falling.

As she sat there, her mind went back and forth. He had to love her. Surely, she wasn't that blind. She couldn't be wrong about the tender caresses or the kindness he showed when she was unhappy or tired. *It's all a big misunderstanding—or my overactive imagination. He loves me. He has to love me. He just has to.*

She looked down at the cup of hot tea and was surprised to find she'd drunk the whole thing while lost in her thoughts. She didn't even remember drinking it, so lost in her thoughts was she. Her throat still felt parched and she poured another cup. The temperature was dropping and steam swirled up, tickling her nose. The past overtook the present and the voice of one of her classmates, supposedly a friend, rang in her ears, "A man that good-lookin' don't marry a gal as plain as you. There's something wrong."

Maybe it was true. She took another sip. *What if he leaves me? What will I do?* She'd almost rather face hell than the pity—or ridicule—of her friends and family. She could hear them now. "We told you so. Miss Goody-Goody wasn't ever going to be divorced—didn't believe in it—ha! Grow up, Brenda. Look at yourself in the mirror. See yourself for what you are..."

She glanced around distractedly as a few snowflakes began to fall. Quickly, they increased in size and quantity. *What a day for a picnic,* she thought. *If it keeps up like this the rest of the day, we could get six inches.*

A squirrel ran across the grass and stopped at the base of a nearby tree. It was foraging for food. *How does he remember where he hid all those acorns?* It spotted Brenda and sat there chattering at her. She wondered if he was telling her his life story or preaching about the evils of divorce. Brenda wished she had something to feed it, but she didn't. Suzy and the boys had finished their sandwiches and Suzy had packed up the remaining food she brought and taken it back with her. All Brenda had was scraps of her tuna sandwich. She started to give it to him but feared she was getting a cold and might pass it on to the little animal.

She sighed and returned to her inner dialogue. *Okay, I'm going to look at this logically. If I divorce Glen, I'll be alone forever and he'll get half of everything I own, even the nest egg I've worked so hard to put together. I'll never get to open the animal sanctuary.*

And the truth is, I still love him. Maybe the best thing I can do at this point is stick with him. Try to help him. If I can train a killer mountain lion to love and trust me, I can do the same with Glen.

He just needs to know that I love him and trust him unconditionally. And that I will encourage him in anything he does to make himself a better person. I know I can do this! I know I can! I will change him by my love. He still loves me and he will not leave me.

She swept a thin layer of frosty crystals from the cover of the notebook she had brought with her and opened the notebook to the center.

She slid her finger along the edge and got a paper cut. "Ouch!" Brenda grimaced and suddenly found herself weeping silently, tears running down her cheeks. *Is Suzy right and I should leave him? Am I in denial?* She took a deep breath and wiped at her cheeks with a tissue she found in her pocket.

This is crazy. Why am I even considering staying with this man? Is my self-esteem that low? Come on, Brenda, why are you setting yourself up for more problems? Do you think you deserve it? No! Are you afraid of having to start over again? Well, yes. Do you fear embarrassment and humiliation? Yes! Are you afraid of losing the only love you've ever known? Yes! Are he and the marriage worth being abused? No...

But I'm the only hope he has. If I can't reach him, no one can and I love him so much that I have to try.

Brenda remembered something she had once read. "Almost all children who feel inferior have a tendency to constantly seek approval and affirmation by being super responsible." Her dad had once told her, "Brenda, you are loyal even when the evidence shows it's undeserved. You need to be aware of this trait and not let it rule you."

Am I doing that now? Is it loyalty or love I feel for Glen now? I honestly don't know. Am I trying to save him because I need his love to affirm who I am?

Back and forth her thoughts ricocheted. *I'm doing it out of love for him! I'm doing it because I want to save my marriage. Save myself from the pain of losing his love! Maybe it's just a compulsion...*

No! I'll be damned if I allow myself to be controlled!

I've got to calm down so I can think clearly and do what must be done to find out the truth.

She looked at the notebook in her lap and wrote at the top of the page: THINGS TO DO LIST. Then she listed several items, beginning with: FIND OUT ABOUT PROTECTIVE ORDER.

It seemed she had been sitting there for an eternity. She got up, feeling foolish as she brushed the snow off her shoulders, and tossed the paper cup from which she'd been drinking her hot tea into a garbage can. She felt numb and knew it wasn't from the change in the weather.

As Brenda got in her car, she noticed the blue Jaguar parked at the end of the block. Quickly starting the ignition and throwing the car in gear, she drove rapidly through town.

When she pulled into the Sheriff's Department parking lot, the blue Jaguar, which had followed behind her all the way, drove slowly past. She stopped her car, stepped out and shouted at Morgan, "That's right! I've come to report you!"

Morgan and the blue Jag sped off down the street, but not before she could see the self-satisfied smile he wore.

Brenda put her hands in her jacket pockets to warm them and went inside. The Sheriff's Department was housed in a typical government building with beige walls, gray metal desks and speckled linoleum that looked like it was left over from World War II.

The deputy was busy typing an arrest form for a hippie-looking man who was handcuffed to the desk.

"Come on, dude. Give me a break. I didn't mean to break probation. I didn't even know my buddy had a pistol," he pleaded.

"Yeah, and my mother's a virgin," the deputy shot back. "Height?"

"Six one. Do you know what this means to me? Seven years. Come on, man. I got a baby son I won't even get to touch till he's eight years old."

The deputy looked up and saw Brenda. "Can I help you?"

She was unnerved and her voice came out squeaky. "I'm Brenda Brumbaugh. I'd like to see Sheriff Gilbert."

"Sorry, ma'am. He's out on a call right now. Can I help?"

"I'll come back later," she said and rushed out the door before he could ask her any more questions.

What was she doing? Her instincts had been, *Go to the sheriff.* But once there, she had doubted her actions. Even if she just inquired about an order of protection, maybe they would put Glen back in jail. That would be terrible. And, being truthful with herself, she knew that she wanted to feel safe, but she didn't want to admit her dreadful dilemma to anyone. What she should have done while she was there was report that lunatic Morgan for harassing her, she decided.

When Brenda stopped at a 7-Eleven to pick up a newspaper, she was stunned to see Morgan pull into the parking lot. *That maniac! What does he think he's doing? That's it—tomorrow I'm calling the sheriff on him.* She strode over to his car, anger fueling her actions. When he saw her coming toward him, he peeled away again. His car was burning oil and the black smoke burned her nostrils. *He thinks we're playing some sort of bizarre game. I'll fix him tomorrow.*

Back on the road, billowing snow clouds were gunmetal gray behind the black skeletons of leafless maple trees. The blue spruces were already wearing tufts of powdery snow and they reminded her of a Christmas card she had once received.

Brenda tried to forget about the annoyance of Morgan and concentrate on her problems with Glen. She could divorce Glen, of course, but she loved him and she believed that deep inside he loved her too. *He's just mixed up*, she told herself. *I have to help him.*

By the time she reached home it was dark. She was surprised to see the sheriff's patrol car parked in front of her house. Had the deputy looked up her address and sent the sheriff here? She stopped the car and walked to the front door. She opened it and gasped.

The room had been trashed, ransacked. The sheriff was dusting black powder on everything, looking for fingerprints, she supposed. Glen was following him around taking pictures.

"What's going on? What happened?" Brenda asked.

"Vandals! I came home and found this mess," Glen said.

She turned to Sheriff Gilbert. "Do you have any idea who it could be? Have you found any fingerprints?"

"A mess of 'em, but they're probably yours and your husband's," he answered calmly, holding her eyes with his.

His scrutiny made Brenda uncomfortable.

"Probably wore gloves, whoever did it. But we'll check for prints anyway," the sheriff said, turning his penetrating gaze toward Glen.

Good Lord, does he think we did this?

Brenda got on her hands and knees and began picking up shards of glass and fragments of her porcelain figurines. She loved these things and now they were destroyed. Unsteadily, she rose to her feet and headed toward the kitchen to get a trashcan. Glen grabbed her arm.

"There's something else you should know, Brenda," Glen said solemnly. "They...killed the lion. She's in there."

"What?" Brenda said, dizzy now with the shock. *This was insane! Who could have done such a thing?*

Brenda pushed open the kitchen door and stepped inside. She gave a low, guttural moan as her stomach twisted and heaved within her. Katula lay on her side, legs splayed out loosely, lifelessly. The lion's big eyes were open, staring vacantly at the ceiling. Her tongue protruded limply from her mouth, which was covered in a froth of foam and vomit, as if she had had a seizure. Blood trickled from her nose. She was dead and so were the cubs she was carrying.

It was too horrible to look at and Brenda ran from the sight sobbing. Glen was standing in the doorway and she almost knocked him down. She raced out the open front door and vomited into the shrubbery bed that flanked the entryway. She was weeping uncontrollably now, her body shaking with every sob. *First Sniffer disappeared and now Katula is dead,* she thought. *What horrible thing will happen next?*

She went back inside, wanting to tell the sheriff her suspicion that this heinous act was committed by Glen or Morgan, but she couldn't with Glen right there. *Katula! Poor Katula.* Her stomach heaved again and she groaned. Dry heaves were worse than vomiting. They made her stomach muscles hurt and her throat burn. She raced to the open doorway again as she heaved and the tea she'd had earlier came out through her nose.

As she sat on the front step, her head in her hands, Glen brought her a wet washcloth and laid it on the back of her neck. It felt good and cool. *But if it was Glen who had committed this heinous act, how could he have the gall?*

"You okay?" he asked.

She wanted to scream, *No, you abusive bastard*! But another wave of dry heaves overtook her. Glen rubbed her back sympathetically.

He couldn't have done that to Katula, then be this sweet to me. He must not have done it. Just because he got rough with me last night doesn't mean he could do something like kill Katula, no matter how much he wanted to punish me.

But then, who would have broken into the house, destroyed everything she loved and killed the lion? *Morgan? Was he that crazy?* She had to face the realities. Either he or Glen must have done this. She didn't believe it was a bunch of crazy vandals out on a wrecking spree. Surely they would have taken the TV or stereo or something.

Glen removed the cloth from her neck and handed it to her, kissed her on the top of her head then turned on his heels and went back in the house.

When the heaving finally subsided, she washed her face with the damp cloth. Her mouth felt like it was lined with tea soaked cotton and she was desperate to brush her teeth. She'd probably never drink hot tea again. How had she gotten herself into such a mess? What had she done to deserve this? Had she loved the wrong man, chosen the wrong profession or was it something else?

Tomorrow she would go to the sheriff and tell him her suspicions—all her suspicions—about Glen and about Morgan. All she had to do now was make it through another night. She heard the sheriff's and Glen's voices and went to the door, cracking it open so she could see and listen.

Glen watched the sheriff work and chatted with him. Brenda was sure he wasn't interested in the investigation, but he did seem to be interested in befriending the sheriff. The thought came to her: *An alliance like that might be useful to him one day.*

She watched Glen as the sheriff dusted the fingerprint powder onto the elk's antler with a fine brush. A fingerprint seemed to emerge out of thin air.

"How'd you learn to do that?" Glen asked.

"Went through FBI courses at Quantico."

"Who do you think did this?"

The sheriff placed the clear tape on the fingerprint and lifted it off. "Hard to say. Odd that they didn't seem to take anything." His eyes narrowed as he looked at Glen. He paused a moment, scratched his head, then went on. "Most likely it was teenagers getting their kicks by tearing things up."

"You think it was more than one?" Glen asked.

"It'd take more than one to tangle with that lion. I still don't get how they got it out of its cage and into the house without it takin' big bites out of 'em."

"Maybe they coaxed it with some meat or something.'

"Poisoned meat, I'll bet. That lion's mouth is foaming; it looks like it went through some bad times before it died," Sheriff Gilbert said. "Well, I'm just about through here." He lifted the last fingerprint, packed his tools and prepared to go. The sound of Brenda slamming the bedroom door vibrated through the room. The sheriff darted Glen an 'uh-oh' look. "Your wife gonna be okay? She's pretty upset."

"Yeah. She'll get over it. She's been real excited about having the lion cubs. You'd have thought *she* was pregnant. You *off-duty* now, Sheriff Gilbert?" asked Glen.

"Sure am. Shoot, I was supposed to be home twenty minutes ago," the sheriff replied, looking at his watch.

"Well, let me give you a beer," Glen offered with a smile.

"Don't mind if I do."

The sheriff followed Glen to the kitchen. Carefully walking around the lifeless mass that had once been Katula, Glen opened the refrigerator door, took out two Heinekens and nudged the door closed with his shoulder.

"These are for company. Brenda would have conniptions if she knew I was drinking." He popped the lids off the bottles and motioned to the corpse on the floor. "I used to have a problem with alcohol, but after what's happened today, I think I deserve one."

Glen handed Sheriff Gilbert the beer, then guzzled about half his own. "I don't understand it. Brenda pokes needles into people all day long, doing blood tests and nursing old, dying people, but she gets squeamish at one drop of animal's blood or seeing wounded or dying animals." He took another gulp of his beer. "Dead animals don't bother me. How 'bout you?"

The sheriff shook his head. "Nope. I got used to it when I started hunting."

"Hey, I'm a hunter, too. Can I repay you for your overtime by taking you huntin'? There's some big ol' bucks right here on my property."

The sheriff pulled at his beer thoughtfully. "Maybe... one day, but I have to get home now." He went into the living room and headed for the front door.

Brenda blew her nose, wiped her tears and walked back into the living room. She could feel the puffiness around her eyes.

"Good-night, Mrs. Brumbaugh. I sure am sorry about your trouble here," the sheriff said as he was preparing to leave. Glen was right behind him.

She said good-bye, noticing again how the man seemed to be studying her. *What could he possibly think?* She could hear the two men still talking as Glen walked the police officer to his car and she went back to her bedroom. She locked the door, took her notebook out, sat down and flipped to a clean page. Quickly, Brenda pulled the pen from inside the metal spiral of the notebook and without much forethought began to write:

Dear Sheriff Gilbert,

If you're reading this, then I'm already dead. I suspect that someone is plotting to kill me. Too many strange things have been happening around my house and to me and I can think of no other explanation.

I am giving the key to the safe-deposit box where I'll keep this letter to my sister. I will tell her to deliver it to you upon my death.

Sincerely,
Brenda Brumbaugh

Shocked, Brenda read what she had written. *Someone is plotting to kill me.* She had never whispered those words to anyone, never even imagined those words in her mind as she lay sleepless in bed or after she was startled awake from a bad dream.

Brenda looked at the blue-lined paper again. *Someone is plotting to kill me.* The words had seemed to write themselves, the pen gliding over the page automatically, with no assistance from her. *Someone is plotting to kill me.* Of course, it was the only logical answer to all the bizarre things that had been happening to her these last few months. Staring blankly into space and absently nibbling on the top of her pen, Brenda began to mentally enumerate the strange events that had recently occurred.

The fire. She had overheard Sheriff Gilbert say it was a chemical fire and that it had probably been set by someone. She sensed he harbored suspicions that she and Glen had planned the fire in order to collect the insurance money on the house. But she had almost died in the blaze and the insurance company was holding up their check while they conducted an investigation of their own. It had been deemed a 'suspicious fire.'

As she had laid in the hospital bed, the thought crossed her mind that Glen had been so desperate to move out of the small ranch on Sunshine Street that he might have set the fire, but she had immediately dismissed it. He loved her and with a little more time and persuasion he must have known he could convince her to put her beloved little house on the market and move further out into the countryside. Her next coherent thought had been that the culprit was her crazy stalker, Morgan. His behavior was so weird, she believed him capable of anything.

Once she was out of the hospital, though, and recovering at her parent's house, Brenda had dismissed these thoughts from her mind. She was just so grateful to be alive and she had confidence that the sheriff's department or the insurance investigators would discover what had really happened.

The car crash. Brenda had always been a good driver with a near perfect record and she knew she had been driving carefully the night of the thunderstorm. The car that had tailed her had come out of nowhere and then disappeared into the night after she had gone off the road and flipped over. Sitting in her bedroom, she shivered to think how close she had come to rolling into the river and possibly drowning in her submerged car. Who were the couple in the other car? Was the driver out to get her or merely dangerous and incompetent at the wheel?

The piano accident. Brenda frowned, thinking of the day she was almost crushed between the car and the swiftly speeding, out-of-control piano. Surely, that was truly an accident. Jane herself had fallen off the truck and gotten a few bruises. Shaking her head briskly, as if to rid it of its growing paranoia, Brenda decided *No, the piano incident was accidental.*

Katula on the loose. She smiled mirthlessly. If she really wanted to give wing to her creeping paranoia, she might suspect that Katula was let out of her cage that dark night in order to attack her. But maybe the unlocked cage was merely an example of Jane's forgetfulness; after all, it was not the first time her friend had inadvertently caused a problem while helping her with the animals. And anyone who really knew Brenda and Katula would have known that Katula would never hurt her.

Thinking of the animals gave Brenda a little stab in the heart. Her darling Sniffer had never returned. After he got out of the house that night, she had posted flyers with his picture, asking that he be returned and even promising a reward. But there was still no sign of Sniffer. *He must have been run over by a car,* she thought. *Otherwise, he would have made his way home.*

Brenda forced herself to turn her thoughts back to what she was now classifying as the strange events in her life.

The poisoning incident. No, not *poisoning,* that sounds so sinister and it was most likely a case of bad oysters. Simple food poisoning. Yet Glen had eaten an oyster and he had been fine, while she had quickly downed two of them and gotten sick immediately. Was her stomach that much more delicate than his? It had been a bad siege. She really hadn't felt like herself for several days after. But anyone could get food poisoning. It was silly to think that everything that happened to her was caused by some malevolent force. *That way madness lies, Brenda,* she told herself sternly. Then suddenly, unbidden, she remembered the dead chipmunk she found in the garbage can.

Had he eaten the food Glen had quickly thrown out after she got sick? Is that what killed him?

And now tonight—*Katula dead and the house vandalized.* What could that possibly mean? It wasn't a direct threat to her life; could it be some sort of warning? By whom? Why? It couldn't be Glen—it couldn't! But who? Who wanted her dead? Morgan? She had rebuffed his clumsy advances and given a negative report on his physical that caused him to lose his insurance policy. Was that enough to justify killing someone? Perhaps to crazy Morgan it was.

Exhausted, she squeezed her eyes shut tightly as she felt tears stinging her eyelids once again. Despite her efforts, the tears escaped and one fell onto the notebook.

When she brushed it away, the blue ink on 'dead' smudged, leaving a pale blue streak as the paper puckered from the moisture. Snapping up a clean tissue from the holder next to her bed, she dabbed her eyes then folded the letter, walked to her chest of drawers and rummaged around looking for an envelope. While she was searching, she found a glittery, heart-shaped valentine covered with pink roses. She opened the card. Scrawled inside was, *Loving you on St. Valentine's Day and wishing you everything in life. Love, Glen.*

Brenda stared at the card. *What happened? What went so wrong that made him hit me, want to hurt me...or is it worse than that? Does he want me out of his life? Is there another woman? Or am I going crazy?*

She suddenly thought of a movie she had recently watched on one of those cable channels that runs old films. *What was it called? Suspicion, that was it. Cary Grant had played a new husband whose wife...what was the actress' name?...well, whatever, she was convinced that her husband was trying to kill her. But it turned out to be all coincidences and circumstantial events; he really loved her and was trying to protect her. But the wife was full of suspicions; she just didn't trust him.*

The thought that she was like the wife in the film, unfairly and irrationally condemning Glen, filled Brenda with guilt. Perhaps he really loved her as much as she loved him. If he was having an affair, she could forgive him. Maybe it was partly her fault. She wasn't home much, what with all her work and studies. If that was what it was—an affair—they could work it out. *But then who was doing all these awful things to her? Crazy Morgan?*

She stuffed the letter to the Sheriff into the envelope and sealed it. She tucked it in to the middle of her biology notebook and closed the book. She would put the note in her safe-deposit box the next morning. Suzy was the co-signer for the box, although she had forgotten to give her a key. She would do that immediately and try not to scare Suzy to death. After her disclosures at the park, she knew Suzy would be anxious. She'd have to handle her sister delicately.

After a sleepless night lying beside Glen, Brenda willed herself to get out of bed the next morning. Glen was still sleeping. Quickly she went to the bathroom, took a shower and put on some lipstick. Then she weighed herself. To her surprise, she had lost seven pounds. Another time, she would have been thrilled. Today, she scarcely paid attention. She dressed for work feeling tired and depressed. The stress of worrying about what fearful occurrence each day would bring was taking its toll.

She got in the car to drive to the bank and looked back at the front door. Glen had walked out of the house and was standing there. He had taken the day off and had promised to clean up the house and bury Katula out in the woods. He smiled and waved. Her heart pounded, but she didn't want to arouse suspicion or anger in him so she smiled and waved back.

As she drove to the bank, her thoughts ricocheted back and forth. Was she crazy or was she being set up? And if she was...she shuddered as it crossed her mind that it boiled down to one frightening question: Would she live through all of this?

CHAPTER TWENTY-TWO

NO IDLE CONVERSATION

Brenda parked in the bank's parking lot. She had been so deep in thought that she didn't even remember the trip there. She was operating on autopilot.

Inside the bank, the attendant opened the vault so Brenda could get out her safe-deposit box. Brenda placed the letter to the sheriff into it and locked it. She took a deep breath and told herself it was only added protection.

When she walked out of the bank vault, Brenda heard two bank tellers snickering and whispering about her. "White trash," Pat Reeves murmured to the other teller. Brenda knew Pat from high school when Pat was a snooty cheerleader and had put Brenda down every chance she got. She'd even called her *Brenda, Queen of the Uglies* behind her back.

Brenda glared at Pat and went to a cute, little blond teller's window, but Pat couldn't resist a chance to ridicule. "How's the animal sanctuary going?" she called loud enough for everyone in the building to hear.

"Fine," Brenda said, pointedly and immediately turned her attention to the blond teller. "I'd like to deposit this into my savings."

Brenda placed $500 dollars on the counter and waited for the teller to do the paperwork. She darted an uncomfortable glance at the other two tellers. "Could I have the balance?"

When Brenda's teller placed the stamped deposit slip on the counter, Brenda looked at it. As she walked away, she heard the two women talking.

"Who's that?" the blond teller asked Pat.

"Oh, that's Brenda Gunn, the homeliest and dimmest girl from my high school class. I bet she can't even spell chimpanzee, even though she looks like one," Pat giggled.

"She may not be able to spell, but she sure can add," the blond teller said. "Have you looked at the balance in her savings account?"

"What is it," Pat asked. "Twelve-hundred dollars?"

There was a pause and Brenda mouthed the answer at the same time the blond teller said, "No, it's $168,526."

Brenda smiled to herself at the thought of her upcoming class reunion. She lifted her head high and just kept on walking.

Though the tellers' exchange gave Brenda momentary satisfaction, by the time she reached her car, she again churned with emotion. She just couldn't get her mind off the note. Somehow just putting it in the safe confines of the bank made her feel secure. *Maybe I'm just overreacting. It'll all turn out alright. It just has to,* she thought. *He has to love me the way I love him.*

Glen took a Tupperware container out of the refrigerator, removed the lid and looked at the luscious steaks swimming in marinade. He fished out a steak and cut it into strips for fajitas, then he sprinkled the strips with seasonings from a bottle labeled *Glen's Special Spices*.

He was humming when Brenda came in.

"What are you doing?" she asked. *That's odd. Glen hasn't cooked for me since the night I got sick.*

"I'm fixing my beautiful wife some dinner."

"What's the occasion?" she asked as she grabbed a Diet Coke from the fridge.

"No occasion. It's just part of my resolution to be nicer to you." He pointed to the Diet Coke and said, "They just came out with a study that says they put antifreeze in diet drinks. Those things will kill you."

"Nice to know you're so concerned for my health," Brenda replied, tapping him on the cheek. She looked at the steaks and sniffed the air. "Looks good and there's plenty of it."

"Uh-huh," Glen mumbled.

"I think I'll invite Suzy and Dave over. I haven't seen them in weeks," she said. She didn't add she had something important she wanted to give her sister.

Glen shot her a dirty look, but she returned it with a sweet smile, then walked out of the kitchen.

Glen was being so kind and attentive, so much like his old self that by the time their guests arrived, Brenda had decided she was overreacting writing the letter to the Sheriff. She was really glad, moreover, to see her siblings together. It was like a holiday gathering and since Suzy was going to be extra busy at work for the next few months, they wouldn't do this again for a while.

She rolled up the oriental carpet in the living room. Suzy and Dave were teaching her to square dance. Country music blared and she was having fun, even though she had two left feet and kept stomping on Dave's toes. Glen came in from flipping the beef over on the grill. Even though he hadn't done it in a while, Brenda knew Glen loved to barbecue; sometimes he had to chip ice off of the grill, but winter weather never stopped him. He was carrying a spray bottle that he used to control the flames. Brenda looked over at Glen with a smile.

"Watch out or you'll throw your bad back outta whack," Glen said to Brenda.

"You better get over here and learn this, Glen. I'm gonna be dancing circles around you at my high school reunion," Brenda said.

"I ain't doin' it," he said laughing.

"Why not?" Brenda asked.

"Cause I might look as stupid as you do," Glen teased.

Brenda stopped dancing, went over to Glen, grabbed the spray bottle out of his hand and started spraying him with it. Glen dodged and ran. She chased him around the living room until he grabbed the bottle from her. Then it was her turn to run. He chased her through the house until she was out of breath, then he grabbed her and kissed her.

For a few moments, it was like the old times. Brenda felt his moist lips on hers and she wanted more, but he released her and flopped onto the sofa, laughing. Dave and Suzy joined them. They both had fresh beers and Dave pulled two packages of peanuts out of his pocket. He handed one package to Suzy.

"Good brother," Suzy said, patting Dave.

"How could I forget the family custom?" Dave smiled and began ripping open the peanuts. He poured them into his beer bottle. The beer foamed and spewed out over the long neck. He covered it with his mouth to catch the mess. When it was done, he touched his bottle to Suzy's, "To the future!" He took a swig while Suzy poured some peanuts into her beer.

Brenda held up her Diet Coke and joined in, "To the future!" She and Suzy jumped off the couch, started dancing and bumped hips.

The country music on the radio stopped and the news came on. Glen reached over to turn it off, but Suzy grabbed his hand.

"Don't turn it off. I want to hear what's new in Mad Man Mulligan's case."

"Who's Mad Man Mulligan?" Dave asked.

"He went to school with Brenda and me. He strangled his wife yesterday," Suzy answered.

"Oh, I heard on the radio that the guy used a piece of barbed wire," Glen said. "How sick is that?"

Brenda looked at Dave and he looked at Glen.

"I don't understand how a woman can be married to a man and not realize he's capable of killing her...or even hitting her," Suzy said, watching Glen.

"I've noticed a lot more of it since O.J. got off. Men think they can get away with it now," Glen said. "But this guy isn't smart enough to get away with murder."

"Would you ever get rid of me?" Brenda asked him, putting her arm around his shoulder.

"What the hell kind of question is that? How do you come up with this kind of crap?" Glen asked in an irritated tone.

"I was just thinking. I'd die for you. Would you die for me?"

"This is stupid!" Glen said and stomped off. He went outside to tend the meat on the grill.

Dave leaned over to Suzy and whispered, "That wasn't a good idea."

Brenda looked miserable. Dave motioned to Suzy, "Let's set the table. It will be like old times."

Suzy laughed. "Yeah, I'll do the work and you'll do the supervising."

"That's what brothers are for, Sis."

Glen stuck his head in the door and said, "I hate to break up the reunion, but the meat will be ready in five minutes. Brenda, can you make sure the beans are hot?"

Brenda nodded and turned to Suzy. "Can you help me in the kitchen?" Suzy finished off the last of her beer and peanuts. They walked into the kitchen together. Once Glen was back at the grill and out of earshot, Brenda pulled the safe-deposit box key from her pocket. "I need a favor," she said.

Suzy was stirring the beans on the stove, but turned to face Brenda. "What kind of favor?"

Brenda's face turned serious. "I put something in our safe-deposit box in case anything ever happens to me."

"You what? Are you alright?" Suzy asked.

"It's okay, Suzy. I'm not suicidal or anything! But if I die, I want you to insist on an autopsy."

"Why are you talking like this?" Suzy asked.

Brenda could hear the fear in her voice and she tried to reassure her sister. "It's nothing to worry about. You know, with my birthday coming up, I just have thoughts of my mortality."

"Right!" Suzy shouted. "You're going to be thirty-six, not sixty-six. You're not ill and you tell me you might die and you don't want me to worry?"

Brenda shushed her, but Suzy continued. "Are you working for the CIA? I think I read a story just like this in the National Enqu—"

Brenda cut her off. "Get serious."

"I am serious," Suzy said placing her hands on her hips. "That's the only thing I can think of—that you'd want to keep a secret."

"Suzy, it's nothing. Just our conversation about abuse made me nervous. You hear about batterers killing their wives and with all the odd things and accidents that have been happening around the house, I'm—" she paused. "Never mind. I'm sure it's my imagination. But..."

"Has Glen been violent again?"

Brenda placed her hand on Suzy's shoulder and stroked a long lock of hair. "Of course not, but I told you he's really moody these days and," she paused and then went on, "Like I told you in the park, he hit me but just the one time."

Glen came in the back door, strolled through the kitchen with a plate of meat in his hand and went into the dining room. He called over his shoulder to Brenda and Suzy, "Hurry up you two! The meat's gonna get cold."

"We're coming," Brenda called after him, never taking her eyes off Suzy. Then she grabbed the bean pot and walked out, leaving Suzy open-mouthed.

Everyone ate the fajitas except Glen which set alarm bells off in Brenda's head. He said he had a stomachache, but Brenda wondered if it was true. The fajitas tasted delicious, but she couldn't help thinking that maybe Glen had put something on the steaks before she'd invited Suzy and Dave. Then, learning that they were coming to dinner, had washed it off. *No! Impossible! Don't be stupid, Brenda! Stop thinking these crazy things. You're as wacky as the wife in Suspicion.* She pushed her fears away and concentrated on her guests.

The dinner conversation was upbeat. When everyone was finished eating, they all started taking dishes and food back to the kitchen. Suzy used this opportunity to corner Dave in the dining room.

"I don't like the situation with Brenda and Glen."

"What situation?" he asked, confused.

"I think there might be trouble."

"What kind of trouble?"

"I can't tell you..." she replied and started to walk away.

"You *can't*—or *won't*—tell me?" Dave pushed.

"I can't and won't," Suzy said defensively. "So don't badger me. We'll talk about it later."

When Brenda walked back into the dining room with Glen at her heels, Suzy and Dave busied themselves with clearing the dishes from the table, each lost in his or her own anxious and confused thoughts.

CHAPTER TWENTY-THREE

A DOUBTFUL
FUTURE

Christmas had come and gone uneventfully, for which Brenda was grateful. Glen seemed to be on his best behavior over the holiday season and had bought her a beautiful black leather, full-length coat, which he wrapped in gold and red paper and placed under the tree on Christmas Eve.

Shopping for gifts and decorating the house, along with her work and studies, kept her exhausted by evening and too busy to do much thinking about her odd situation. She and Glen had thrown a small New Year's Eve party—at his request—and he had been a superb host, drinking nothing but non-alcoholic sparkling cider and dispensing charm and good will to their friends and Brenda's family. Standing side by side in the doorway and waving their guests good-bye in the frosty predawn hours, Brenda had rested her head on Glen's shoulder and he had placed his arm around her waist and held her close. Brenda prayed that this was the beginning of a return to the earlier, happier times of their marriage. She allowed herself, once again, to relax in his company and she firmly pushed aside any negative thoughts that occasionally bedeviled her.

They both worked long hours at their jobs that winter and didn't see much of each other. Frequently, Glen was in bed and snoring when she came home or she was already asleep by the time that he made it home from the dealership. Their weekends together, though, were pleasant and Brenda began to think that alcohol was at the root of all their problems. If Glen just stayed away from booze, everything would be alright, she decided.

Early one morning, before Brenda left for work, Suzy called.

"You know what's getting close, don't you, Brenda?" Suzy asked teasingly.

Brenda was stumped. "What?"

"Your birthday! Thirty-six and holding, right, Sis?"

"Suzy, it's the first day of February today. My birthday isn't until the end of the month." Brenda laughed into the phone. "Don't rush it, please."

"Well, the problem is I just realized I'm going to be in the Bahamas on vacation on your birthday. Would you mind if we celebrated early this year?"

Brenda felt warmed by her sister's thoughtfulness. "Of course, I wouldn't mind. But really, you don't have to do anything special for my birthday."

"Hush, now. Of course I'm going to do something special," Suzy scolded. "Matter of fact, I've thought of the perfect surprise. Now, can you possibly take a day off from work this week? I promise you it will be worth it."

Brenda thought for a moment before answering. She didn't want to disappoint Suzy and she had been working extra hard these past couple of months. "Okay, you've got a date," Brenda told her sister. "Would Thursday be good?"

"Thursday it is," Suzy said gaily. "Come to my house for lunch first, then we'll do the surprise."

Thursday was a gray, cloudy day, but Brenda felt cheerful and she hummed absentmindedly as she drove her Mustang past the only buildings in town—Stahl's Specialty Aluminum Foundry, the Foundry Restaurant, the Post Office and the Quick Stop. Brenda smiled. The town seemed right out of *Little House on the Prairie*.

When I was younger, I always told myself I'd get married and move away, but now I am married and what did I do? Brought my husband here. I guess I'm a country girl at heart.

Brenda came up behind a farmer driving his tractor. He crept along at a snail's pace and, of course, she was in a No Passing Zone. She checked her hair in the rearview mirror and adjusted the collar on her new gray suit. Noticing the blue Jaguar behind her, she frowned, then seeing a side street, she made a quick turn down it and smiled. She'd lost him.

Suzy had told her they'd meet at her house. Her first clue that she was overdressed was when she opened the front door and saw Jane and Suzy in their designer jeans.

Suzy served her a delicious lunch with champagne. Afterward, Suzy said, "Don't ask any questions. We've got a surprise to help you with any qualms about the future that you might have."

Brenda was so glad to see her friend and her sister getting along for once, that she didn't object.

Suzy and Jane had paid for a psychic reading for Brenda. She was skeptical, but it would have been impolite to tell them so. It wasn't that she didn't believe that some people had the *gift*. No, she *believed*. In fact, she'd had her own premonitions throughout the years. There was the time she'd been barreling along Highway 2 and a voice said, "Slow down. Over the next hill there's an accident." Brenda slowed and sure enough, there was a wreck. The voice scared her, but the fact it had been right scared her more. And, there was the time her childhood dog, Tippy, visited her after his death to let her know he was okay. She'd had a lot of unexplained experiences, but Brenda figured anybody who used a neon sign probably was a charlatan.

As they made their way up the sidewalk, Brenda imagined a woman with a turban and a crystal ball. She was shocked to find *The Psychic Doctor* was a man. Doc was in his early thirties and dressed like an escapee from the Don Ho show. That afternoon, he wore a colorful Hawaiian shirt with Bermuda shorts and Birkenstock sandals.

Although his appearance was somewhat quirky by Missouri standards, his home was not. The walls were a pale teal and framed with a classy teal and tan border. Instead of a card table with a crystal ball, they sat at a designer table made of faux ancient Roman columns and thick, beveled glass. The place reeked of good taste and Brenda decided Doc must be a big success.

He chitchatted with the women for a moment, then set about telling them how he worked.

"I cannot control your destiny, only *you* can do that. All I can tell you is what will happen if you remain on the same path that you're on right now. Do you understand?"

The women nodded and he continued. "This is very powerful stuff. Whether you're a believer or an atheist, I always start with a prayer. Anybody got a problem with that?"

They all shook their heads and Suzy squelched a giggle. Doc asked them to sit around a table and joined them. He reached over and took hold of Brenda's hand and his head jerked back like he had a received a jolt of electricity.

"Something wrong?" she asked, pulling away her hand.

"You have very powerful energy. I wasn't expecting it, that's all," he replied and took her hand again. His hand was soft and smooth—*more like a rich girl's*, Brenda thought. They all held hands in an unbroken circle and Doc bowed his head. "We call upon *The Great One* to guide us in our search for truth and happiness. Reveal the knowledge we need to know to make us stronger, better people and protect us from evil. We pray our Spirit Guides will talk to us today to shed light upon the paths that we walk on. Amen."

There was a moment of silence. Brenda got a whiff of the soft scent of bayberry. She opened one eye and peeked around the room for the origin of the fragrance. On a table at the end of a plush sofa was a candle. It flickered and licked the air, sending out the mild aroma. Doc released Brenda's hand and the others followed suit. Then he turned to Brenda.

"Birthdays are a time when we all reassess our accomplishments, our purpose in life and dream about our future. I sense you are most interested in two areas—your love life and your career. Am I right?"

Brenda, her face guarded, nodded.

The shadow of a smile tickled the edge of his lips and he continued, "I like skeptical clients. It offers a challenge. It's true, I haven't told you anything that anyone at this table couldn't have guessed at and come up with the right answers."

Although Brenda's face was free from expression, she was reeling inside. She'd been thinking that very thing just a second before he said it. *But, I bet he says that to everybody. Ninety-nine percent of the people that come in here probably think the same thing.*

"Yes, they do," Doc said answering her thoughts. Without missing a beat, he turned her hand over and began looking at her palm, and then he placed his palm on top of hers.

It was damp and hot to Brenda and before long her palm was tingling. It felt like someone was dropping thousands of tiny straight pins into her hand. After a moment, Doc removed his hand. Suzy and Jane watched in anticipation.

He pointed to a line in Brenda's palm, "This line means you're stubborn—"

"Worse than a mule!" Suzy interrupted.

Brenda kicked her under the table and Suzy grimaced. Doc ignored them and continued, "—stubborn yet sensitive. You're the type who loves every living creature and can't stand for them to be hurt."

"That's for sure," Jane said. "You ought to see her animal menagerie. Well, before it got decimated, anyway."

Suzy shot Jane a dirty look for her insensitive comment and quickly asked, "Do you see the man in her life?" She wasn't spending her time and money to have Jane rub salt in Brenda's wounds. She wanted to get to the bottom of Brenda's relationship with Glen.

Brenda shook her head and darted Suzy a "stop it" look. *Now we're getting down to the real reason Suzy brought me here.*

Suzy took a lemon drop out of her purse and popped it in her mouth. Brenda's throat was dry and she tried to swallow, but couldn't. Suzy's lemon drop smelled divine.

"Please give me one of those," Brenda said.

Suzy took out the package and offered them to everybody, but only Brenda accepted. Suzy got back to the subject at hand, "Let's talk right now about this man in Brenda's life."

"Suzy, your manners."

"Never mind, Brenda. That's what we need to know and not any other crap."

Brenda colored.

"It's alright," Doc said soothingly.

Suzy went on, "Doc, Brenda took long enough to find someone. Now it better be someone who's right for her."

Brenda knew her sister was looking out for her but past memories flooded her mind. She would never forget the day Suzy told her that everyone in town called her "Billy Gunn's old-maid daughter." She bit her lip.

"For you," Doc said slowly, "I see the fairy tale and the nightmare," Doc said. "A man you think of as your soul mate, the man of your dreams is in your life. Are you married?"

Brenda shook her thoughts away and tried to focus on what Doc was saying.

Brenda nodded. He could have just seen her wedding ring. She frowned.

Doc gave her a side-glance. "Ah, you really are an unbeliever." She held up her hand so he could see her ring. "I see you are wed."

"Thank you," Suzy replied. "Now that's settled."

He ignored her and continued, "At first things were wonderful, but now you wonder about him, because strange things have been happening."

"Yes, that's true," Brenda felt her pulse begin to race.

"You must remember," Doc said looking at Brenda, "things are not always the way they appear. Keep your wits about you."

"She doesn't have time for chitchat," Suzy grimaced. "And neither do I." Suzy lowered her eyebrows and decided to get right to the point. "What about her future?" she asked Doc.

They all laughed, especially Doc, but Brenda was serious-faced and failed to see the humor.

"Well, Doc, the future?" Suzy prodded.

He sat with his eyes closed, mumbling over and over to himself, "Her future." Then with his palm outstretched and raised, he looked up toward heaven. Suddenly, his body shook for a moment and then he said, "Your future is in doubt."

"What the hell does that mean?" Suzy interrupted.

Doc was silent for a while, then he said, "There is no more coming." He looked at Brenda. "I'm sorry. Sometimes I only see a short revelation," he shrugged.

"It's alright," Brenda said a bit shaken. "What about the others?"

Doc smiled at Jane and Suzy. "I know you didn't pay for a reading for yourselves, but this was such a short one, I'll give you a little peek into your futures for free."

He took Jane's hand in his and studied her palm. "This is your love line," he said, pointing to one of the tangles of lines in her palm.

She offered him a flirtatious smile, but he ignored it and continued.

"What *you* think is true love will only cause you great pain," he said to Jane.

"I told you about the new guy," Brenda said. Brenda shook her head towards Suzy and added, "He's married."

"So I see."

Doc looked deep into Jane's eyes and told her in a serious tone, "You must keep your emotions under control."

Then he turned to Suzy and took her hand. He rubbed a line in her palm with his index finger and closed his eyes as if to concentrate. "You will be even more successful. A new job soon. Possibly, you'll be the boss."

Suzy jumped out of her seat and cheered, "Alright!" Then she sat back down, leaned over to Brenda and gave her a high five.

He turned to Brenda, "When trouble comes, call me," he said quietly.

Brenda was taken aback. "Yes, of course," she murmured not knowing if he was real or a fake.

As they walked out the door, Jane scowled. They climbed into Suzy's car and started back to her house. They were oddly silent after they'd said good-bye. Brenda got in her own car and started home to think about the afternoon.

Since it was after six, Brenda drove quickly. She was anxious to get back and prepare dinner for Glen. He had specifically told her he would be home early tonight.

When she arrived, she saw Glen's truck parked at the curb, but the door was ajar. "That's strange," she murmured. She got out of her car and walked over and closed the open door. Glen was usually so protective of that truck. She looked around and then noticed a few yards down the road Glen's friend Manny's car. *What's he doing here?* she wondered.

As she walked up the path to the house, she was surprised to see there were no lights on in the house. Feeling unsettled, she moved more quickly to the front door. It was unlocked. *What in the world was Glen thinking?* Once inside, she walked all around the house calling Glen's name and flipping on the lamps. Only silence greeted her.

Where was Glen? What if something has happened to him? Her heart raced. "Brenda, get a hold of yourself," she murmured, but she had a strange feeling in the pit of her stomach. Maybe he'd forgotten to close the truck's door and he was visiting a neighbor. But what if he was hurt and bleeding somewhere? *Stop it! Stop thinking that way,* she told herself. *He's probably showing Manny the property. Everything is fine. I have to stop letting my imagination run wild.*

Trying to get her mind off it, she walked into the library and sat down to do some paperwork. An hour passed. She was getting more nervous. The sound of the clock ticking above her desk distracted her. She looked out the window and feeling warm from the house's central heat, got up and opened the window a crack. Angry voices floated on the night air towards her.

She ran to the front door and opened it. Glen's and Manny's loud voices accosted her. *They must be in Glen's workroom.* She ran outside towards it in time to see Manny cursing to himself as he strode to his car and sped away. She ran through the darkened garage.

"Glen, are you in there?" she pounded on the workroom door. "Glen?"

Opening the door, she saw only darkness. Hearing a moaning sound, her heart pounding, she looked around. "Glen, are you in here? Glen? Glen?"

Another moan. Then she saw him sitting in the dark, holding his head down in his lap, which held a revolver. She flipped on the light and saw his bruised face and cut lip. "Oh my God! Glen, what happened? Are you okay?"

"Go away, Brenda," Glen snarled as he waved the gun. "Leave me the hell alone."

"Glen, I'm not going to leave you here with that gun, not in your mood. You'll have to kill me first."

He gave her a bitter laugh. "And go to jail for the rest of my life or get the death penalty? I don't think so, but don't tempt me." He jumped up and pushed Brenda into the door. "Now, get out."

"Glen, talk to me. What's wrong? What happened between you and Manny?"

"Turn off the lights and get the hell out of here."

"I won't leave you like this. You have to talk to me."

Glen lifted his head and yelled, "Did you hear me? Don't come near me. Get the hell out of here and leave me alone. It's none of your business. It doesn't concern you."

"Glen, you're my husband. What concerns you concerns me. Please tell me. What's going on?"

"He wants the twenty thousand dollars he loaned me for the down payment on our house right now. Is that what you wanted to hear? Now turn off the light and get out of here." He jumped up and pushed Brenda into the wall. "Do you hear me? Get out before you get hurt."

Twisting away, Brenda ran out of the workshop and back into the house. She paced back and forth. *What do I do? Who do I call? Should I call the sheriff? Should I have Manny arrested? Should I take Glen to the hospital? How can I do that? Who will help me? Who won't make it worse?*

As the night wore on and he didn't come in, she finally picked up the telephone and dialed a number. "Mom, is Dad there?" When her dad came on the line she said, "Something's wrong with Glen. I think he's going to kill himself. I don't know what to do. He's become violent and I can't talk to him. He's out in his garage workshop sitting in the dark with a gun on his lap. Glen's acting crazy. Please come quick."

Brenda sat curled in a ball on the sofa watching the front window, waiting. Finally, she saw her parent's car stop in front of the house. Her mother, father and brother Dave got out. Her parents headed up the front path, but Dave went towards the garage.

Crying uncontrollably now, Brenda opened the door. Hurriedly, her parents embraced her. "Dave's gone to see if he can reason with Glen," her mother said, looking worried.

"Wait. Does he know Glen has a gun?" Brenda said.

Her mother nodded. "We told him. Don't worry, Dave can handle himself."

Her father frowned.

They sat in the living room while Brenda explained. "I wasn't going to tell you this, but Glen and I have been having some problems. I think he's..."

Just then, Dave burst in. "Brenda, what in the world were you and Glen fightin' about? He's a real wild man," Dave said.

"We weren't fighting. This isn't about me. I came home and heard him arguing with his friend Manny. When I went out there, I saw his bruised face and the gun."

"Well, I think he's on something," Dave grimaced.

Brenda's dad interrupted, "Brenda, I've been wanting to tell you the same thing. Glen has been acting and looking really strange at work lately. He quit today, but if he hadn't, I would have had to fire him. He's late half the time, he doesn't show up for meetings and when he does, he's disoriented."

Brenda nodded. "I'm afraid he's going to do something to himself, he's so depressed."

"I'm afraid, Brenda, he's going to do something to you," her father said softly.

"He's drunk, that's what he is. And I'm not so sure he isn't on drugs, too," Dave interjected.

"What are you saying? Glen doesn't drink anymore. He did take a drink from Jane a few weeks ago, but that was her fault for taunting him. He's sworn to me he hasn't touched a drop other than that in years and he won't do it again."

"Wake up, Brenda. You're too gullible. He's got an empty liquor bottle in there. He's drunk a full fifth plus some beer as a chaser, and I don't know what else. But I've gotten that much out of him."

"No, Dave, you have to be wrong. Glen couldn't be drunk. That would be the final straw."

Dave shook his head. "Brenda, have you seen his eyes? He looks half-mad."

"No," she cried, pushing past Dave and running through the garage into Glen's workshop. She found him lying on the floor beside the wood-burning stove.

"Glen, have you been drinking?"

"Get out of here. It's none of your business."

"I've been worried sick about you, thinking you could be deeply depressed and all the time you were breaking your promise to me. Where have you got it stashed?" She began to open the cabinets.

"What the hell do you think you're doing?" He jumped up from the floor and screamed. "You bitch! I ought to—" He slapped her face hard.

Just then Dave burst through the door and pushed Brenda aside. "Get out of here and go back in the house," Dave said.

The two men grappled.

"Let me at her. You don't know who you're fucking with, bitch."

"Brenda, get back in the house!" Dave yelled. "Damn it, Glen, calm down," Dave said, subduing him.

"Let me at that bitch."

"No, Glen, you don't want to do that. You're just upset right now. Brenda, get the hell out of here now! I mean it," Dave said with an iron edge in his voice.

Sobbing, she ran back inside the house. She locked the door behind her. A few seconds later she heard the sound of a motor. She looked out the window to see Glen leaving. Dave got in her parent's car and started after him.

Her dad rushed to her side. "Brenda, come with me. Let's sit down. We need to talk," he said, leading her to the couch where her mother was sitting.

Brenda sat down and he pulled up a chair. "Brenda," he began sadly.

She was crying again. "I don't know, I don't know what to do. One minute he's the Glen I married and the next I'm looking into the eyes of a stranger. One night he's yelling and threatening or he doesn't show up until midnight and won't tell me where he's been. The next he's loving, apologetic and kissing me. And now the drinking...Am I the cause of his drinking? Have I pushed him away? Have I become so obsessed with work that I have pushed him into the arms of someone else? Why is everything falling apart?"

Billy Gunn began again with a heavy sigh. "I know we haven't been the best parents, but we love you and have to tell you that this guy's no good. I hear he's been screwing around on you. Suzy says he's pushing you around and now he's drinking. He's going to destroy everything you've worked so hard for. You'd better divorce him before that happens."

"Don't you see I'm trying to give him a chance?"

"You've given him too many chances already. I think we all have. So far, all he's done is hurt you. You can't help him. He has to help himself and he doesn't appear to want to do that."

"I have to try, Daddy," she said. "I meant my wedding vows. If I don't try to help him, who will? And I'd never be able to forgive myself."

"Brenda, you always were stubborn," her father said.

"You know who I get it from, don't you?"

Her father laughed for a moment and then turned serious again. "Honey," he said to his wife. "Go get that satchel we brought."

Brenda's mother nodded, went into the foyer and then came back. "Here it is, Billy."

He reached in and took out a gun. "This is a .38 police revolver. Brenda, I'd feel better if you kept it," he said.

She shuddered. "I hate guns. I don't want to hurt anything or anyone."

Her mother, who had been quiet, spoke up. "It's so he won't hurt you. If he comes after you, shoot for his legs. Bill," she said, turning to her husband. "Are you sure she knows how to use it?"

"Dave will show her tomorrow," he said grimly.

"No, Daddy, I can't," Brenda said quietly. "I could never use it. I think it would be better if you all go home when Dave comes back. And please, take the gun with you."

Her dad put the gun back in the bag. "If that's what you want." Brenda thought she saw the glint of tears in his eyes.

She nodded and walked over to the window. "I think I hear a car."

Dave rushed in and told them breathlessly, "He really took off. I couldn't catch him."

"It will be all right," Brenda said. "Thank you for coming, but please go home. He'll only be angrier if he sees you all here when he returns."

"Promise you'll call if there's more trouble?" her dad said.

"I promise," she said.

CHAPTER TWENTY-FOUR

A CALL
IN THE NIGHT

She took a sleeping pill and went to bed. She couldn't be sure how much time passed. Brenda thought she was awakened from her dream by Glen coming into the bedroom. When she awoke, she looked around and saw no one was there. She decided it must have been the sounds of Glen's voice that woke her. He had returned to the house. She could hear him on the phone. Brenda looked at the clock as the digital numbers clicked from 3:14 to 3:15 A.M. *What on earth is Glen doing on the phone at this time of night?*

Brenda got out of bed and very quietly tiptoed toward the living room. She crept as close as she could to the living room doorway. If she got any closer, the light would expose her. She could see Glen sitting in the easy chair, a drink in one hand, the phone in the other. She strained to hear, but all she got were bits and pieces.

He finished his drink while the person on the other end of the line spoke. He shifted the phone from one ear to the other and plopped his feet up on the coffee table. He poured Johnny Walker Red Label over ice into his highball glass. Brenda could smell the whiskey odor as she watched him swirl it around. Something the other person said must have upset him. Glen looked perturbed. He turned, pulled his feet off the coffee table and placed them on the floor. The shift in his posture was just enough to make what he was saying crystal clear.

"I know, sometimes part of me wants to just get rid of her. She holds the purse strings too tight and she's always telling me I should do 'the right thing.' But another part of me wants to protect her." He paused again, then continued. "I know it's weird. Here I am, plotting to kill her and wanting to protect her at the same time. Man, what would a shrink say about that one?" The ice cubes clinked in his glass as Glen took a sip of booze. "Ah-h," he sighed, obviously enjoying the whiskey.

"After the fire, the 'accidents' with the car and the piano, the loose lion and the poisoned cocktail sauce didn't work, I thought my subconscious was getting in my way. That's why I had to kill the dog. It was a practice run." Another pause. "Because I knew if I could kill something Brenda loved so much and get away with it, then I could kill Brenda without chickening out."

Brenda couldn't believe what she was hearing. This had to be a nightmare she was having. She pinched her arm to see if she could feel it and she did. *But it has to be a dream. I'll wake up in the morning and Glen and I will laugh about it.*

Quietly, she walked back to the bedroom and carefully picked up the extension. She sat on the edge of the bed motionless, barely breathing. Brenda listened in shock.

Glen was begging now, "Don't leave me, Baby. I couldn't stand it!"

And then she heard a muffled voice say, "I can't wait any longer," she said. "I hate her! She's all we talk about anymore!"

It sounded like a woman's voice to Brenda but was strange, as if the woman was disguising it by holding something over the phone.

"I know," Glen responded, "but doing it now increases our chances of getting caught. I think she and her family are getting suspicious. Murder will get us the *big bitch*."

"The *big bitch*?" she asked.

"It's prison lingo for Death Row."

"Glen, the way I see it, you traded Algoa Prison for Brenda's prison. She has you where you can't leave."

"But, Death Row?" he said, half under his breath. "I've seen guys make that long walk to the *death room*. The death room is where they'd get either a lethal injection or lethal gas. Some of the toughest men I've known became hysterical and wet their pants. I've seen the realities of it up close and it scared me shitless."

"Your little *accidents* haven't worked, Glen! First the fire, the car and then the lion. Hell, you can't even poison someone right! Am I going to have to do this myself?" she asked.

"Shut up! I'll do it."

"Are you sure?"

"I said I'll do it!" he thundered.

"Remember, it has to be an accident, Glen. That way, the insurance money automatically doubles," the woman reminded him.

Now Brenda heard the woman entreat, "Glen, you've got to do it. If you don't—"

Glen spoke softly, "I will darlin'. I will, but *accidents* don't just happen."

"Yes, they do. Make this one happen soon. I love you," she said.

"I love you, too." Brenda heard Glen guzzle the rest of his drink and then hang up the phone.

There was no time now for Brenda to think about what she had to do. She gently placed the telephone back in its cradle and slid under the covers and pretended to be asleep.

Glen tiptoed into the room, removed his black, silk robe and eased into bed, being careful not to wake Brenda.

She may have been pretending to be asleep, but her mind was racing. It all started to make sense—Glen's mood swings, his disinterest in sex...*accidents*...He'd said, *"Accidents don't just happen."*

Brenda lay there too afraid to move a muscle and too afraid to go to sleep. Finally, Glen's snores drifted into the cool night air. She could smell his whiskey breath. She stayed another five minutes to make sure he was in a deep sleep before she slipped out of bed and crept to the living room.

Sitting on the edge of the sofa, she picked up the phone. She was going to hit *69, but a terrible feeling of dread flashed through her like a bolt of lightning and she hung up the phone.

What if the woman was someone she knew? What if it was someone she didn't know and would never be able to find? What if it was really a man? The voice had sounded strange. Glen had been in prison an awfully long time. Maybe he was bisexual? "No!" she heard herself whisper. She was sure she'd have known *that* about him. But she hadn't known so many other things. *My God!* Her head was spinning.

She shoved the thought from her mind. *This is crazy. I have to know who it is so I can protect myself.* Brenda picked up the receiver. Her hand shook as she punched *69. The computer-generated voice announced the phone number of Glen's lover. Brenda couldn't believe her ears.

She recognized the number immediately, though her heart was telling her, *It can't be.* But her mind knew differently. It was Jane's home number. Her husband and her best friend were having an affair! And not only were they having an affair, they were planning to kill her! Brenda quickly returned the telephone to its cradle and sat on the sofa thinking. She was horrified to have her worst suspicions of Glen confirmed, but Jane! She never once thought her capable of something like this. She never once doubted her friendship. *All those times I confided in her about my worries and fears...and she sat there listening, the dependable friend, telling me Glen could never cheat on me or hurt me...And all the while she was sleeping with him and plotting my death!* Brenda felt herself gag and thought she was going to be sick, but she stifled it.

Finally, when she got her emotions under control, Brenda stood up and went back to bed. She pulled the covers up to her chin, but could not sleep. She lay in the darkness staring at the ceiling. She looked over at Glen. *He looks so sweet and innocent when he sleeps*, she thought sadly. She thought back to their wedding day and how beautiful he was to her then. Now she looked at him and saw a lying, cheating would-be murderer. How had she fallen in love with this man? How had she been so easily fooled? But he really did seem to love her. She felt sure there was a time when he did, but what went wrong? When did things change for him? *Stop it, Brenda. You can't dwell on the past. You have to worry about your future. What are you going to do now?* The police. She had to go to the police without arousing Glen's suspicions.

"You're up early," Glen said, as he walked past Brenda. She shrugged him off and gulped down her vitamins. She was so nervous one caught at the back of her throat. She gagged, then drank a big gulp of sweetened grapefruit juice. The vitamin washed down completely.

"I have to go feed the animals," she said and started for the door.

"Those damned animals! Why are you so crazy about them?"

She turned to face him. "They don't lie or cheat or turn on me without warning." She wanted to say, *"And they don't try to kill people unless they're attacked."* But instead she said, "I just love them. I always will, I guess."

Glen looked at her with angry eyes. Then he grabbed a doughnut and flew past her out the door. The slamming door fanned a cool breeze onto Brenda and felt like an Alaskan wind. Glen stomped off without another word.

Brenda ran into the living room and watched him from the window as he drove away. Her legs were shaking; she wanted to smash something. She picked up the crystal candy dish and slammed it against the wall.

"Damn you! Damn you, Glen!"

The sound of the shattering glass opened the floodgate of emotions. She couldn't control her heartbreak and rage any longer. She climbed onto the sofa and grabbed Glen's elk head off the wall. It was heavy and she toppled backward off the sofa and on to the floor. Dust flew from the animal's hair and it made Brenda sneeze. She stood up and threw the beast on the floor. Its glassy eyes stared at her.

She'd always hated it. Hated the idea that he'd taken a life and now proudly displayed his cruelty to the world. *Maybe after he kills me, he'll have me stuffed too.*

She began stomping the head with her heel, digging into its hide, smashing its nose...She wished Glen was here to see her destroy something he loved; the way he'd destroyed something she loved. One of the antlers broke off under her foot.

"How could you do this to me? I hate you! I could kill you! Both of you!"

The impact of her words echoed through her head, *I could kill you!* She froze. The depth of her rage scared her. At that moment, she really wanted to kill them. Brenda caught the reflection of her face in the glass of the curio cabinet. What was she thinking? She hated violence. She could never kill anyone!

She couldn't let them turn her into a cold-blooded killer—like they were. Her knees went weak and she fell to the floor. The adrenaline rush was subsiding and her body felt weightless. She lay there for a few minutes trying to pull herself together, to think clearly.

The phone began ringing, but she didn't want to answer it. Whatever the person on the other end had to say wasn't important. Nothing mattered now. Nothing. The answering machine picked up and Brenda could hear her cheerful voice telling people to leave their number. What a fool she'd been. That girl on the answering machine couldn't really have been her. *Was it?*

Then, taking a deep breath, she got up. There was only one thing to do now. She had to go to the police.

CHAPTER TWENTY-FIVE

PROOF POSITIVE

Brenda sat in the sheriff's office waiting for him. The female deputy who Brenda had once gossiped about with Mrs. P. and who'd come to ask questions when Brenda was in the hospital walked in holding a cup of coffee.

"I radioed the sheriff," the deputy said. "He'll be here in about twenty minutes."

"That's fine. Thank you," Brenda said.

It took so much of her energy to get the guts just to come in that she didn't want to leave. Afraid she wouldn't come back if she left, she sat in the brown leather chair across from his desk. The sheriff's office smelled of stale cigars, but she waited there just the same.

The deputy handed Brenda the cup of coffee. She took one sip of the bitter liquid and decided that the coffeepot must not have been washed since the day they bought it.

The deputy saw her reaction. "I don't make the coffee. Never drink the stuff myself."

"I can tell. It needs a woman's touch—a couple of tea-spoons of Drano would help," she joked.

They laughed. The deputy's chrome name tag caught the light and glimmered her name, Elizabeth Hanson. Brenda thought she looked a lot more attractive than she'd remembered. She was a buxom woman and Brenda could tell that beneath her baggy uniform, she was a shapely woman.

Deputy Hanson leaned on the edge of the desk and said, "If you decide you want to talk, I'm here."

"Thank you, but I need to talk with the sheriff," Brenda said.

"Some man doing you wrong?" the deputy persisted.

"What makes you think that?"

"I don't know...After a couple of years of police work you get to where you can spot 'em. The counselors call it the 'victim mentality,' but I call it 'the man takeover.' The man takes over you and tells you what to say, who to see, where to go, how to think and before you know it, you don't know which ideas are his and which are yours. And he's telling you the good ones are his!"

"You just described my—" Brenda stopped herself and sat quietly looking at the coffee cup.

"If you change your mind, I'm here," Deputy Hanson said and left the room.

Brenda picked up the only magazine in the room, *Field and Stream*. Since she didn't have an interest in reading about how to *Be a Sure Shot: Ways to Set Your Sites*, she put it back on the table. The squawk of the police radio in the other room made her edgy. How was she going to tell him what she knew? What if she told him and he didn't believe her?

Brenda looked at her wedding ring and twisted it on her finger. It no longer seemed romantic or even beautiful. The plain platinum band now reminded her of handcuffs. It tied her to a man that wanted her dead.

Sheriff Gilbert walked in. "Mrs. Brumbaugh, I don't have anything new on the fire." He took off his western hat, hung it on the hook and smoothed his hair with his palms.

"I'm not here about that, Sheriff," she said.

"Oh, well I'm afraid I don't have anything on the vandals who broke into your house, either. Guess I'm battin' zero right now. You want some coffee?" he asked as he took a seat at his desk.

She smiled and pointed to the first dreadful cup. "I already have some."

He punched the intercom button on his phone and talked, "Could you bring me a cup from that tar bucket?" He laughed, released the button and turned his attention to Brenda. "Tell Glen I sure do thank him for the venison he gave me."

This wasn't going well at all. Brenda nodded and said, "I'll tell him."

"What was it you wanted to talk to me about?"

"I...uh...I...I'm not sure where to start."

"Well, Mrs. Brumbaugh, everybody that comes to see me has a problem. Why don't you start by telling me yours?"

"Okay. My husband is planning to...to...kill me."

The sheriff frowned and leaned forward, "What makes you think that?"

"Well, I heard him talking on the phone. He's having an affair..." She couldn't bring herself to say "with my best friend." She closed her eyes and continued in a trembling voice. "He and his lover are planning to kill me."

"Are you alright?" the sheriff asked.

"How do you think I feel? I thought he loved me."

Deputy Hanson tapped on the door, came in and set the cup of coffee on the sheriff's desk. Brenda and the sheriff waited until she was gone before they resumed talking.

"Do you have any proof?" the sheriff asked.

"Proof? I heard it from his own lips," she said.

"Yes, Ma'am. But...*I* didn't hear it and I need something tangible before I can do anything," he said.

"That's crazy. I come in here, tell you my husband's going to kill me and you can't do anything?"

"Well, you have to see it from the law's side. I need proof positive. Let's just say you're fighting with your husband over some dent you put in the car. He says, 'Shut up or I'm gonna break your damned neck.' Now you take that to mean he's going to kill you. If I go out and arrest him, he'll say, 'I didn't mean it. I was just mad.'"

"But this isn't like that!" Brenda said.

"I can't arrest every man that threatens his wife."

"You could arrest him if he threatened to shoot the President."

"Yes, but that's the President," he said, slurping his hot coffee.

"I don't see the difference. If somebody says they're going to kill somebody, you ought to be able to arrest them," Brenda said, growing more agitated.

"I don't make the laws. I just enforce them. What you need to do is get me something tangible—like a letter or plans, or him on tape talking to his accomplice."

"I thought you people did that. I doubt he's going to let me stick a microphone under his nose and he's not dumb enough to leave murder plans sitting on the coffee table!"

Brenda was furious and she slammed her palms on top of the desk, then leaned across and got right in his face, "How many times have you seen or heard of a person who has had her house burned down with her in it, her car run off the road, a lion released in her backyard and then later killed, her dinner poisoned and her new house broken into and vandalized? And, to top it off, this person heard her husband on the phone plotting to kill her!"

"I know what you're saying, but my hands are tied. It's all coincidence until I see some hard evidence to the contrary. You'll have to get some first."

Shaking, Brenda got up. She went to the door, then suddenly turned around. "I'll get your stupid evidence for you or you'll have my dead body. I guess that will be proof enough." She walked out and slammed the door.

CHAPTER TWENTY-SIX

IN HER OWN HANDS

Her father had been right. She needed protection and the police weren't going to provide it. Brenda sat in her car and watched a man dressed in black leather come out of the gun shop, mount his Harley and roll away. *How does he stand riding that thing in the cold? I've got a heater and I'm still cold.* She flipped the switch to turn up the heat.

It was hard to tell if she was numb from the cold or if she was still in a daze. Her thoughts were swirling in her mind. She looked up at the neon sign, which read "Gun Heaven."

What was she doing here? She was the one that picketed the NRA conventions. She'd always said *she* would never have a gun in her house. She refused the gun her father had offered her. They frightened her. But now she was more frightened of dying.

Brenda brushed a stray curl off her forehead and back into its proper position. *I don't even know what to ask for. They'll think I'm stupid.* She touched the door handle. It was cold to the touch. *A gun's just metal like this.* She jerked her hand off the handle as if it were a snake and continued her pep talk to herself. *It can't hurt anybody unless it's loaded. Oh God! I can't do this! Yes, you can,* she told herself. *They're planning to kill me. I have to stop making excuses.*

She opened the car door and the winter wind nipped at her face. There was a big patch of ice on one of the steps and she hurdled it. She opened the door and slipped meekly into the gun shop. The air inside carried the heavy smell of gun oil. She'd never seen so many guns. The walls were lined with racks of every kind imaginable. She didn't know what they all were, but she recognized a few—rifles and double barrel shotguns—the others she just classified as big ones and little ones. It was amazing that just one store could have so many. Then she thought about all the stores like this one in every town in America and the sheer volume paralyzed her.

She wanted to run outside, but she couldn't move, so she stood there transfixed by her surroundings. Below the racks on the walls were waist-high glass cases that formed a U around the room. All the cases had five terraced racks. Each shelf had a pole that ran through the triggers of the guns and held them in place. They were lined up like dominoes with their barrels down. Over the door leading to the back room was obviously the owner's prized possession. Encased in an oak shadow box, lined in purple velvet was an old-fashioned machine gun. It looked like something right out of a movie. A brass plate on the frame was engraved with the words: "This belonged to Bonnie Parker."

Something about it struck Brenda as funny and she laughed out loud. It just seemed so ludicrous that out of all these macho guns, the most prized was one that belonged to a woman.

"May I help you?" Brenda heard a deep voice ask and she looked at the clerk. She offered him a nervous smile. He was a big man with a beer belly who looked about nine months pregnant and he wore a T-shirt with a bulls-eye on it. Scrolled across the top was written: "Go Ahead Asshole. You're On TV." He saw Brenda looking at the shirt.

"I've been robbed so many times, I thought I'd let the *bastards* know they can't get away with it," he said, pointing to the security camera behind him. "What can I do ya for?"

Brenda made her way to him and put her hands on the glass case in front of her. It had a film of glass cleaner and felt slick. She looked down at the hundreds of handguns in the case.

"I want a gun," she said and her voice cracked, but she tightened her jaw in an attempt to make him realize she was determined.

His bushy eyebrows furrowed and he gave her a suspicious look. She didn't look away. Instead, she leaned forward as if to speak in confidence and caught a whiff of his breath. It was a rank mixture of garlic and onions.

"It's for my own protection. Someone's trying to kill me," she whispered, then backed away from the counter.

Brenda was surprised that the clerk didn't seem alarmed at all. If someone had told her something like that, she'd be all over them trying to find out why...

She must have had an "I don't believe this" expression because he said, "Lady, I hear that story at least fifty times a day."

He pulled a square piece of velvet out of his hip pocket and set it on the counter. Brenda thought he acted more like he was going to sell her diamonds than a gun.

He reached into the case and pulled out a .38 Special handgun. It was nickel-plated and he set it on the blue velvet. It seemed bright and shiny and huge to her, although she could see it wasn't as big as the other guns in the case. He offered it to Brenda and she instinctively backed up a few more steps.

"My dad has one of those. He wanted to give it to me."

"This here's just what a little lady like yourself needs. This is what most policewomen use." He popped the latch and flipped out the cylinder. "If you hit him once with this, he'll be screamin' for the ambulance." He showed her the cylinder so she could see there weren't any bullets. "Go ahead and touch it. It ain't loaded."

Brenda touched the barrel. It was cool on her fingertips. He gestured for her to take the handle and she did. It was heavy.

"How can I aim anything this heavy?"

"You don't want one too light or too little. The weight cuts down on the recoil." He pretended his finger was a gun and showed her how the gun would recoil or flip up when it was fired.

"Do you give lessons?" she asked.

"No, Ma'am. We sell 'em. We don't baby-sit 'em."

"I'll take this one," she said and started to put it in her purse.

"Whoa! You can't take it with you today." He pointed to the bright orange sign behind him. "There's a three day waiting period."

I can't take another three days of this. Even if I do manage to survive, I'll be Looney Tunes soon! She tried to calm her voice, but it didn't work. "But I told you there's someone trying to kill me."

"Tell it to your congressman. Those damned people that picket the NRA got the laws changed. I can't do nothing about it. Do you still want it?"

Brenda nodded.

She filled out the paperwork, paid him with cash, stuck the receipt in her purse and left.

As she walked out the door, the fresh air hit her and she stopped to get her bearings. Brenda took a deep breath and noticed it was beginning to snow. Fluffy, dime-sized flakes floated all around her. It was lovely and she thought of herself in some giant snow globe that had just been turned upside down. The thought was comforting, but she was still edgy. Her hands shook when she pulled a Tic-Tac box out of her pocket. Trembling hands were a new experience for her and she almost missed her mouth with the Tic-Tac. She finally got it in her mouth and began to suck on it. She didn't want her breath to smell like the salesman's or the gunshop itself.

It was then Brenda noticed the blue Jaguar sitting across the street. Even through the haze of the snow, she recognized the driver. It was that nutty Morgan. Why was he still following her? That's another reason she'd feel better when she had a gun. A thought then flitted through her mind that maybe Glen had hired this whacko to kill her.

By the time she got in the car, her hands were trembling so badly that she could barely adjust the rearview mirror to watch him. He was just sitting there.

Brenda pulled the receipt for the gun out of her purse, folded it and hid it in the crease where the seat and the seat back came together. The only way Glen would find it there was if he cleaned out her car. She didn't have to worry, because he would *never* do that.

She started the car and drove away. The blue car followed her at a safe distance.

On the way home she stopped at the hardware store and bought a lock. She needed to have a safe place in the house where she could lock herself inside if she had to. The place she picked was her closet.

When she arrived home, Brenda quickly cleaned up the mess she had left in the living room. *Glen'll never even notice that my treasured glass candy dish is gone*, she thought miserably. Then, as she looked at the mangled elk head that lay on the floor, her sadness turned to disgust. She quickly grabbed it, not wanting to look at it a moment longer, and dragged it outside. She put it at the bottom of an trash bin, then poured the garbage out of another bin over top of it.

When Glen came home later that night, Brenda told him the elk head had fallen off the wall. "It must have been too heavy for the hook," she told him. "The antler broke and the whole thing was ruined." Glen looked at her angrily but said nothing.

CHAPTER TWENTY-SEVEN

WATCH AND WAIT

The next morning, to Brenda's surprise, Jane called and asked her to lunch. Not wanting to arouse suspicion, Brenda decided to go.

Her mind was racing as she walked into the café. Brenda waited for her eyes to adjust because the place was dark and there was a thick haze of cigarette smoke hanging in the air. The smell of grilled onions and hamburgers was almost as thick. The once white walls were yellowed with grease and dust. *I bet those walls haven't been washed since 1952 and the jukebox is probably just as old.* Hank Williams' *Your Cheatin' Heart* was playing just below the chatter of the customers. *What an appropriate song*, Brenda thought.

Brenda removed her coat and hung it on the chrome coat rack next to the cashier.

Jane waved to her from a booth near the back and Brenda joined Jane at the table. "Hello," Brenda said coolly. Her heart was pounding.

"How's it going?" Jane asked in a casual and too friendly matter. "Have you ever eaten here before?"

"No," Brenda answered, glancing around the room. *This is not the kind of place I'm used to.*

A skinny brunette walked over to the table. She shifted her weight to her left leg and stood with her hand on her hip. "Do you know what you want?" she asked, sucking on a Tootsie Pop. She slurped and swallowed, then grabbed the sucker's stick between two fingers and pulled it from her mouth. She held it like a cigarette in her writing hand while she took their order.

"I think I'll just have a chef salad with ranch dressing, Nancy," Brenda answered, reading her name tag.

"Anything to drink?"

"Do you have Coke in a bottle?" Brenda asked, wondering how long it had been since Nancy washed her uniform.

"Yeah, but they're the little bottles. And you don't get refills."

"That's fine."

"Same for me," Jane said.

The waitress scribbled on her pad and walked away.

"Brenda, I'm glad you came. I've been worried about you."

You should be more than worried. You should feel like the scum of the earth! I know just what are you up to Jane. "I'm fine," Brenda said, tensely watching her friend.

"Listen, it was wrong of me to ask you to finance all my whims. I'm sorry for all the times I did that," Jane apologized.

"It's just your way," Brenda said quietly. Her heart flip-flopped as she spoke.

The waitress slung the salad plates in front of them. "Is there anything else I can get for you?"

"Not right now," Brenda answered.

The waitress laid the check on the table and stomped away.

"Well, I think it's pretty clear she won't be coming back," Brenda said.

"I bet she won Miss Congeniality at her high school prom," Jane said sarcastically.

They laughed, then Jane turned serious.

"Is Glen acting better?"

It's probably a good idea to let her think everything's alright. "Don't worry about it. We're doing fine," Brenda said.

"Well, if you need my help, just let me know."

"That's really nice of you," Brenda said.

They made some inconsequential chitchat, finished their lunch and paid the bill. Standing up, Jane said sweetly, "Let's get together again real soon. Just us girls." Jane gave Brenda a light kiss on each cheek, and in that moment, Brenda was assaulted with the familiar scent of Jasmine. She fought the bile that rose in her throat.

"Yes, let's." Brenda forced a smile, and reflecting on Jane's kisses thought, *Isn't that what the mafia does just before they kill you?*

Somehow, Brenda got through the next few days. She tried to be home as little as possible. On the fourth day, she went to pick up the revolver in the evening, after a long series of appointments. Luckily, the store was still open.

The veil of night was thick as Brenda drove home. The only light she had to guide her came from pinhole-sized stars. It always amazed her how much darker it was in the country than in the city. She pulled slowly into the driveway and turned the motor off. Quietly, she got out of her car and headed toward the darkened house. Instead of entering, she walked up to a frosted window and tried to see in. All was dark and quiet.

Where is Glen? He should have been home long ago. I wonder if the Sheriff told him about my visit. Maybe it's a trap? What if he's waiting inside to shoot me and planning to claim he thought I was a burglar?

There were no signs of life coming from within the house, but she wasn't taking any chances. As she headed to the door, Brenda pulled the .38 from her purse and took the safety off. The metal felt warm compared to the cold night air. She fumbled with her keys, tried to find the keyhole and made a mental note to buy a tiny flashlight for her key chain. Finally she found the hole, slid the key into the lock and turned it slowly, trying to make as little noise as possible. She heard the tumblers rotate and fall. Brenda turned the knob, opened the door and stepped inside. The hardwood floor creaked and she cringed, paused and listened. All she heard was the solitary cry of a distant coyote. It sounded lonely and sad.

She went from room to room searching the dark house—the bedrooms, closets, bathrooms and living room. The last room she went into was the kitchen. She looked around. Now, certain there was no one home, she was about to holster the gun when behind her there was a crash. She spun around, ready to shoot, when she realized it was the ice-maker releasing a new load.

Brenda sighed with relief, turned on the lights, locked the doors and hid the gun under the sofa. With that ritual out of the way, she went to the kitchen, reached in the cabinet where she kept the cooking sherry and poured herself a drink.

Brenda's hand shook as she picked up the glass and took a gulp. Her nerves were frayed. *It's horrible when you're afraid to enter your own house. I feel safer in a big city with the druggies, pimps and muggers than I do here! Something's got to give.* She swallowed the rest of the jigger of sherry. It burned her throat all the way to her belly, but she knew it would relax her. *I almost shot the refrigerator. How would I have explained that to Glen?* She chuckled. *This is getting weird. I actually can laugh about all this insanity.*

Suddenly, her emotions turning on a dime, she began to sob. She stopped herself. *I have to be calm,* she told herself, *or I'll never get out of this.* Brenda leaned over and was putting the sherry back under the sink when she noticed boxes of rat and bug poisons. *Oh my God, he could use one of those on me,* she thought. She scooped the boxes of poison up and dumped them into the trash can. Then she covered them over with crumpled paper towels.

She forced herself to focus. *What else do I have around here that he might use?* She rummaged through all the kitchen drawers and dumped all the butcher knives into a lobster pot. *Why hadn't I thought of these before?* She placed the pot full of knives in her closet and locked it.

While in her closet, she took out her manicure set. Although she prized her slender fingernails, the long nails would have to go. It would be impossible to fight anyone off with them and they made it difficult to hold the gun. She took the clippers and *snip, snip, snip.* She cut her fingernails down to nubs. And somehow, once again, she got through another night with Glen.

The next day was a teasing taste of the spring soon to come: 60 degrees, sunny and clear. Yet the peaceful woods behind Brenda's cottage erupted with the sound of gunfire. A flock of wild geese took to the sky, squawking.

Brenda's dogs and other animals went wild from the noise, bouncing around in their cages.

As soon as Glen had told her he was leaving and wouldn't be home till late, She had called her brother, who now stood behind Brenda, holding her hands in place over the .38 Special. Dave had a clean, cool smell like Crest toothpaste, Brenda noticed as he talked into her cheek.

"You have to sque-ee-eze the trigger. Don't jerk it," he explained.

Brenda squeezed the trigger and the gun fired. The recoil knocked her back into him. She squinted to see where the bullet went into the target. There were no holes.

"I missed completely. Again!" she barked.

What was she going to do if she couldn't learn to shoot the damned thing? She needed to learn quickly! *Hell, who knows when Glen and Jane's plans are going to be enacted.*

Brenda fanned her hand in front of her face to clear her breathing space of gun smoke.

"It's going to take some time. Don't be so hard on yourself," Dave said, making her correct her stance by shoving his knee into the back of hers, forcing her knees to bend.

"And remember, if you want to stop somebody, but not kill 'em, shoot him in the leg."

Aim for the leg, Brenda repeated her mother's and brother's words to herself.

She squeezed off another shot and completely missed the target again. *I'm screwed*, she thought bitterly, but she didn't let it show on her face. Instead, she smiled and said to Dave, "I'm just going to have to practice this. Thanks for showing me."

Dave took the gun, opened the chamber and dumped the bullets into his hand. He showed the chamber to Brenda so she'd know it was empty and handed it back to her.

"Are you sure you and Glen are getting along now?" he asked, casually scratching his head.

"Sure I'm sure." She wasn't going to have her brother implicated in this.

"Then why didn't you ask him to teach you?" he asked.

"I just can't be sure of him after what happened, so I decided to take Dad's advice. Only I don't want you to tell the folks. They'll only worry." She could tell by the look on his face he didn't quite buy it.

"Is anything wrong?"

She shook her head. "No. Why?"

"I think Dad's wrong. You and guns don't mix," Dave responded.

"Well, it's just for protection." She closed the chamber, flipped the safety on and holstered the gun. "It gets spooky out here at night, especially since Sniffer disappeared and the house got broken into."

"And here I was, thinking you're turning into a rough, tough, backwoods woman who wants revenge when her man gets violent and all you are is a fraidy cat," he laughed.

Now, that was something he'd believe. Her family had always considered her timid.

"Well, let's just keep this between us," she told him.

The tension within her mounted. She hardly thought of anything else now. It was a deadly game of cat and mouse. She remembered the sheriff's words. He had to have proof positive. Well, she was going to get it. When Dave left, she went to a store which sold cell phones. She stood in front of a counter holding several types of cellular telephones. Three other models were resting between her and the salesman.

Brenda flipped each one open and closed, with one hand. A streamlined black one seemed the easiest, but the numbers were small. If she were wounded, it might be difficult to use. She finally settled on a larger size because it had a glowing keypad.

"Will this phone work if I'm in a closet?" she asked the salesman who was waiting patiently for her to decide.

"Sure will. My teenage daughter hides in the closet all the time. She likes to talk to her boyfriend in private. Her brothers won't leave her alone. Why are *you* in the closet?"

Brenda ducked her head, as if ashamed, "When my husband drinks, he hits me. Next time, I plan to hide in the closet and call the sheriff."

Embarrassed he'd asked, the salesman patted her hand and said, "There's a women's shelter here in Kansas City if it ever gets to be too much on you."

"Thanks," she said. It was surprising how compassionate strangers could be. Too bad the police, who were supposed to protect the innocent, weren't. She paid for the cellular phone, thanked the salesman again and left the store. She walked three blocks down to Missouri Highway 7 to the library. A cold wind had picked up since earlier in the day and it stung her chafed cheeks. She wished she'd brought some face lotion. *Well, maybe I'll stop at the drug store when I'm finished here. How strange,* she thought, *in the midst of such turmoil to think of such a banal, normal thing like dry skin.* She hurried past the chrome sign that read "Mid-Continent Library" and walked into the lobby. It was a new brick building with double glass doors and a diamond-shaped pattern of dark and light gray tiles on the floor and walls. As Brenda looked around for the Reference Desk, she noticed that above the bookshelves were copies of famous paintings. Finally, she saw the reference sign in the far corner.

She walked past a row of computers and stopped in front of a cute college-aged boy with red hair. He was on the phone and held up one finger to indicate he'd be off in a moment. "Can you wait?" he mouthed. Brenda nodded and looked around. Straight ahead of her were rows and rows of books and to her left were tables where people could read and do research.

The librarian hung up the phone and asked, "May I help you?"

"Yes," Brenda said. "I'd like to look up articles on cases the District Attorney has prosecuted recently."

"That would be on microfilm." He typed into his computer. "Any specific subject?"

"Wife abuse."

He typed it in, scribbled some numbers on a scratch pad and said, "Come with me and I'll get you set up."

He led Brenda to a room that had a row of microfilm machines. There was only one machine not in use. The librarian fished through the drawer marked *Kansas City Star* 1995, plucked out several reels of microfilm and brought them to Brenda. As he bent over to show her how to load the machine, she smelled the fresh scent of lemon. He appeared to be such a wholesome young man, it seemed to be a very appropriate smell. She watched his freckled hands thread the film through the viewfinder and realized why he smelled of lemons. The freckles on his hands were at least two shades darker than on his face. She figured he must use lemon juice to lighten his facial freckles.

He finished his demonstration, showed her how to make copies and left her to her research. After reading through some of the articles, she found the headline she remembered. *DA Sets Up Battered Women's Hotline*. Brenda wrote down the telephone number that was given in the article and stuck it in her purse.

Back in the car, Brenda punched the numbers of the abuse hotline into her new cell phone. She was on Highway 50 driving home.

A sweet-voiced counselor answered, "Hotline for battered women. How may I help you?"

Brenda paused. She wasn't sure if she wanted to report Glen or not. The counselor must have been used to women being uncertain when they called because she filled the void. "It's okay. Anything you say is confidential."

How she hated begging for help from strangers. When she spoke, Brenda had a tear in her voice. "I think my husband's planning to kill me. What do I do?"

"Leave home right now!" the counselor snapped back.

"Why should I have to leave? He's the one who's evil!" Brenda said.

"You can't afford to stay there. If you wait until he chokes you unconscious, it'll be too late!"

"I know..." Brenda began to cry. "Hold on a minute. I need to blow my nose."

Brenda didn't think she'd be this emotional, but now she was finding it hard to drive. She pulled onto the shoulder of the road and stopped. Turning off the ignition, she pulled a tissue from the travel pack above the visor and blew her nose. She peered out the window at the field beside her. There were about fifty metal barrels lying on their sides and just as many roosters strutting around crowing. She picked up the phone.

"Okay, I'm back," she said quietly.

"You're wedding vows do not mean until he kills you," the counselor said sharply. There was an uncomfortable silence. Then the counselor spoke softly into the phone. "Look, your gut told you he's serious or you wouldn't have called. Get out and get a divorce before it's too late."

"Isn't there anything else I can do?" Brenda cried.

"Do you want to die?"

"No," she answered. *What did I expect from this call? Did I think they'd solve the problem in any other way than having me leave?*

"What if I just confront him?" Brenda asked hopefully.

"If you do confront him, make sure you're in a public place. That way he can't harm you," the counselor warned. "Look sweetie, if you even suspect he wants to kill you, your marriage is already ruined." It was another dead end, no more real help than seeing the sheriff had been.

When Brenda got home, she called 911, but all she got was a recording. "Your call cannot be completed as dialed..."

"Damn!" she muttered under her breath. She dragged out the phone book and looked up the emergency number for the Sheriff's Department. She found it: 747-5511.

"747-5511...747-5511...747-5511." She repeated the number over and over like a mantra in order to memorize it. She knew if she needed to make the call, she wouldn't have time to look up the number and she wanted to be able to remember it no matter how anxious or frightened she was.

A short while later, she heard the sound of an engine in the garage. Brenda ran to the side door. She saw Glen drag himself out of his truck. He moved slowly, his shoulders slumped as if he were depressed. *He's never looked so old.*

"Glen, where have you been?" she asked. "Are you alright?"

He didn't respond. Standing near the front of his truck, he blinked as if it took a moment to register what she'd said. Finally he replied with a sharp, "None of your business."

"I think it is," she said just as harshly.

He tripped on a wrench lying on the garage floor and grabbed the side of the truck to keep from falling. When he did, the oversized zipper on his winter coat dug into the side of the vehicle and scratched the paint. He looked at the tiny comblike scratches on the fender. "God dammit!" he shrieked. "Look what you made me do to the truck!"

"How is it my fault?" Brenda asked.

He picked up the wrench and said, "You didn't put the wrench away."

"I haven't been using the wrench," she shot back at him.

Glen was furious and he slammed the wrench against the fender to vent his anger. Then he threw the tool to the ground. Now the fender had a large dent to go along with the scratches.

"Glen, I don't know what's going on, but we need to talk." *Maybe I can change his mind. Maybe...*

"Aww, Brenda, you always want to talk, but it doesn't change anything," he said wearily. They went into the living room where he slumped onto the sofa. She sat on the coffee table squarely in front of him. Looking directly into his eyes, she asked, "Do you want to go to a marriage counselor?"

"It won't do any good," he said, looking away.

"Why?"

"Because it doesn't change anything."

"What do you want to change?" she asked.

He sat there in silence.

"Please talk to me," she begged.

He didn't say anything. She became angry. He was just using her. He had solicited her love just so he could smash it apart and break her heart. The thought of that enraged her even more.

"Say something! Anything! Tell me to go to hell!" she screamed as she shook her fist at him. Suddenly, he grabbed her hand and pulled it toward him.

"Shut up! Who the hell do you think you are?" he said angrily, shoving her backward. While she struggled to regain her balance, he punched her in the face several times. Brenda finally steadied herself and darted for the closet. She was running down the hallway toward her bedroom when she felt him grab her shirttail. She kept on running. She'd barely made it to the closet when he caught her by the arm. She grabbed the closet door with her free hand and slung it between her and Glen. Her body was inside the closet, but he still had her one arm. She had to get away from him. Instead of continuing to pull her arm away, she stopped resisting. She let him pull her toward him and then struck him in the face. The slap caught him off guard and he instinctively grabbed his cheek. Free of his grasp, Brenda snapped the closet door closed and locked it. She felt in her pocket for the cell phone. 747-5511. Dialing the sheriff's department, she told the officer who answered, "My husband is beating me up." Then she gave him her name and address.

The palm of her hand was bright red. It hurt like the devil. She could only imagine what her face looked like.

Glen was pounding and kicking the door and screaming obscenities at her. "Open this fucking door, bitch! If I have to break the door down, you're going to be sorry. I'm going to get the wrench and my rifle. I mean it, Brenda!"

The door shook and she was afraid he would knock it off its hinges. She heard the wood splinter and crack. *Oh my God! He's going to break the door down!* She crouched in the corner until she heard the sound of a police car siren. Suddenly, Glen stopped beating on the closet door. Seconds later she heard the doorbell ring and pounding on the front door. She could barely make out the voice of the female deputy calling, "Mrs. Brumbaugh, Mrs. Brumbaugh!" She slowly crept out of the closet and, with her heart pounding, she looked around. Glen was no where in sight. She quickly inspected the door. It was smashed on the outside and looked ready to cave in. *That was close!* Brenda ran as fast as she could to answer the front door. As she opened it and tried to catch her breath, she saw Glen dashing to his truck.

CHAPTER TWENTY-EIGHT

No Protection

O ut on the front porch, Brenda watched as one of the deputies ran after Glen and caught him just as he was about to get into his truck. The deputy brought Glen back to the house, where Deputy Hanson was waiting.

"I'm going to take a look in his truck," the other deputy announced. "He looks like he's been drinking."

"There's nothing there. Save yourself the trip," Glen said.

"Are you Glen Brumbaugh?" Deputy Hanson asked.

"Yes Ma'am, I am."

"May I see some I.D.?"

Glen took out his wallet and handed his driver's license to Hanson, who looked at it and then handed the wallet back to Glen.

"Mr. Brumbaugh, did you strike your wife?"

"No Ma'am, I did not."

"How can you lie like that, Glen," Brenda said. She removed her glasses and pointed to her nose and face. Brenda, crying now, said, "He hit me right here with his fist and it pushed my glasses into my face and cut my nose."

Hanson stared at Brenda and shook her head. The second deputy, who had been driving the patrol car, walked up after he'd finished searching Glen's truck.

"Does it look like he hit her?" the burly, dark haired deputy called out.

"Yeah," Hanson said. "The cut on her nose is bleeding pretty hard and she's going to have a heck of a shiner." Hanson turned to Brenda. "I guess my next question is for you, Mrs. Brumbaugh. Do you want to press charges?"

Glen gave Brenda a glowering look, but she knew now what she had to do. She took a deep breath.

"Yes, I do."

Hanson looked at Glen. "Mr. Brumbaugh, we're going to have to arrest you for assault. Would you please turn around and put your hands behind your back?"

Glen took the money out of his wallet and threw it on the ground. "Keep that for me," he spat at Brenda. "I'll be coming back." Then he turned and put his hands behind his back.

As the male deputy put the handcuffs on Glen and lead him away, Brenda walked over and picked up the money. With tears rolling down her cheeks, she went into the house. Deputy Hanson followed her.

"He will come back to kill me. You know that, don't you?"

"Do you have a weapon?" the deputy asked.

Brenda nodded.

"I shouldn't say this, but you know you have the right to protect yourself."

"I know that," Brenda shivered, "but with all the guns he has, and being the marksman he is, I doubt I'll see him coming."

"That's why," Hanson said, "you have got to get a lawyer first thing tomorrow morning and get an order of protection."

After they left, Brenda couldn't fall asleep. At dawn, she drank some coffee and looked in the mirror at the purple bruise on her nose. It looked even worse today and now her eye was black, blue and swollen. She thought about trying to camouflage it with makeup, but even putting on makeup hurt too much. *I'll call the office and tell them I need at least two days off.* She made the call then hurriedly dressed. She knew she had to act quickly if she was to survive.

First, she called a locksmith. He responded immediately and changed all the locks. Then she called her parents to tell them what she was doing. Afterward, she called an attorney, then headed downtown.

The brass sign on the door read, Jim O'Neill, Attorney at Law. Brenda had heard he had a reputation for being above reproach—just the kind of attorney she needed. She pushed open the door and sank into a rich, forest green carpet. The office reeked of money and power.

She paused at the receptionist's desk and waited to be noticed. The dark-eyed beauty behind the desk was pulling a file for someone on the phone. She had perfect posture and long slender legs that were flattered by a flowing jersey skirt. She wore big rings on every finger and Brenda could tell that they weren't fake stones.

When she hung up, turned around and saw Brenda's bruises, she gasped. Then, realizing what she'd done, she tried to make excuses for her reaction.

"I thought I was alone. You startled me."

Brenda gave a worn smile and said, "I have a noon appointment with Mr. O'Neill."

"Just take a seat. I'll let him know you're here. Can I get you anything to drink?"

"I'm not thirsty, but this bruise is beginning to throb. Could you put some ice in a baggie?" Brenda asked.

"Of course," the receptionist said and scurried off to the office lounge two doors down.

Someone in the lounge ordered the receptionist to usher Brenda into O'Neill's office immediately. Brenda heard him say, "We can't have other clients see her. They might get the wrong idea and think we're ambulance chasers."

Brenda didn't have to wait long to see Mr. O'Neill. She could tell by his demeanor how he'd become so prominent. He was a ball of energy.

The man can't sit still. I bet he's a continuous blur of motion from the time he rises in the morning until the time he collapses into bed. The entire time she was telling him about her suspicions and about the beating leading up to her visit to his office, he was busy. He made them both some coffee, watered his plants, cut a wayward string off his shirt cuff, adjusted the thermostat, cleaned his reading glasses and completed a myriad of other minor tasks.

Normally, Brenda would have been offended by such activities when she was talking about something so traumatic, but she could see that he was soaking up every word. He'd stop her from time to time and ask her to elaborate on a detail or two. When she finished, he put his hand on her shoulder in a fatherly way and said, "You are a very strong woman to have endured all that you've been through."

"Will you handle my case, come with me to get an order of protection and then file divorce papers?" Brenda asked.

"Yes, Ma'am, I will. But first, I'll need a retainer."

"How much?"

"Five thousand dollars."

Brenda opened her purse, grabbed her checkbook and quickly slammed it shut. She didn't want him to see the gun.

As she wrote him a check for his services, despite her resolve to stay calm, she burst into tears. "I really loved him... I never wanted to do anything like this, but I have to."

"I've seen this kind of thing before and I'm sorry to say the men usually don't stop," he said in a sympathetic voice while handing her a tissue.

"I know. That's why I came to you," Brenda said as she signed the check and handed it to him. She leaned closer and spoke in a hushed tone.

"Can we get the order quickly?"

"We will, Mrs. Brumbaugh," the attorney said and walked her to the door. He had his hand on the doorknob, but instead of opening it, he turned to her and said, "First, get pictures of your face made and then come back here. We'll go to the courthouse together."

She nodded her head. He opened the door for her and she stepped out. As she was leaving, she thought she saw him glance at her purse suspiciously.

Brenda left O'Neill's office and went straight to Wal-Mart. Walking into the portrait studio, she was met by a fat woman with an even bigger hairdo than Tina Turner. She wore bright purple eyeshadow and orange lipstick.

"Can I get some pictures made?" Brenda asked the woman.

The woman lowered her eyelids, exposing even more purple shadow. "Is it for you?" she asked suspiciously, obviously not wanting to be involved in a brawl or a police matter.

Brenda nodded.

"Mind me asking why you want it made with that big ol' bruise?"

"My husband did this," Brenda said. "And I'm going to mount it on the wall in the living room to remind him of what happens when he loses control."

"Sugar, that's wonderful. You come right on back. I'll take your picture."

The photo session took about fifteen minutes because the photographer wanted to get the lighting just right. As Brenda watched her, the thought came to her that capturing the gruesomeness of the bruise was a challenge for her. It made Brenda realize how boring the photographer's job must be day in and day out.

When they finished, Brenda thanked her, left Wal-Mart and drove to a large hardware store nearby. She bought a tiny flashlight for her keychain, a steel door for the closet and a new lock for it in the building supplies department. The door was supposed to be used as an exterior weatherproof door and the salesman thought she was crazy for using it on her closet. Brenda didn't tell him what Glen had done to the last one.

Then she headed back to O'Neill's office. He was as good as his word and took her down to the courthouse for an emergency hearing. But there were others ahead of them. They waited hours, finally seeing Judge Engleheart, who issued an Order of Protection. The Sheriff's department promised to serve it immediately. Unfortunately, neither the sheriff not Deputy Hanson were on duty yet, and the deputy who received the Order of Protection didn't tell her that Glen had already been released and that the officers would have to find him first.

Not knowing, Brenda went home feeling safe. Getting out of her car, she never saw his truck stashed behind some trees and didn't see him hiding behind one of the evergreens until he jumped out at her.

"Come here," he yelled.

"What are you doing here? The police arrested you. You should be in jail," she said, alarmed.

"Good 'ol Jane bailed me out. Come here a minute."

She kept walking, quickening her pace.

"I don't see any bruises."

She was silent.

"Where are all the bruises you're supposed to have?"

Brenda took off her dark glasses and turned her face towards him for a moment. Then she ran into the house and locked the door. She went into the library.

She took out her cell phone and called the sheriff's office. "Yes, I was there today with my lawyer and the judge granted me an Order of Protection. I was told to call immediately if my husband came near me. Well, I just got home and he's here now." She paused and listened for a few moments. "What do you mean you haven't served him? Well, you have to get out here quickly. I don't know how long he'll stay."

Brenda hung up and called her parents, who she knew would be waiting to hear what had happened. Her dad answered.

"I just wanted to let you know I got the order, but it took nearly all day and before we could serve Glen, they released him," she reported breathlessly. "He's outside right now. I got the locks changed this morning; so I hope that keeps him out. The sheriff's on his way here to remove Glen from the property."

Suddenly, from the direction of the kitchen, she heard the sound of the wood door being sawed. *What the heck is he doing? Sawing down the door? Has he completely lost his mind?* "Hang on a moment, Dad. I think he's trying to get in.

I'm not going to hang up. If something happens to me, I want you to know." She put down the cell phone, but left it turned on just as Glen walked in.

"What the hell are you doing?" Glen angrily asked.

She tried to keep her voice steady. "I was just getting ready to schedule some work."

He stared at her. "I'm going to take my hunting dogs, get a few of my clothes and then I'm leaving."

"I just want to ask you one question," she said softly. "Why?"

A siren sounded outside.

"Did you call the police?" he growled.

"Why should I call the police? I'm trying to do my work."

"I hear a siren. If I knew you called them, I'd strangle you right here."

Someone pounded on the front door, then began shouting, "Mrs. Brumbaugh, this is the police!"

Glen looked in the direction of the front door then turned back to Brenda and hissed, "I should have broken your damn neck. And I will. And when I get done, there will not be a member of your family left 'cause I'll kill every damn one of them. And that's a promise."

He strode to the back door as Brenda ran to the front one. "Thank God you're here, Deputy Hanson," Brenda cried with relief as she threw open the door.

"I just got on duty when your call came in. Where's your husband?"

"Glen's going out the back way right now. He's been threatening me and my family."

Just then, the second deputy, who had run around to the back of the property, came around the corner of the house escorting Glen.

Hanson walked over to him. "Mr. Brumbaugh, we're here to serve you with an *ex parte* order of protection. Would you please take a seat in the back of my patrol car?"

"Officer, my wife, she's sick. She needs help." He glared at Brenda. "Oh, why do you do things like this, darling?"

Hanson cut in. "Mr. Brumbaugh, you can go get in the back of my car or I can handcuff you and put you there myself."

Glen left meekly. Hanson shook her head.

"Mrs. Brumbaugh," Hanson said, "You do understand the *ex parte* and how it works, right? Your husband is not to set foot on this property. The first time he does, it's a misdemeanor and the second time it's a felony."

Brenda looked at Deputy Hanson. Her heart was racing and she felt clammy all over. "You mean he gets two chances to kill me? After the first one, you know, it may be too late."

CHAPTER TWENTY-NINE

OF DREAMS, DELUSIONS AND NIGHTMARES

Brenda smelled the fresh baked biscuits and fried potatoes with onions. *Glen doesn't usually fry potatoes. He must be fixing me a special breakfast.* She was hungry and hightailed it toward the kitchen. As she drew closer, she heard voices. *Glen isn't alone. I wonder who's visiting? Why didn't he wake me? Oh, I told him to let me sleep late.*

"I love you, Sweetie," she heard Glen say.

Sniffer must be back. "Sniffer?" she called, walking into the kitchen. Then she remembered—Sniffer was gone.

Brenda was aghast to find Glen and Jane in each other's arms. They were in a passionate embrace and she thought for a second they were going to crawl onto the table and complete the act. They were enjoying deep French kisses and she could tell one was doing a tonsillectomy on the other. She just wasn't sure which one.

"What the hell's going on?"

Glen and Jane paid no attention to Brenda. They continued to kiss and paw at each other's crotches. When Jane finally released Glen, she said, "Your breakfast is getting cold."

They sat down at the kitchen table.

"Hey, this is my house. That's my husband you've been groping. And... What the hell?" Brenda was appalled. Jane was wearing her Victorian nightgown. It was her favorite. She liked the way it flowed in layers of antique chiffon. It was white with pearls sewn to the bodice and Brenda thought it made her look slim and sexy. Glen had taken Brenda out of it many, many times.

Upon closer scrutiny, Brenda realized Jane was wearing the ruby necklace and ring that Mrs. P had given her.

"Get the hell out of my clothes and out of my house!" Brenda screamed. She was outraged. "Glen, how could you do this to me?" she shrieked. "Answer me."

They didn't so much as blink an eye to acknowledge Brenda's presence.

"I'm going to be a more attentive wife to you than Brenda ever was," Jane told Glen. She picked up a bite of biscuit, sopped it in honey and fed it to him. The honey dripped off the biscuit and ran down his chin. Jane seductively licked it away.

Was? What does she mean was—Oh my God. Am I dead? That's the only thing that makes sense. No wonder they're ignoring me. They can't see me.

"What happened to me? Did you do something to me? How did I die?" Brenda shouted, still not getting their attention. Tears ran down her face as she walked away from the kitchen. She hadn't noticed it before, but she didn't really walk. She sort of half-glided, half-floated because she was completely weightless.

Suddenly, Brenda was surrounded by darkness. It was a state blacker than anything she'd ever seen before. She tried to plow through it, but she was awakened by the insistent sound of the phone ringing. Brenda turned the bedside lamp on and groggily answered the phone. It was Deputy Hanson.

"Mrs. Brumbaugh, I thought you'd probably still be very upset after what happened so I wanted to tell you personally that we've officially served your husband the papers. He was pretty angry when he left here. I'd be careful if I were you."

Hanson's words snapped Brenda fully awake. "You mean he's probably coming to kill me and you can't do anything to stop him." She was so frustrated with the way the damned justice system worked that she slammed the phone down, then got up and banged her knuckles against the wall, screaming just to vent her anger. *I'm going to force them to play their next hand. I'm so tired of all this. I'd rather be dead than live the rest of my life this way.*

She picked up the phone and dialed Jane.

Jane picked it up on the first ring.

Brenda didn't wait for "hello;" she just began talking. "I know what you're up to."

Jane feigned innocence. "I don't know what you're talking about."

"You and Glen have been planning to kill me."

"You're nuts!" Jane said.

"I heard you two on the phone, so don't play innocent with me!"

With a thud that echoed in Brenda's ears, the phone went dead. *I'm going to call her back and this time, I'll get it all on tape!* Brenda went to her desk and retrieved her tape recorder. Then she sat back on her bed, and just as she reached for the phone, it rang, causing her to jump. She took a deep breath and answered it. Glen's angry voice shot, "Listen up,

Brenda." Before he continued, she quickly held the recorder up to the earpiece of the phone and pressed *record*.

Glen's voice was sharp and clear. "You bitch, get this damned straight. I'm coming to kill you! And very soon!" Then the phone went dead.

With a chill running down her spine, Brenda flipped her tape recorder to *off* and ran around the house rechecking all the windows and doors to make sure they were locked.

Walking into the living room, Brenda looked around. It was too familiar. It would be too easy for Glen to chase her, even in the dark. She pulled the sofa into the center of the room and began to rearrange the furniture.

When Brenda finished, nothing was in its original place. Brenda checked her gun for bullets and replaced the spent cartridges. *It's going to be a long night*, she thought as she pulled the drapes closed and turned on the television. She sat down on the couch and pressed the mute button so she could hear every sound, knowing that Glen could show up at anytime.

For hours, Brenda waited. She'd never noticed before how the house creaked and groaned as if it breathed like a living organism. She made it through the *Late Show* and the *Late, Late Show*, but somewhere along the way she began to doze. She was soon fast asleep clutching her gun.

Suddenly, Brenda heard the sound of glass shattering. Half awake, she panicked, aimed the gun in the direction of the sound and shot wildly at the door. She blinked away the sleep and focused on Glen. He swung himself through the upper window of the front door and landed like a gymnast who'd just completed an exercise on the parallel bars. He seemed confused—either his eyes hadn't adjusted to the dark yet or the rearrangement of the furniture was throwing him off kilter. She adjusted her aim and mustered a strong voice. "Go away, Glen, or I'll shoot you."

"You wouldn't shoot an unarmed man. I left my rifle in the truck."

"What do you plan to do? 'Break my damn neck' like you threatened to do so many other times?"

The flickering light from the television screen danced across his face, giving him a sinister look even though he was grinning. It was the same grin that had won her heart, talked her into giving him money and made her want to die for him. He took a couple of steps toward her.

She waved the gun at him, indicating for him to stop where he was. "Do you have any idea how much it hurt when I found out you were having an affair with Jane and were planning to kill me?" She waited for a response but none came. She continued, "I was so angry I wanted to kill you both."

Glen released a sarcastic sigh, "You won't kill me. You can't even chop the head off a dead fish."

His remark made her mad and she gripped the gun tighter. She wanted to pull the trigger just to show him she could, but *how* could she? Here was the man she'd given her heart to, the man she'd wanted to father her children.

The thought of it now sickened her. She tightened her finger on the trigger, aware that her hand was sweaty and slick.

She could kill him.

She wanted to kill him.

She had every reason. He'd broken in the house to kill her. She had his confession on tape... All she had to do was squeeze the trigger.

But she couldn't do it. Someplace deep, deep inside her, she still loved him and didn't want him dead. She pleaded with him, "Glen, I know you don't want to do this. You're not a killer. Inside you're a good person. If you kill me, it's going to eat away at you and you'll never be happy with Jane."

He chuckled. "That just shows how little you know about me. You live in a fairytale, Brenda, where everyone is good and they all do the right thing. Well, in my fairytale, killing you is the right thing so Jane and I can live happily ever after."

"I'm begging you, Glen. Please, don't make me shoot you!"

"Jane's right. You are pathetic," he said with a sneer.

"Why don't you just run away with Jane? I'd rather lose you to another woman than shoot you."

"Sorry, Brenda. We need your money. That's why we've gone through all this. We planned it after I first met Jane on visiting days at Algoa Prison. I was her ex-husband's cellmate for a while."

Brenda flinched from the harsh words. *Oh my God! He and Jane had set her up from the get-go.*

It seemed to Brenda that Glen was delighting in hurting her. He smiled and continued, "I want it all—Jane, the money, freedom... And there's only one way to get it all."

Suddenly, he lurched at her. She grabbed the first thing that was at hand and threw it. It was her grandmother's vase. He caught it, then smashed it on the floor. Brenda rushed to the phone and held it to her ear but it was dead. *He cut the phone line!*

She couldn't get to her cell phone. How could she have been so stupid to leave it on the counter? Now it was behind Glen.

"The only way you'll get it all is over my dead body and I'm not going to make it easy for you," she screamed.

"You're dead, bitch!"

Brenda's only hope was to escape and darkness was her only friend. She shot out the television screen and bolted across the room.

Glen laughed at her and pulled a flashlight from his hip pocket. Brenda crawled behind a large wing chair. A gust of wind blew through the broken door and the drapes across the room fluttered. Thinking she was behind the draperies, Glen attacked and ripped them off the wall only to find she wasn't there.

"Oh, goodie. Let's have a suspenseful game of hide-and-seek," he said sarcastically.

Glen searched the area with his flashlight, but didn't see Brenda cowering behind the chair.

She had to get her cell phone; so she inched out from under the chair and picked up a lamp. She threw it blindly. Purely by luck, it went sailing across the room and knocked the flashlight out of Glen's hand. The lamp and the flashlight crashed to the floor and Glen was left fumbling around in total darkness. Brenda ran to the counter, grabbed the cell phone and stuck it in her pocket. Then she took off half-crawling, half-walking toward the shattered door. She pulled the house keys from her pocket and poked the gun into her waistband. If she could get the door unlocked, maybe she could escape. She pressed the tiny flashlight she had attached to her key chain, but in her haste she pushed too hard and the switch broke off. Her heart pounded so loudly she thought he might hear it. In the dark, she fumbled with the keys trying to feel the right one. The dogs outside must have caught her scent, because they started barking and gave away her location.

She could hear Glen's footsteps and knew he was coming toward her. Finding the right key, she searched for the keyhole with her fingertip. A loud crash pierced the darkness and she knew Glen had stumbled over the coffee table.

"Dammit! I cut my leg. You moved the furniture. You bitch!" he shouted, stumbling around and cursing.

Trembling, she finally found the keyhole, slipped the key inside and turned.

"You won't think you're so fucking smart when I get a hold of you!" Glen yelled.

Brenda wasn't used to the new door lock and turned it the wrong way. She pulled on the door, but it didn't open, so she turned the key 360 degrees. Finally, the bolt snapped back. She threw open the door and was darting out when Glen caught her by the hair. It felt like thousands of tiny needles were stabbing her scalp at once. She screamed, but kept struggling forward despite the pain. She thought he was literally going to pull all her hair out, leaving her bald.

He threw her against the wall and began beating her head against it. She felt the Sheetrock give and her head sunk into the foamy insulation. She struck Glen hard on the shoulder blade, but it didn't phase him. She pawed her waistband trying to find her gun as he continued to drum her head against the wall. Then, letting herself go slack for a moment, she saw her chance and bit into his forearm. He pulled away so hard she thought she might lose some teeth, but she hung on.

"Let me go! I'm going to get my rifle and finish you off!"

Brenda finally retrieved the gun from her waistband and tried to move away enough to point it. She had a clear shot of his chest but once again couldn't bring herself to pull the trigger. Finally, she pointed the gun barrel down toward his leg, closed her eyes and squeezed the trigger. *BLAM!*

Glen stepped back and looked at her in bewilderment for just a second. Then he made a move and fearing he was going to attack her again, Brenda squeezed the trigger a second time. *BLAM!*

Glen was turning from her and stopped for a second before moving away. *Oh my God! I can't believe I actually shot him!* Then, like a bolt of lightning, he was running toward his truck. *What the...? Where is he going?* Brenda looked around and seeing no signs of blood or bulletholes began to panic. *There's no blood and he's running! How can he run if I shot him in the leg? Oh my God—I missed him and now he's really mad! Oh Lord, he's going to get his rifle! If he gets his gun, I'm finished. Oh God, help me! Please help me!*

As panic set in, Brenda tried desperately not to lose control of her emotions. *Think, Brenda, think.* Then she remembered where she could go for safety—the closet! *He's really going to do it. He's going to kill me.* She started running. Suddenly, she was flipping through the air and landed with a thud. The wind was knocked out of her. She gasped to catch her breath. She'd tripped over the coffee table, too. The sharp corner of the coffee table cut her knee. The pain sent an aching sensation down her calf, but there was no time to check the wound.

Even though the dogs were barking like crazy now, she heard Glen's truck door slam shut. She staggered to her feet and took off running again. Nothing in her life had prepared her to be hunted like a deer. She was looking over her shoulder when she ran into the bedroom door. Her body banged into it and bounced backward. She kicked open the door and kept running. *Just a couple more feet and I'll be in the closet.* Finally, she was there.

Brenda ran into the closet, locked the steel door her brother helped her install and unscrewed the light bulb. *I'm not going to make it easy for you.* She pulled the cell phone from her pocket. "Please work!" she whispered, crouched in a dark corner. The only light came from the glowing key pad. Even though she'd memorized the sheriff's number, she was so scared that her brain misfired and she couldn't remember it. "747-55... 757-444... 747-5511... That's it." Her hands were shaking and she had trouble making her fingers hit the right buttons. She dialed 747-5551. The phone rang, then squealed and a recording said, "We're sorry, but the number you've re—." Brenda hung up and dialed again, 747-5511. When she pushed the last digit, the phone began to ring... once... twice...on the third ring, someone picked up.

"Johnson County Sheriff's Department," said a voice from the other end of the line. "May I—"

In a hoarse and trembling voice, Brenda gasped, "For God's sake, help me! My husband's going to kill me!"

"Okay, Ma'am, can I have your name and address?" the dispatcher said automatically.

"Brenda Brumbaugh." She quickly gave her address then frantically added, "You have to hurry! Please. Please, he's gone to get his rifle! I might've shot him. I don't know!" Her voice was filled with terror.

"Ma'am, Ma'am! I need you to calm down," he said.

"You don't understand. He's coming back to kill me!"

"You said you think you may have shot him?" the dispatcher said in a calm tone.

"I'm not sure. It all happened so fast," she moaned.

"One moment," the dispatcher said. It seemed an eternity that Brenda waited, but then the dispatcher was back on the line.

"Mrs. Brumbaugh, the sheriff is on his way. He'll be there very soon. Where do you think you may have shot your husband?"

"Maybe in the leg. I can't be sure. I couldn't see any blood," Brenda said as she tried to calm herself. She gulped in big breaths of air.

"Are the windows and doors locked?"

"No, the front door was left open when he ran out," she told him.

"I need you to go shut that door," the dispatcher instructed her.

"No! You don't understand. If I go close to the door, I'll be where he can see me. I'm a sitting duck. Please, tell the sheriff to hurry! Please!" Brenda begged.

"Where are you right now?"

"I'm hiding in my bedroom closet."

"Alright. Sit tight. The sheriff will be there right away."

After she put the phone down, in an attempt to make herself small, Brenda curled up on the floor, bringing her knees up to her chest. She pulled her new long, black leather coat from the hanger above her. She hid herself under it, only subliminally aware of the irony of using Glen's Christmas present to her to hide from him. The leather was cold against her skin. *Maybe he won't realize I'm under here.* She bowed her head and got a strong whiff of the gun powder on her hands.

She sat there motionless, praying. *I'm trapped. My life is in your hands, God.*

"Mrs. Brumbaugh, are you there? Hello. Hello? Mrs. Brumbaugh? Mrs. Brumbaugh?"

Brenda jerked her head up in shock. She looked around and realized she was hearing the voice of the dispatcher coming from her cell phone. *If Glen comes back here, I don't want to be given away by this idiot yelling at me.* She turned the phone off, laid it back on the floor and hugged her gun.

She lowered her head again under the coat. Resting her forehead on her knees, she closed her eyes. *I'm scared, God...but I'm ready if this is what you want. I only ask one thing. Please make it quick. If it be Thy will...*

Sheriff Gilbert pulled his patrol car alongside Glen's truck. He shined his spotlight at the vehicle and that's when he saw it—a bloody hand print on the window. On closer inspection, he noticed that there was a smear of blood on the door handle and drops of blood leading to the house. He got on his radio and spoke to his dispatcher.

"This is the sheriff. Charlie, you better send me an ambulance and some backup. I think somebody's been hurt out here at the Brumbaugh place."

"Ten-four," the dispatcher responded.

The sheriff started walking toward the house. He did not want to drive all the way up to the residence for fear he might contaminate evidence. When he neared the house, he saw something lying in the driveway. He couldn't make out what it was so he squinted to see better and kept walking toward it. When he saw the patch of blood, he was pretty sure it was a body. The sheriff expected the crumpled heap in the driveway to be Brenda. He was shocked to see it was Glen.

His instincts told him Glen was dead, but he felt for a pulse—just so he could say that he had in court. He looked at his watch. It was 8:12 P.M.

He stuck his head in the garage and looked around. No one was there. He backed up and headed for the front door. Glass crunched beneath his feet.

"Mrs. Brumbaugh, you need to come on out here. It's Sheriff Gilbert," he called.

He waited. There was no reply. He unhooked his holster and took out his .45. With his pistol in one hand and his flashlight in the other, he searched the house room by room. When he found the bedroom closet was locked, he became suspicious. He'd never seen a steel door *inside* a house before. Since he could not unlock it from the outside, he knew the lock and a person had to be inside. He knocked on the door.

"Mrs. Brumbaugh, come on out here." There was no answer. He knocked harder on the door and repeated his demand. Still, there was no answer.

He went back to his car and got a Slim Jim to open the door. Deputy Hanson drove up, stuck her head out the window of the patrol car and asked, "What've we got?"

"Glen Brumbaugh's dead and I think his wife is in the bedroom closet. It's locked from the inside. I've knocked on the door, but she ain't answering. I'm afraid she might have killed him, then killed herself."

"My God almighty!" the young deputy said.

He sighed and said, "You stay out here, take pictures and direct the ambulance attendants. Don't let them contaminate the crime scene. I'm going in and see what's in that closet."

The sheriff tried to get a response from Brenda one more time without success. He jimmied the skinny metal strip between the jamb and the door and slid it down to the lock. It took about ten minutes and some fancy maneuvering before the Slim Jim finally snapped the lock. The sheriff heard the sirens of the ambulance pulling up outside. He drew his gun and slowly opened the closet door. When he peered inside, he saw only blackness and a trembling foot poking out from beneath a black leather coat in a heap on the floor.

Brenda was in such a state of shock and fear she never even heard the sheriff's calls to her. When she heard the scraping noise on the door lock, she thought it was Glen trying to get in. She'd contorted her shaking body, trying to get even smaller, trying to disappear. She had tried to block her thoughts but they wouldn't stop. *My time has come. He's found me!*

As the door creaked open, she didn't dare allow herself to even breathe. *I can't watch. I don't want to see it coming.* In an instant, images of her family, her pets and her wedding day flooded her mind. She tried to make peace with Glen and the world and braced herself for the worst.

A moan escaped her lips as she felt the leather coat being lifted off her.

"Mrs. Brumbaugh, it's the sheriff."

Huddled in the corner of the closet, she looked up at him like a frightened child, speechless. He edged closer with his gun drawn. "Mrs. Brumbaugh, are you okay?"

It took her a moment just to register the fact that she was still alive. "Sheriff?" she finally said in a tone of disbelief. Tears began falling down her face. She felt momentary relief at the sight of the sheriff, but almost immediately, she was again gripped with fear. "Glen...where's Glen? He is coming to kill me..."

Deputy Hanson entered the bedroom and pulled her gun, too.

"Where's your gun?" asked Deputy Hanson, ignoring Brenda's question.

"Here," Brenda said and held it up for them to see. "But where's Glen? Did you get him?"

This time the Sheriff spoke. "Put the gun on the floor and let us see your hands."

My hands? What for? What is going on? They're acting like they're afraid of me when Glen's the dangerous one! Brenda was so dazed that everything seemed like a surreal dream and she did as she was told. She feared she was in shock and needed medical attention, but she couldn't seem to form the words to tell the sheriff. She had the strange feeling she was actually outside her body, watching these events take place.

"Come on out of the closet, Mrs. Brumbaugh," the Sheriff said as he picked up her gun and put it in a plastic bag.

Brenda tried to stand, but her knees felt like they were made of Jell-O and she collapsed. Deputy Hanson holstered her gun and came to help Brenda off the floor.

Brenda held onto Hanson and stepped out of the closet. "Where's Glen?" she repeated. "You have to get him before he gets his rifle," she said to the sheriff, the pitch of her voice escalating with fear. "He's going to kill me."

"We need you to tell us what happened," the sheriff said, ignoring her question. "I want you to go into the other room with Deputy Hanson and she'll take your statement." Sheriff Gilbert gave the deputy a nod and walked out.

He went out front and supervised the removal of the body. The headlights of the ambulance picked up the glint of metal on a long rifle barrel out in the woods and he yelled, "Whoever is out there better lay down his firearm and come on out."

"Don't shoot, don't shoot!" cried the voice. "I'm puttin' down my gun."

The bushes shook and out stepped Morgan. He made his way to the sheriff with his hands in the air.

"Don't shoot. I'm unarmed," Morgan repeated.

"Who the hell are you and what are you doing snooping around out here?" Gilbert demanded.

"Russell Morgan's the name, sheriff. I was going to my deer stand and I heard some shots. I decided I'd check it out. What happened?"

"Did you see anything?"

"No sir-ee. I heard four shots though. What happened?"

"That's none of your concern right now," the sheriff replied.

Morgan inched closer to the sheriff and almost stepped in a small pool of blood in the driveway. His eyes got big. "Oow-ee-ee! I better get outta here!"

"No, you'd better hang around. We may need you as a witness. Go over to one of the deputies' cars. Give them your name and address. Then sit in the backseat and wait till one of us can interview you," Gilbert ordered.

Morgan nodded and walked to the closest patrol car, his hands still in the air.

Brenda and Deputy Hanson went to the kitchen and sat at the table to talk. Although Brenda didn't tell Hanson why, she refused to sit next to the window for fear Glen was out in the yard or the woods and would shoot her in the back. Deputy Hanson made them both cups of hot chamomile tea and draped a blanket around Brenda's trembling shoulders. Then Brenda told the officer what happened. Deputy Hanson asked few questions but took a lot of notes. When Brenda finished, the officer spoke in a hushed tone.

"I can't help but feel sorry for you," Hanson confided. "Remember when I saw you earlier at the station I told you to get an attorney and an order of protection?"

Brenda nodded and tried to smile. "I did. But it didn't help."

The sheriff walked into the room. Brenda looked into his face. "Please, will you tell me now? Did you find Glen or not?"

Gilbert narrowed his eyes and said, "We found him in the driveway."

"In the driveway? That's crazy. What was he doing—standing out there in the open just waiting for you? Didn't he even try to hide from you?" Brenda ran her hands through her hair and said shakily, "Never mind. It doesn't matter. I don't really care what he was doing. I'm just glad you found him. I want to press charges."

A strange look swept across the sheriff's face. "You can't, Mrs. Brumbaugh."

This sheriff's going to fiddle around until Glen kills me! "Well, why can't you do it this time?" she asked angrily.

"Glen is dead."

"What? No!" Brenda said in disbelief. She slumped back in the chair. "No, he's not dead. That's impossible! I aimed for his leg. I didn't even see blood. I thought I didn't even hit him!"

"He's dead!" the sheriff repeated curtly.

"No! No! NO!" Brenda screamed. "I didn't want him dead! I loved him! I only wanted to prevent him from killing me!" Brenda's sobs grew louder and more hysterical. She fell to her knees, wailing. "Oh my God, I killed my husband!"

They let her sob for a few more minutes, exchanging glances over her prostrate form. The sheriff reached down and put his hand on her shoulder. "Ma'am, you have to get up. Please get hold of yourself. I have some questions I want to ask you."

Brenda couldn't stop crying. *How did this happen?* She hadn't wanted him to die. What would she do without Glen? She loved him—despite it all, she still loved him!

"I can't answer questions right now," she said through her tears. "Please, just leave me alone," she begged. She had a gaping wound inside her heart. She didn't know how she could go on. How could she live with herself...with what she had done?

"I'm afraid, Mrs. Brumbaugh, I need to talk to you right now," the sheriff said firmly as he helped her to her feet.

"I have to call my parents to tell them what happened," she managed to gasp between sobs.

"Okay," he relented. He watched her carefully.

Brenda dialed her parents' number. "Glen's dead," she said when her father answered, then broke into a fresh round of sobs. "I...I killed him." Billy Gunn didn't ask any questions but simply said, "I'll be right there."

She hung up the phone as the Sheriff sighed. "Mrs. Brumbaugh, since you admit you killed your husband, I have to read you your rights." Solemnly, he began to intone, "You have the right to remain silent. Anything you say can and will be used against you in a court of law. You have the right to an attorney. If you cannot afford an attorney, one will be appointed to you..."

CHAPTER THIRTY

FATAL DECEIT

Brenda stared at the sheriff in disbelief. *Read me my rights? Why would I need an attorney? Is he going to accuse me of a crime?* "Why are you doing this? It was an accident!" Brenda cried.

"We'll see," the sheriff replied.

Brenda tried to calm herself, but she couldn't stop shaking.

"I'm not going to waste a lot of time here. Let me tell you what I think happened. I believe you knew what you were doing when you shot him!"

Brenda was paralyzed with fear. *Is he accusing me of murder?* This was too much to comprehend. "I had no choice," she cried. "I had to do what I did or he would have killed me."

She suddenly realized she was going to have to defend herself against the sheriff. The same sheriff she'd tried to get to help her before. She didn't understand. She'd always thought the law was supposed to help people. She rubbed her forehead. Her head was spinning. She simply couldn't process all the events of the last few hours.

"You read a lot of those true crime stories?" the sheriff asked.

"No."

"I saw a lot of books in your office. How about those murder mysteries?" he asked, but didn't give her time to answer. "This scenario you're cooking up sounds a lot like a book that writer, Ann Rule, wrote. You ever read her books?"

"I haven't had time to sit and read an entire book since I was nineteen years old," she replied tersely.

"Maybe you set up your husband," he said, not taking his eyes off of her. "That could be your story. You claim that he's trying to kill you, but really you're planning to kill him.

Brenda stared back at him, trying to gather her composure and her wits about her. "If I wanted to kill him why would I shoot him in the leg?"

"How do I know you were aiming for his leg? Maybe you're just a bad shot."

"What makes you think I set him up? There must be a reason."

"For one thing, there's no blood on the floor where you claim you shot him. Maybe you murdered your husband in cold blood in the driveway, as he was walking up to the house," he said, shaking his finger in her face. "And if you did and it's the last thing I do, I'll see that you spend the rest of your life behind bars. Now, what about the blood?"

"I don't know how to explain why there's no blood on the floor," Brenda sputtered the words out.

He continued to talk, but Brenda was in shock and tuned him out. She watched him wag his finger in her face, as tears spilled from her eyes.

"Now, why don't you write down everything you remember." The sheriff thrust a pad and a pen at her.

Brenda took them and, with tears still coursing down her cheeks, began writing. After she was finished and had given the pad back to him, the sheriff finally said, "I'll be watching you. Don't take off for anywhere."

Right after he left, her dad and Suzy arrived in separate cars. She told them all that had occurred.

"Did the sheriff ask you a lot of questions before I got here?" her dad asked.

"I think I've told them the story three times already, then he had me write it all down."

Suzy shook her head. "They're not supposed to do that with what you're going through. They don't know what state your mind is in. They could have been endangering your life."

Brenda's dad wanted to bring her back home with him, but Brenda declined. "There's nothing to be afraid of anymore," she said sadly.

"I hope that's true," her father said. "But I don't like how the sheriff acted. If your mother wasn't ill I'd stay here with you, but I have to get back to her."

"I'll stay the night, Dad," Suzy offered.

Her dad gave Brenda a kiss and Suzy a hug and left.

"Okay, but I have a call to make and I want to be alone to make it," Brenda said quietly.

Suzy's eyebrows went up, but she was strangely reticent. "Whatever you say, Brenda," she said. "I'll be waiting in the living room."

Brenda dialed a number and heard it ring. It rang three more times before the answering machine picked up. "Hi, this is Jane. You know what to do," the recorded voice said. There were a series of beeps, then nothing. Brenda waited and listened. She heard breathing on the line.

"I know you're listening," Brenda said angrily. "Your affair with my husband got him killed. If I ever see your face again, I'll make sure you get the gas chamber."

Jane got busy throwing her clothes into a suitcase. When she ran out of space, she got a roll of plastic trash bags from the kitchen and started throwing shoes, clothes, makeup and everything she owned into them.

With her bags stuffed in her car and a plane ticket in her hand, Jane looked around her house one last time. Then she stepped out the door, got into her car and drove away, never to return.

Getting into the shower, Brenda scrubbed herself for hours, trying to wash away any trace of what she'd done this evening. After she'd used up all the hot water, she let the cold water run on her as she silently sobbed. Finally, Suzy came in and made her get out of the shower.

"You've been in there long enough to have taken four showers, Brenda. Now, come on and go to bed," Suzy told her handing her a fluffy bath towel. "Rest is what you need, Honey."

Brenda let Suzy lead her to the bed and tucked her in like a small child. She thought she could not, but fell into an exhausted sleep within minutes.

In the morning, she asked Suzy to drive her to the district attorney's office. "I don't think I'm in any shape to drive myself." In truth, she needed the moral support. Her brother Dave called and when he learned that Suzy was going, he offered to drive them both to the courthouse. "Afterward," he said, "I'll drive you two to the funeral home to make arrangements for Glen's burial."

There was a knock on the door and Brenda heard Suzy on the other side. "Dave's here, Hon. We'll be waiting in the car. Don't take too long."

Getting her jacket, Brenda looked in the mirror. She barely knew the woman starting back at her with tired, blue eyes. "I'm a murderer," she murmured. "I killed the man I would have died for." Tears formed in her eyes. *But I had no choice. If I hadn't, he surely would have killed me.*

"Okay," Brenda answered softly. She heard the clack of Suzy's high heels and knew she'd gone to the kitchen. She looked back at the mirror. "It's almost over," she told her reflection.

Walking into the courthouse's second floor conference room, Brenda recognized the District Attorney instantly, because she looked just like her pictures in the newspaper stories Brenda had seen. The DA, Sheriff Gilbert and a man introduced as the pathologist were seated around a long table. The DA indicated that Brenda should sit down. Suzy, who was carrying a sealed paper sack, sat down next to Brenda in an empty seat. Dave who hadn't wanted to come in, waited downstairs.

The District Attorney soon got down to business. "I know this is a difficult time for you, Mrs. Brumbaugh. I'm sorry, but we have to go over a few things while they're still fresh in your mind."

"I understand," Brenda replied. "I have some questions, too."

"You first," the DA said.

"Well," Brenda cleared her throat, "I tried to shoot Glen in the leg. That shouldn't have killed him. I have to know what I shot that killed him."

The sheriff scratched his head and cut in. "Well, I think the first bullet hit him in the leg. He fell and while he was down on his knees, I think you stuck the gun in his back and shot him."

"Sheriff Gilbert, please," the DA said reprovingly.

"You're wrong," Brenda said sighing, "and I think you know it."

The pathologist spoke. "The facts are, one bullet hit his femur. The bullet lodged in the bone; it never exited the body. That's why there was no blood at the spot where you shot him. Only if the bullet had gone through the leg and exited on the other side would there have been blood. The second bullet did not go in straight, mind you, which tells us he was in the middle of a turn."

"That's exactly what I told the sheriff. He was going out to his truck to get his rifle," Brenda said.

The pathologist went on. "That bullet hit his liver, kidney and lung. Neither bullet exited. He bled to death internally. It was relatively quick."

"Now Mrs. Brumbaugh," the District Attorney said, turning to Brenda, "as I said on the phone, this isn't a formal hearing, but I need to know if you have any other evidence to substantiate your story. I've already read the sheriff's report and your written account and I have a copy of Mr. Brumbaugh's arrest record."

Brenda motioned to Suzy who handed her the paper bag. Brenda dumped the contents of the bag on the table. She riffled through the stack, nervously pulling out papers as she talked.

"Here's my diary of the past year and a copy of the restraining order." She handed the District Attorney a brown leather book with a broken clasp.

"And this is the phone bill documenting my call to the Battered Women's Hotline." These she handed to the sheriff and frowned. "I believe you have records on my calls to your department seeking help against my violent husband."

Brenda picked up a yellow form. "This is my payment for the gun and the two white strips are register receipts for the cell phone and the steel door. This green receipt is from the locksmith who changed all my locks."

She picked up the picture of her bruised face she had made at Wal-Mart. "This is what he did to my face," she said and handed it to the DA

She saw the District Attorney shoot a look at the sheriff.

"And here is the original tape of..." Brenda's voice faltered and the muscles in her face grew tense. Suzy patted her hand. Brenda cleared her throat and continued, "...Glen telling me he was going to kill me."

The District Attorney walked over to a cabinet behind the table and pulled out a tape recorder and inserted the tape. She played the tape and they all listened as Glen's angry voice filled the room. Afterward, Suzy opened her handbag and pulled out a key. "Oh, and here's the key to her safe-deposit box."

"What's that for?" the sheriff asked warily.

"You'll find a letter inside dated last November, saying that I thought someone was trying to kill me," Brenda explained. "I know you think I'm a murderer," Brenda continued, staring at the sheriff, "and I guess I am. I killed the only man I ever loved, but there was nothing else I could do. Not if I wanted to live." She burst into tears.

Suzy pulled a tissue from her handbag and handed it to Brenda.

"I think the moral of his sorry life, as one young sage

said," Suzy interjected, "is that sometimes when you're out to screw someone, you get screwed."

The DA half-smiled, but Sheriff Gilbert glared at Suzy.

Brenda sniffled. "I'm sorry," she said, dabbing her eyes. "It just hurts so much."

The DA gave Brenda a sympathetic look and the sheriff rolled his eyes. The District Attorney ignored him and closed her notebook.

"You've been through quite an ordeal, Mrs. Brumbaugh," she said and began picking up the papers on the table. "I can see it's clearly a case of self-defense."

"Hold on a minute!" the sheriff objected, rising out of his chair.

"I've never seen a case so cut and dried. Look at all this evidence. I am not going to put her through anymore torment," the DA told the sheriff. Then she turned to Suzy and said, "You can take her home. This case is closed."

Epilogue

Time had passed. Tulips were sprouting green buds and the daffodils were in full bloom. Brenda loved spring. It was the season of renewal. The earth, the trees and the bushes all had fresh, tender, light green growth. Brenda longed for renewal also and prayed for an end to the heartbreaking memories that plagued her. She was working hard to put the past behind her. Some days she was successful and some days she was not. The nights were, of course, the most difficult of all. In some of them, she still relived the pain and then she told herself it would take more time to get beyond the hurt, past the painful betrayal she had endured. But sometimes now she dreamed of a happier future.

She parked her car at the entrance gates, threw her keys in her tote bag and climbed out of the vehicle. This was such a pretty place at this time of year with all the shrubs and spring bulbs in bloom. She began to walk to her destination, enjoying the warm sunshine. She pushed up the sleeves of her nurse's uniform so she could feel the heat of the sun on her arms.

Slowly, she made her way up the gently rolling hill, greedily gulping in deep breaths of the fresh spring air. It smelled so sweet. *There must be a honeysuckle vine nearby*, she thought. As she walked, she practiced the resolve she had learned with the assistance of counseling and time. *I'm going to take the time to really enjoy spring this year. I think I'll make sure to get home at least an hour before sundown so I can sit in the yard and look at the flowers. I am not going to dwell on what could have been. I will look forward.*

As she reached the crest of the hill, she saw the monument she had chosen right after she and Glen had bought insurance together and purchased the grave site for what she had supposed would be their family plot.

Brenda had chosen a double headstone—she would one day be buried there, too—with two large, red granite intertwined hearts sitting on a base of gray marble. Their surname—Brumbaugh—had been inset in a band of gray granite spanning the two hearts. Now there was a mound of earth where Glen was buried. Right after his death, his name, date of birth and date of death were inscribed. On the other side, Brenda's name had been inscribed, along with her date of birth and an empty space where her eventual date of death would one day be added. Between the two hearts was the date of their marriage.

No one, certainly not her family and friends, understood why Brenda had kept the dual headstone. They were especially perplexed that Brenda would want someday to be laid to rest next to the man who had tried to kill her.

Brenda tried to explain to those she cared about how she felt; how Glen had been the love of her life, how happy and contented he had made her feel in the beginning of their relationship, how beautiful and feminine she had then felt in his presence and how seriously she took her wedding vows, though the horror of what had happened was always with her. After a while, she realized that no one understood and she stopped trying to justify to others keeping the headstone. She would simply smile and steer the conversation to another subject. Brenda knew what they did not. If she was to get on with her life, she had to forgive and leave Glen's judgement to God. So she had separated the good memories from the bad and now was beginning to feel at peace.

Brenda removed a pot of lavender hyacinths from her tote bag, breathed in their heady aroma then placed the clay pot on the grave. She sat down next to the headstone, legs crossed, and watched as a bright red cardinal perched on the top of one of the granite hearts. He chirped his lovely song and Brenda smiled.

Quietly, in a soft murmur, she began to speak. "Dearest Glen, I ask God everyday to forgive me for killing you and I will continue to ask His forgiveness every day of my life. I think He has forgiven me and now I am learning to forgive myself. It has taken me much thought and prayer, but I have forgiven you, Glen, because you were my husband and I loved you. I will always love the good that was in you and the hopes and dreams we talked about during those long, romantic nights we shared. But now I am ready to move on."

As the cardinal flew away, Brenda pulled her notebook out and began writing down the poem she had been composing in her head for so long.

HER STRENGTH

In a small community
Neighbors thought they had a clue,
Only to find out about the neighbor man they never knew.

Her pride wouldn't allow her
To speak of the abuse;
You didn't see it on TV or hear it on the news.

The gun she had to buy
Little did they know,
How much strength it took to fire the deadly blow.

Her family said it was meant to be
She had a lion's heart;
That's why she survived and didn't fall apart.

Still why'd he try to kill her, why did he lie?
Why had he gone when she only meant to wound him?
So many questions why.

She walks into the chapel
To kneel down and pray,
Asking for 'forgiveness' for the life she took away.

And suddenly she feels it,
God's love of her so strong
That His eternal mercy, restores her heart's sweet song.